Thoreau's Democratic Withdrawal

D1547659

◆ STUDIES IN AMERICAN THOUGHT ◆
AND CULTURE

Series Editor
Paul S. Boyer

Margaret Fuller: Transatlantic Crossings in a Revolutionary Age
Edited by Charles Capper and Cristina Giorcelli

Emerson's Liberalism
Neal Dolan

Observing America: The Commentary of British Visitors to the United States, 1890–1950
Robert Frankel

*Picturing Indians: Photographic Encounters and Tourist Fantasies in H. H. Bennett's
    Wisconsin Dells*
Steven D. Hoelscher

*Cosmopolitanism and Solidarity: Studies in Ethnoracial, Religious, and Professional Affiliation
    in the United States*
David A. Hollinger

Thoreau's Democratic Withdrawal: Alienation, Participation, and Modernity
Shannon L. Mariotti

Seaway to the Future: American Social Visions and the Construction of the Panama Canal
Alexander Missal

Imaginary Friends: Representing Quakers in American Culture, 1650–1950
James Emmett Ryan

The Trashing of Margaret Mead: Anatomy of an Anthropological Controversy
Paul Shankman

*The Presidents We Imagine: Two Centuries of White House Fictions
    on the Page, on the Stage, Onscreen, and Online*
Jeff Smith

*Unsafe for Democracy: World War I and the U.S. Justice Department's Covert Campaign
    to Suppress Dissent*
William H. Thomas Jr.

Thoreau's Democratic Withdrawal

Alienation, Participation, and Modernity

Shannon L. Mariotti

THE UNIVERSITY OF WISCONSIN PRESS

This book was published with support from
SOUTHWESTERN UNIVERSITY
and the
ANONYMOUS FUND OF
THE COLLEGE OF LETTERS AND SCIENCE
AT THE UNIVERSITY OF WISCONSIN–MADISON

The University of Wisconsin Press
1930 Monroe Street, 3rd Floor
Madison, Wisconsin 53711-2059
uwpress.wisc.edu

3 Henrietta Street
London WCE 8LU, England
www.eurospanbookstore.com

1   3   5   4   2

Printed in the United States of America

Library of Congress Cataloging-in-Publication Data
Mariotti, Shannon L.
Thoreau's democratic withdrawal : alienation, participation, and modernity /
Shannon L. Mariotti.
p.   cm.—(Studies in American thought and culture)
Includes bibliographical references and index.
ISBN 978-0-299-23394-5 (pbk.: alk. paper)
ISBN 978-0-299-23393-8 (e-book)
1. Thoreau, Henry David, 1817–1862—Political and social views.
2. Solitude—Political aspects.   I. Title.   II. Series.
PS3057.P64.M37   2009
818'.309—dc22   2009008143

*To
David*

❖❖

Contents

Acknowledgments

I am very happy to have this opportunity to publicly acknowledge those who have helped bring this project to fruition. First, I would like to thank the community of people in Ithaca, New York, at Cornell University, who supported this project in its initial stages. My advisors, Anna Marie Smith, Susan Buck-Morss, Jason Frank, and Isaac Kramnick, had early faith in my sense that there were important sympathies between Thoreau and Adorno and encouraged me to follow this line of thought through to its conclusions, always making themselves available to meet with me, talk to me, and give me new things to read and think about. The Political Theory Workshop, organized by Jason Frank, and the group for advanced graduate students, organized by Richard Bensel, gave me forums to present my work to a larger audience and receive helpful suggestions and feedback from a wider range of scholars. My work also benefited from the Cornell political theory reading group, especially Banu Bargu and Jeff Selinger.

I would like to thank my colleagues at Rollins College and at Southwestern University for their support of political theory in general and me in particular. Ed Royce, a sociologist at Rollins, was especially generous with his time, reading my work and talking with me about Thoreau, Adorno, Emerson, and also Du Bois. Eric Selbin, at Southwestern University, has also given me helpful advice and always makes time to talk about theory with me.

I am especially grateful to Jack Turner, who has been an incredibly thoughtful and informed reader and critic of my project: this book has benefited from Chip's knowledge, care, and attention in ways large and small and I count myself fortunate that Thoreau afforded us an opportunity to become acquainted. I would like to thank Tom Dumm, who gave me valuable suggestions and encouragement. I would also like to acknowledge Jane Bennett; her book *Thoreau's Nature: Ethics, Politics, and the Wild* opened my eyes to new possibilities for reading and thinking about Thoreau.

I would also like to thank Gwen Walker, at the University of Wisconsin Press, and Paul Boyer, the editor for the Studies in American Thought and Culture series, for their enthusiasm and support for my project. Thanks also to both Adam Mehring and Mary Sutherland for help with editing and useful suggestions.

Samuel Frederick and Maryam Murday Frederick have been an important part of my life from the beginning of this project to the present day: I would like to thank them for making Ithaca a wonderful place to live and for their easy, unique, and constant friendship. I will persist in thinking that they named their child Henry after Henry David Thoreau. Sam was also one of my German instructors, helping me work through Adorno's difficult prose: he continues to provide help on demand whenever I need an expert on the language.

I would like to thank my parents, Robert and Jeanne Mariotti, who raised me in a space apart from cities and strip malls, enabling and encouraging my love of reading, thinking, and not watching television: in ways large and small, your influence is between the lines of this book.

Finally and most importantly, I would like to thank my partner and my best friend, David Rando, for our everyday life and for representing home to me, in the best sense. Our togetherness has truly been the vital background for my thinking and writing since we met, way back then.

Preface

Reclaiming Spaces of Withdrawal
for Democratic Politics

Theodor W. Adorno was a German intellectual, one of the chief architects of the critical social theory of the Frankfurt School, as the thinkers associated with the Institute for Social Research were called. He was also part Jewish, escaping "by accident" from his homeland during the Nazi years.[1] Adorno left Germany for England in 1934, moved to New York in 1938, then Los Angeles in 1941. He was in exile for nearly twenty years and did not return to Frankfurt permanently until 1953. The bulk of Adorno's writing was undertaken during these years: "In a 1957 letter, Adorno wrote of his eleven-year exile in America: 'I believe 90 percent of all that I've published in Germany was written in America.'"[2]

One text he wrote in Los Angeles, but published later, was the collection of essays titled *Prisms*. Unexpectedly, in a piece on Aldous Huxley, we see Adorno's thoughts turn to Henry David Thoreau. It is somewhat surprising to learn that Adorno was aware of Thoreau, given their different contexts, but it is even more striking to see the fellowship he establishes with Thoreau: in this essay, Adorno, the twentieth-century German social theorist, identifies Thoreau, the nineteenth-century American Transcendentalist, as a like-minded critic of "Americanism." Adorno sees himself as a skeptical visitor to the United States but notes a paradox—with a few notable exceptions, such as Tocqueville, the sharpest insights into America's unfreedom have come from her own native sons. As he writes, "a visitor like De Tocqueville, who a century ago already perceived the element of unfreedom in unrestrained equality, remained the exception; opposition to what in the jargon of German cultural conservatism was called 'Americanism' was to be found in Americans like Poe, Emerson, and Thoreau rather than in the new arrivals."[3] Writing from Los Angeles, exiled from his native Germany, Theodor Adorno reaches back in time to Thoreau.

This brief quotation dramatizes a sympathy analyzed more fully in this book: Adorno's sense that he shared common ground with Thoreau runs deeper than he himself may have appreciated.

Given these affinities, I reread Thoreau's writings through the lens of Adorno's critical theory to make three related arguments that at first glance might seem counterintuitive, paradoxical, or at least surprising. First, I make a case for the democratic value of practices of withdrawal, where we distance ourselves from the public sphere, from collective spaces, and from the participatory, intersubjective engagements that typically define democratic politics. Second, I show how Thoreau's unique politics of withdrawal are best illuminated by exploring his so-called nature writings, not necessarily his more overtly political pieces such as "Resistance to Civil Government" or other "reform" essays. Third, I argue that reading Thoreau with Adorno helps us understand how and why these practices of withdrawal have positive democratic value, given certain persistent features in the landscape of modernity stretching from Thoreau's nineteenth-century New England to Adorno's late-modern twentieth-century context. Reading Thoreau with Adorno, rather than through the more traditional lens of his neighbor Emerson, helps illuminate aspects of Thoreau's work that have historically been missed, misunderstood, or maligned. There are unexpected sympathies between Thoreau and Adorno and also previously unrecognized divisions between Thoreau and Emerson. In short, Thoreau's unique democratic politics of withdrawal is best understood by analyzing his nature writings through the theoretical lens of Adorno.

But how can withdrawal be democratically valuable? And how could Adorno, a German critical social theorist and member of the Frankfurt School, help us better understand the political richness and theoretical importance of Thoreau, a thinker usually categorized as an Emersonian Transcendentalist? I first became interested in the benefits of reading Thoreau with Adorno when I recognized similarities in their critiques of modernity, despite their different theoretical categories and contexts. Thoreau and Adorno make a similar diagnosis of how modernity contributes to a sense of alienation understood as a loss of critical capacity and the ability to think against conventions. These losses are dangerous, given that critique and negation are central to their understandings of what it means to be human and to have a self. Further, for both Thoreau and Adorno, these capacities are central to the idea of democracy: we cannot truly have democratic self-government without this kind of critical self. As Adorno says, "Critique is essential to all democracy. Not only does democracy require the freedom to criticize and need critical impulses. Democracy is nothing less than defined by critique."[4]

There are forces in modern society, however, that work against this possibility of a more truly democratic politics, arranging instead to shape citizens into machines who thoughtlessly bend to the force of the collective. This is where practices of withdrawal enter the picture as democratically valuable. For Thoreau, the conditions of modernity demand practices of withdrawal that are outside the normal parameters of conventional, public, participatory, intersubjective notions of democracy. By confronting wild nature in the woods and fields around Concord, by huckleberrying and walking, Thoreau cultivates a critical distance from Main Street and tries to dislodge conventional ways of thinking: he courts a feeling of dislocated homelessness to counteract tendencies of modern alienation that pull us to think in terms of what he calls the "common sense." While walking, Thoreau also trains his eye on what he calls "little things" and their wild qualities stimulate him to think against the conventions of Main Street and all it represents. Adorno helps illuminate the political significance of the practices of withdrawal that Thoreau exemplifies in his nature writings. Enacting his practice of negative dialectics, Adorno employs a "microscopic gaze" that pays attention to particular things and draws out the "nonidentical" qualities that resist categorization and systematic logics, toward a critique of the illusory harmonies of modern society. Adorno helps us see how Thoreau's excursions into nature are not apolitical retreats but ways of confronting particular objects that stimulate dissonant, rupturing, negative critiques of modern society and allow him to recuperate the capacities that define truly democratic citizens. Because of their sympathies, reading Thoreau with Adorno helps illuminate Thoreau's own expansion of democratic politics, beyond conventional participatory imperatives.

Is it dangerous to associate political value with such practices of withdrawal? In a political climate where American citizens are often seen as apathetic, self-absorbed, lazy, and victims of malaise, it might seem counterproductive to talk about the political value of withdrawal. Are people too concerned with their private lives to worry about the common good, if such a thing can even be identified? Given this diagnosis, is anything that engages people and brings them together to participate in public spaces in common cause, by definition, a good thing and of political value? Such concerns motivate several strains of contemporary political theory. Because of fears of apathy and a lack of civic engagement, there is a participatory imperative in contemporary political theory that extols the virtues of collective engagement, contestation, and deliberation. Democracy cannot thrive, the argument goes, if citizens withdraw from public spaces. We see this sentiment undergirding several different strains of political thought.

Robert Putnam, for example, worries about the health of a democracy where citizens have relinquished political participation, retreating from public life into a privatized existence in front of the television.[5] While for Putnam, Americans today are "bowling alone," for Robert Dahl they have gone shopping, abandoning a culture of citizenship in favor of a culture of consumerism. To work against rising political inequality and a weakening of democracy, Dahl calls for Americans to reject the prevalent "competitive consumerism" and devote more time and energy to civic activities.[6] Robert Bellah and Michael Sandel make similar claims regarding the need for greater public-spiritedness and community-mindedness. In *Habits of the Heart,* Bellah et al. chart the negative side effects of the individual pursuit of happiness and call for greater commitment to the community to ameliorate the rise of an autonomous yet alienated individualism in modern American society.[7] Sandel's "public philosophy" emphasizes the insufficiencies of the liberal focus on the atomistic, unencumbered individual and calls for a return to the principles of republicanism, calling on Americans to be more community-oriented and civic-minded in their decision-making.[8] In all these formulations, despite their differences, democracy is defined in terms of public participation and democratic vitality is associated with coming together in shared social and political spaces.

Jürgen Habermas and later generations of deliberative democrats also emphasize engagement in the public sphere, consensus-building, and intersubjective deliberation. Employing a definition that has widespread support today, Habermas insists "on the original meaning of democracy in terms of the institutionalization of a public use of reason jointly exercised by autonomous citizens."[9] Habermas sees intersubjective communication as the best response to the "alienation phenomena" that stem from the "colonization of the lifeworld," to use his terminology.[10] Later generations of deliberative democratic theorists pursue valuable variations on this theme, placing more emphasis on ensuring presupposed substantive rights, on strengthening collective action, or shifting and de-centering the location of the public sphere.

But the tendency to define democracy in terms of publicity and participation does not just characterize civic republican and deliberative democratic theories, though it may be most directly advocated there. It is also represented in more radical understandings of democracy. For Sheldon Wolin, for example, democracy is not an institution, political system, or form of government: instead, he characterizes it as "a mode of being." He sees democracy as a rebellious moment, as "a political moment, perhaps *the* political moment, when the political is remembered and re-created."[11] But what is the space for such a moment? Where does it occur, and with whom? For Wolin, "the political" is "an expression of the idea that a free society composed of diversities that can none-theless enjoy moments of commonality when, through public deliberations, collective power is used to promote or protect the well-being of the collectivity."[12] The political is imagined as a shared, common space where we engage with each other, even if the definition of democracy is de-institutionalized.[13]

If deliberative democratic theories oriented toward reconciliation and building consensus make up one major strand of contemporary theorizing about democracy, the opposing camp might be agonistic pluralism. In Greek antiquity, the *agon* was a public celebration of contests at games; it also denotes a verbal dispute between two characters in a Greek play.[14] The image of the *agon* as a public celebration of contest lives on in these theories: difference, conflict, and pluralism are seen as markers of democratic vitality.[15] For example, Bonnie Honig is critical of the ways that republican, liberal, and communitarian theories tend to "displace" politics: instead of confronting the inevitable remainder that arises from every attempt to secure order and settlement, most political theories define success in terms of eliminating "dissonance, resistance, conflict, or struggle" and seek to expel, deny, or assimilate difference.[16] Those who displace politics in these ways are charged with "closing down the agon" while for Honig democratic politics is about opening up unstable, uncertain, contentious spaces for the public, popular contestation of difference.[17] She defines democratic vitality in terms of "the tumult of politics," "activism," "political contest," and "social democratic struggle."[18]

Difference is an inevitable part of our own identities, as well as our relationships with each other: it is both "*intrasubjective* and *intersubjective*," as William Connolly puts it.[19] But for Connolly, the two are linked: the politics of personal identity makes us rethink our democratic politics. We must cultivate an ethos of critical responsiveness, because "affirming" the relational, constructed, and collective character of identity, can "make a difference to the ethical quality of political life," understood in terms of our collective life together. Ultimately, difference serves to revitalize, energize, and engender robust public contestations, opening "political spaces for agonistic relations of mutual respect" "between interlocking and contending constituencies."[20]

These agonistic theories, in their emphasis on the political value of dissonance, destabilization, rupture, and a kind of uprooting homelessness, share valuable common ground with Thoreau's and Adorno's critical practices. And yet, even agonistic theories of democracy cannot fully capture the political practices of withdrawal that both Thoreau and Adorno see as so valuable to a democracy. Agonistic theories also tend to measure democratic politics in terms of the vitality and robustness of our engagements with each other: the kinds of interactions that define democratic politics are still likely to be collective, public, and participatory. The image of the *agon* as a public celebration of contest is still evident in these theories in ways that render Thoreau's and Adorno's practices of withdrawal less visible at best and pathological at worst.

Thus despite their many differences, all of the theories discussed in the preceding paragraphs—from civic republicans to agonistic theorists—place parameters around democratic politics in ways that tend to exclude Thoreau's and Adorno's practices of withdrawal; consequently, the dominant frameworks of contemporary democratic theory do not go very far in helping us recognize and comprehend the unique politics of Thoreau and Adorno.[21] When we limit our definition of democratic politics to public spaces where we engage in collective action in common, we render any politics that occurs in spaces of withdrawal *by definition* undemocratic, unrecognizable, or even dangerous and pathological. When we reckon withdrawal only in terms of apolitical apathy, there is also a danger that we may too readily become cheerleaders for anything that seems to draw people together in a public space. Fearing apathy, we may tend to become uncritical proponents of participation. We may fail to see how some forms of political engagement do not serve genuinely democratic purposes, failing also to appreciate how some forms of withdrawal may in fact be valuable to democratic politics. In addition, we will be likely to misunderstand attempts to expand the parameters of the political beyond its usual participatory, public, shared boundaries.

Dana Villa's *Socratic Citizenship* shares this concern with the tendency to equate participation and civic engagement with citizenship as such: further, there are important sympathies (as well as significant differences) between the dissident, subversive, critical mode of philosophical inquiry he calls "Socratic citizenship" and the democratic politics of withdrawal that I find in Thoreau's and Adorno's work (which I discuss further in the next chapter).[22] But as both of our studies show, given conventional notions of politics, any political practices that happen in spaces of withdrawal seem especially fragile, prone to being lost, forgotten, misunderstood, and maligned. These practices must be remembered as possibilities, as potentials, over and over again. Bob Pepperman Taylor says "Thoreau is, on the whole, the political thinker scholars of American political thought love to ignore or hate."[23] We might say the same about practices of withdrawal: they tend to be ignored or hated, which might account in no small part for how Thoreau and Adorno have often been received by students of politics. This project seeks neither to champion political apathy nor to criticize all forms of public engagement. I do not want to idealize withdrawal, but instead to shine a spotlight on the democratic politics of withdrawal we see in the work

of Thoreau and Adorno and show how withdrawal need not necessarily be
equated with apolitical apathy. As long as we rely on an understanding of democratic politics that privileges collective engagements in public spaces, we will
obscure the unique and valuable politics of withdrawal that exists in the work
of Thoreau and Adorno. To withdraw typically means to pull back, to retire,
recede, quit, and disengage. But Thoreau and Adorno withdraw from public
spaces, in fact, to engage in an alternative form of democratic politics. Negative dialectics, walking, and huckleberrying instantiate, perform, and enact the
critical negation that democracy depends upon and is defined by. And yet, for
both Thoreau and Adorno, the power of conventional ways of thinking is so
strong that they must withdraw from mainstream society to see the nonidentical and wild qualities of particular objects that hold the potential for broader
social critiques.

These practices are not just pathways to a new kind of politics. They are
not just tools to make eventual changes in conventional politics, though they
hopefully also have this effect. Their practices of critical negation are not pre-
requisites to get under our belts *before* we rejoin the polity to engage in conventional politics. In their practices of withdrawal, Thoreau and Adorno are not
putting politics on hold until a future moment where it becomes possible to engage in politics as it is more commonly understood. Negative dialectics, walking, or huckleberrying are immanent: they enact a democratic politics by their
very practice. Without citizens who possess the capacity for critique, a democracy exists in name only. Without the capacity to think against conventions, to
break apart logics that seem smooth and harmonious at a distance, to see particularity instead of just identity, the individual is little more than a machine
made up of moving parts, a powerful image of modern alienation for both
Thoreau and Adorno.

If we wonder how this kind of coercive power can exist even in a democracy, Alexis de Tocqueville reminds us that it exists *especially* in such govern-
ments. Tocqueville describes the "tyranny of the majority" as a peculiar danger
of democracies because their emphasis on equality and popular sovereignty
can lead to an unthinking and unquestioning allegiance to the power of the
majority, to popular opinion. Multiplicity and individuality are eclipsed by conformity with the majority. Tocqueville says "I know of no country where there
is generally less independence of thought and real freedom of debate than in
America." In American democracy, "the majority has staked out a formidable
fence around thought." Tyranny is not a euphemism, here. The tendency in
American democracy that Tocqueville describes acts violently, but not upon
the body: "Princes had, so to speak, turned violence into a physical thing but

our democratic republics have made it into something as intellectual as the human will it intends to restrict. Under the absolute government of one man, despotism, in order to attack the spirit, crudely struck the body and the spirit escaped free of its blows, rising gloriously above it. But in democratic republics, tyranny does not behave in that manner; it leaves the body alone and goes straight to the spirit."[24]

In a passage that sounds eerily as if Foucault might have written it, Tocqueville describes the internalization of the power of the majority. This tyranny acts on our intellect and our spirit, shaping the ways we think and act. The majority is sovereign and all-powerful, like a king who cannot be opposed, but it operates *inside* us. Fortunately, for Tocqueville, Americans possess a unique enthusiasm for assembling, for associating, for practicing politics in their daily lives, all of which also keeps this tyranny in check. But for Thoreau and Adorno, there is no such safeguard. The individual is too easily lost to the collective in public political practices. This is a problem that Adorno identifies in Nazism, but which also persists in democracies: he did not think he left the roots of fascism behind when he moved to Los Angeles.

For these reasons, Thoreau and Adorno give us a valuable language for articulating the political value of withdrawal itself.[25] They give us compelling reasons to hesitate, to refrain from uncritically accepting the imperatives of contemporary democratic theory, cautioning us against automatically equating participation and publicity with democratic politics *as such*. How can *more* participation and engagement help when the thinking individual is so easily lost to the collective and conventional ways of thinking? If we define democracy only in terms of intersubjective action in a public sphere, we cannot see the political value of their practices. Given historical forces of alienation, Thoreau and Adorno call for a more expanded notion of the political that extends beyond engagement in a public space. Given modern conditions, we must cultivate resistance to alienation via different methods: these thinkers show how withdrawing and distancing oneself from intersubjective encounters and contestations in the public, shared spaces usually associated with democratic politics can itself be democratically valuable. In this way, Thoreau and Adorno help us recover a previously denigrated space for democratic politics and help us reclaim a previously neglected mode of democratic practice.

Thoreau's Democratic Withdrawal

Introduction

Reading Thoreau with Adorno

Pursuing Thoreau's politics can be as frustrating and maddening as chasing a loon—or a white whale; he was a grand apolitical, political-like man who resists tidy summations.

Michael Myers

Thoreau as a political theorist is a remarkably apolitical writer.

Philip Abbott

Thoreau is, on the whole, the political thinker scholars of American political thought love to ignore or hate.

Bob Pepperman Taylor

Thoreau and Democratic Politics

Historically, Henry David Thoreau has been a problematic figure for students of politics.[1] At best, he has been read as a marginal member of the political theory canon known for the stinging critiques of American politics we see in his essay on civil disobedience. At worst, Thoreau has been maligned as a misanthropic and excessively withdrawn hermit with nothing but scorn for conventional politics: after all, he wrote "my thoughts are murder to the state and involuntarily go plotting against her."[2] Furthermore, the book for which he is most famous, *Walden,* has often been regarded as nature writing, with little to contribute to political theory. In general, students of politics have found it difficult to reconcile this "hermit of Walden Pond" with our dominant understanding of democratic politics as a public, participatory, collective endeavor: how can Thoreau, who withdraws away from Main Street, into the woods and huckleberry fields, be conceived of as a political thinker? This question captures the conflict between our predominant images of Thoreau (often melancholy and misanthropic, a passive dissenter, withdrawing into nature) and our most powerful images of politics (a public, intersubjective realm of positive action, based on engagement and participation).

Given this conflict, those who wish to redeem Thoreau as a political thinker typically downplay his solitary withdrawals into nature and his pessimistic attitude toward society. More emphasis is placed on his active engagement and public participation in Concord life or his moments of fulfillment and creation. Within this broad category, scholars differ greatly on how Thoreau's politics are manifested. But overall, those who wish to make a case for the political significance of Thoreau's work tend to emphasize his participatory, public, positive, and creative sides; we are presented with images of Thoreau speaking at the lyceums, giving advice, spectacularly performing his conscience, and creatively engaging in self-culture.

For example, Mary Elkin Moller writes a corrective to what she perceives as a misleading overemphasis on the image of Thoreau as "the hermit of Walden Woods"; instead, she reads Thoreau as primarily a warm friend, neighbor, and member of the human community whose misanthropic moments simply reveal disappointed desires for more authentic relationships.[3] For Bob Pepperman Taylor, Thoreau is a bachelor uncle, giving political advice to future generations of Americans to help them better recognize the gulf between their ideals and practices.[4] George Kateb calls Thoreau a "democratic individualist" who can dissent and negate because he has been positively shaped by the ideals of the American electoral system.[5] For Jack Turner, Thoreau's politics is captured in his performance of conscience, aesthetically, creatively, spectacularly, and theatrically in public civic spaces (town halls, town squares, the free press) to inspire ethical action in others.[6] Jane Bennett focuses on a different kind of positive, creative moment: charting Thoreau's postmodern sensibility, she sees Thoreau as an artist, a sculptor engaged in techniques of self-fashioning and self-creation aimed toward cultivating a heteroverse sensibility that better enables us to resist the conformist world of "the They" and be open to "the Wild."[7] Brian Walker also emphasizes creative self-culture: for him, Thoreau is engaged in a democratic political project aimed toward advising post-aristocratic citizens immersed in a market society about practices that might help them cultivate heroic, noble, happy, and free dispositions.[8] Exploring Thoreau's ethics of self-making toward a different end, Morris B. Kaplan shows how Thoreau's acts of civil disobedience and his critiques of conventional social arrangements can inform queer citizenship.[9]

On the other side of the spectrum are scholars who acknowledge Thoreau's political ambitions but show how they could not completely or adequately be fulfilled because of his personality flaws and psychological problems. Some have argued that Thoreau's excessive, exaggerated, paradoxical, and contradictory style of rhetoric is evidence of a troubled mind. The most infamous example is a highly ad hominem and vitriolic essay by Vincent Buranelli published in 1957.[10] Other thinkers, such as Philip Abbott, focus on Thoreau's isolation and rejection of community as evidence of a personal crisis.[11] Richard Bridgman's book *Dark Thoreau* explores the many pessimistic, hostile, resenting, depressed, frustrated, and anxious moments in Thoreau's work and concludes that the problems Thoreau experienced were rooted in his own subjective psychology.[12]

Other writers see Thoreau's politics as limited by less negative, but still damaging, qualities of his idiosyncratic personality and way of life. In her essay "Civil Disobedience," Hannah Arendt argues that Thoreau's politics are limited by his need to act from conscience; she says that "conscience is unpolitical" in that it is action from self-interest that cannot be generalized. For Arendt, Thoreau is more concerned with the goodness of the self and withdraws from the world.[13] Nancy Rosenblum thinks Thoreau's democratic politics are limited by his Romantic militant conscience, rooted in a sense of anger, insignificance, and powerlessness that limited his abilities for coexistence.[14] In later writings, she argues that Thoreau's Romantic militarism and what she sees as his apolitical withdrawals into nature are constantly being inhibited and chastened by his democratic desire to expose and exhibit his heroic individualism in public spaces, to give others "a strong dose" of himself.[15]

Others have argued that Thoreau was forced, for various reasons, to retreat away from history and politics into nature and the realm of individual consciousness. For Joel Porte, Thoreau's "political dream was finally a government which would leave him alone" to pursue his solitary aesthetic experiences, searching for sublime epiphanies in nature.[16] In *American Romanticism and the Marketplace*, Michael Gilmore argues that Thoreau had to sacrifice his ambitions to use his writings as a platform for reform because he refused to sell his work as a commodity, to adapt it to the market and popularize it for a wider audience.[17] In his classic text *The Machine in the Garden*, Leo Marx argues that because

Thoreau could not reconcile the contradiction posed by the machine (burgeoning industrial modernity) in the garden (the pastoral sublime) in reality, he was forced to retreat from history to his creative art: Thoreau must instead try to restore unity poetically, "in his craft, in *Walden*."[18] In different ways, these thinkers show how Thoreau's political aspirations, positive political action, or proposals for alternative social orders had to be sacrificed and abandoned. As the story goes, he withdrew from the public realm and from politics to Walden Pond in order to engage in such solipsistic pursuits as walking and huckleberrying.

Something is missing in these opposing ways of reading Thoreau. To buy wholly into either story, there are many moments in the text that we must ignore. In this project, I take into account *both* the undeniable evidence of Thoreau's moments of withdrawal *and* the importance of his political concerns. Thoreau's moments of negativity and estrangement are not limiting but, in fact, give rise to a unique mode of democratic political practice. Thoreau's melancholy does not yield apathy or apolitical retreat into nature. Instead, his experiences of pain, suffering, frustration, and estrangement motivate productive, political, democratic practices. But these experiences are not purely subjective, psychological, and rooted in his idiosyncratic psyche. Instead, by situating Thoreau in his context, at the heart of the most intense period of nascent modernization in New England, we can understand how his sense of alienation and his withdrawals respond to the social changes taking place in Concord.

We can reach a fuller, deeper understanding of Thoreau by analyzing his nature writings in conjunction with his more conventional political writings such as "Resistance to Civil Government." When we explore his nature writings along with his reform essays, Thoreau's paradoxical thought pushes us toward an uncommon understanding of democratic politics, where a sense of loss motivates activities such as walking and huckleberrying that aim to recover and recuperate the critical qualities we must have to be real democratic citizens. We can best address the paradoxes that arise from Thoreau's work when we appreciate how his political practices move beyond conventional participatory imperatives and seek to reconfigure our notion of democratic activity. Given modern conditions of alienation, Thoreau finds that practices of withdrawal can constitute democratic political practices. His thought pushes us to break apart this binary opposition between democracy and withdrawal, between politics and nature, and between a dark sense of alienation and valuable political practices. Instead of highlighting all the ways that Thoreau is a round peg who does not comfortably fit into the square hole of conventional democratic politics, we should appreciate that Thoreau tries to reshape the hole itself. How does he expand the parameters of democratic politics to even encompass practices of withdrawal?

Leigh Kathryn Jenco's article "Thoreau's Critique of Democracy" provides an especially illuminating foil to my own interpretation of Thoreau. Jenco argues that Thoreau's thought is incompatible with democracy. But in making this assertion, she relies on the same traditional notion of democratic politics that Thoreau is trying to unsettle through the alternative politics of withdrawal he enacts in his excursions in nature. Jenco sees representation, an obligation to promote the common good, and participatory endeavors in the public sphere (such as voting) as the core principles that are "constitutive of liberal democracy." But for Jenco, Thoreau is primarily concerned with individual morality: his thought is grounded in a deontological moral philosophy "that renders impossible the mediation of justice through democratic institutions." Thoreau's only duty, as Jenco sees it, is to "perceive and perform right," but this is incompatible with democracy; he cannot support the political obligations that "representative democracy imposes." In sum, she sees Thoreau as deeply concerned with the "moral damage produced by the democratic process." For Jenco, Thoreau issues a larger challenge regarding the viability of democracy *as such* when he asks: "Is a democracy, such as we know it, the last improvement possible in government? Is it not possible to take a step further toward recognizing and organizing the rights of man?"[19]

But Jenco misses what I take to be the central thrust of the passage above: here, Thoreau is distinguishing the incarnation of democracy that he saw in his own day from its greater possibilities. Thoreau qualifies his discussion in two important ways to indicate that he is looking for an alternative form of democratic politics, as opposed to an alternative *to* democratic politics *as such*. First, he asks whether "*a* democracy" is the last improvement in government, as opposed to asking whether democracy itself is the last improvement in government. Second, Thoreau asks his question with regard to democracy "such as we know it"; again, this signals his recognition of the flaws in his current form of democratic government, but indicates the possibility of a more truly democratic politics.

But because of the traditional way she defines democracy, Jenco cannot help but say that Thoreau's writings are incompatible with democracy as such. Jenco is right to highlight Thoreau's criticisms of the representative democracy of his own day, of the hollowness of voting, of the superficiality of many conventional efforts at social reform, of a politics concerned primarily with offices and institutions, instead of individuals. Thoreau is indeed issuing a warning about the dangers of a commitment to conventional notions of democracy. But the better possibilities Thoreau enacts, especially in his nature writings, are part of his central project of reconfiguring our notion of *what counts* as a democratic practice. The traditional notion of democracy that Jenco relies upon is exactly the one Thoreau is pushing us to see past, with his practice of a democratic politics of withdrawal designed to sharpen our threatened critical capacities. Thoreau finds the roots of true democratic self-government in the capacity to think against conventions, to critique, to think for one's self. Because of the alienated nature of modernity, we must withdraw from mainstream society, into nature, to recuperate the capacities that are the basis for true democracy.

Jenco is certainly not alone in reading Thoreau through the lens of traditional notions of democracy. In fact, even those who argue the opposite side of the coin and say that Thoreau is ultimately committed to democracy also tend to define that concept in conventional ways. Here, Thoreau's withdrawals into nature are still cast in opposition to publicity, concern with the common good, and engagement with others. For example, Nancy Rosenblum sees Thoreau as constantly going back and forth between apolitical romantic withdrawals into nature and spectacular self-assertion of his heroic individualism in public forums, but these two realms are still strictly separated. For Rosenblum, Thoreau is invariably being pulled away from nature into the public sphere by his democratic concerns: his commitment to democracy "inhibits" his romantic withdrawals into nature. But her reading also suggests that self-distancing and withdrawing into nature is dangerous to democratic politics and must be chastened and tamed: "Tortuously but decisively, democratic inhibitions recall Thoreau from imaginative flight to neighborly concerns, from exceptionalism to equality" and, by implication, from Maine's Mount Ktaadn or Walden Pond to common concerns in the public sphere, from nature to democracy.[20]

To highlight the often missed theoretical dimensions of Thoreau's nature writings, to capture his democratic politics of withdrawal, I draw from another thinker situated at the other end of modernity—Theodor W. Adorno, the twentieth-century German social theorist. Adorno helps illuminate the theoretical and political richness of Thoreau's excursions into nature. These are two thinkers who are typically not spoken of in the same breath, separated by time and space and typically placed in wholly different theoretical categories. Thoreau's unique brand of New England Transcendentalism responds to an intense period of nascent industrialization in nineteenth-century Concord, Massachusetts. Adorno, on the other hand, is a twentieth-century German intellectual, a Marxian social theorist and critic of late modernity. Because of these differences, their deep sympathies are all the more compelling. Through their political practices of withdrawal, Thoreau and Adorno remind us of a forgotten mode of citizenship, but they are not its only practitioners nor even its innovators. In fact, they might be reminding us of what Socrates taught us in the first place, as thinking and politics were first being connected into the practice of political philosophy. Though this project focuses on Thoreau's and Adorno's politics of withdrawal, we might also draw another connection across space and time to another thinker who shares common ground: Socrates. Dana Villa's *Socratic Citizenship* illuminates another politically valuable withdrawal that resonates in important ways with my readings of Thoreau and Adorno. Villa shows how Socrates' "fragile" idea of citizenship was lost, given the way Western political thought persistently values collective, participatory action over individual, critical thought. The political value of withdrawal is, it seems, an idea that is especially prone to being forgotten, consistently needing to be recalled, remembered, recovered.

Similarly concerned with the uncritical participatory imperative in contemporary politics, Villa recuperates, in the figure of Socrates, a mode of citizenship practiced in an "alternative public sphere" beyond the "boundaries of the 'official' public realm." For Villa, Socrates challenges notions of citizenship that rely only on civic engagement, public deliberation, devotion to public service, and associational participation. Socrates brought a dissident form of citizenship into the city, based on a negative, disillusioning, dissolving, skeptical, disenchanting rationality. Or, avoiding the law courts and assemblies, he practiced his philosophical inquiries by withdrawing from traditional public spaces. Socrates saw Athenian public spaces as dominated by the multitude, by conformity to convention, by moral self-satisfaction, and hubris. As Villa notes, because of the distortion, domination, and injustice that characterized the public stage, to truly "think what we are doing," to use Arendt's phrase, and to engage in moral reflection, withdrawal was often necessary. But Villa argues that Socrates' withdrawal was not apolitical: "the very terms in which Socrates casts his withdrawal from the 'official' public realm make it clear that his philosophical activity has a distinctly political dimension." He engages in a new form of citizenship in alternative public spheres, by acting as a gadfly and "irritating the moral and intellectual conscience of his city," by "maintaining rigorous moral and intellectual integrity as an individual," by "undermining authorities, purging opinions, and creating a general puzzlement where previously there had been a firm faith in the soundness of 'traditional values.'"[21]

Many of the critical, dissenting, withdrawing qualities that Villa identifies with Socrates also apply to Thoreau, and Villa briefly discusses these resemblances. But Villa ultimately does not see Thoreau as engaging in a form of Socratic citizenship (and Adorno does not figure into the analysis at all). Though there are important differences, the resemblances between these thinkers are greater than Villa appreciates. But this failure to fully appreciate the sympathies between Thoreau's critical practices and Socratic citizenship likely stems from the fact that Villa draws only from Thoreau's "Resistance to Civil Government." It is typical for students of politics to focus only on this text, but it problematically skews our understanding of Thoreau's politics to read this essay outside the context of his so-called nature writings such as "Walking" or *Walden*. Villa's portrait of Thoreau is rendered too absolute, too militant, too violent, too imposing:

> Thoreau's essay extends and, in many respects, deepens the Socratic idea of conscientious individualism, yet it also goes beyond that idea insofar as it is an unabashed call to action and—in the last instance—to arms. . . . [I]t straddles the distinction between an activist absolute morality . . . and an abstentionist absolute morality. As a result, its connection to the disillusioning political art of Socrates is tenuous at best. For Thoreau, conscience is not simply the nay-saying voice that results from the thinking dialogue with oneself, or the product of the perplexity produced by the dialogue with others. . . . Thoreau's conscientious "no" to complicity with an unjust state leads to an impassioned "yes" to demonstrative, perhaps even violent, action.[22]

Villa seems to conclude that Thoreau's withdrawal from conventional politics is not complete *enough*. Villa argues that Socrates wants only to continually break down unthinkingly traditional, conformist and unjust opinions, whereas Thoreau wants to refill this empty space with an alternative kind of action that is positive, public, even revolutionary—and that, consequently, would be subject to the problems Villa identifies with conventional society and politics.

But Thoreau's call to action is not, as Villa thinks, a call to engage in revolutionary action in the public sphere. Thoreau does indeed issue a call, but he asks us to engage in a politics of withdrawal to recuperate the critical capacities that are vital to democratic citizenship. In this way, Thoreau mirrors Socrates' mode of citizenship. In addition, Thoreau's and Adorno's understanding of the power of thinking as a fundamentally important political capacity that unites us as human across race, class, status, gender, et cetera, is deeply sympathetic to Villa's notion of Socratic citizenship.[23] Even the way Villa characterizes Socrates sounds like Thoreau. For example, Villa calls Socrates a "truly 'bad' citizen" by contemporary standards: compare this with Thoreau's statement, in his essay on civil disobedience, that he wishes to be a "bad subject" but a "good neighbor."[24] Further, like Thoreau, Socrates' seemingly insignificant withdrawals made him, "in the eyes of his fellow citizens, the archetypal philosophical good-for-nothing, someone who failed to actively contribute to the public good" while "Socrates saw himself as performing an invaluable service to his city through this (apparently self-indulgent) behavior."[25] The same charge was made to Thoreau and the same response came from Thoreau.

At the same time, there are important differences between Socratic citizenship and Thoreau's and Adorno's politics of withdrawal. Most importantly, Villa presents Socrates' dissolvent rationality as an end in itself, based on a skepticism of all society, all forms of intersubjective engagement. Social life, for Villa, has an "essentially mimetic character," an "automatic or intrinsically conformist quality."[26] In contrast, both Thoreau and Adorno see withdrawal as politically valuable given a specific kind of modern society, but these acts are necessary coping mechanisms given specifically modern historical conditions: withdrawal is not an end in itself and they do not describe all society as essentially problematic. Further, both Thoreau and Adorno withdraw in ways that maintain a yearning for (and aim toward) the possibility of greater neighborhood, greater community, and the possibility of a less alienated form of fellowship. But, aside from these differences, Thoreau, as well as Adorno, have more in common with Socrates and with the mode of withdrawal called Socratic citizenship than Villa seems to appreciate.

Alienation in Modernity

Before we can understand Thoreau's withdrawals, we must understand what motivates him to distance himself from Main Street and from the shared spaces of traditional politics. Thoreau's writing contains a deep and sustained critique of the alienating nature of nascent modernity in New England. The sense of loss and dark moments of melancholy that Thoreau experiences are not the products of a flawed psyche, but are responses to nineteenth-century modernization.

This is the first way that Adorno illuminates the political value of Thoreau's withdrawals. Adorno can help us appreciate how Thoreau's experiences of loss do not limit, but in fact motivate, his unique political practices. Adorno's writings on alienation show how psychic states of melancholy and angst are not purely subjective but can be understood as important responses to social and political conditions. As he writes in *Negative Dialectics*: "The smallest trace of senseless suffering in the empirical world belies all identitarian philosophy that would talk us out of that suffering. . . . The physical moment tells our knowledge that suffering ought not to be, that things should be different. 'Woe speaks: "Go." '"[27]

For Adorno, suffering can stimulate political practices, unconventional though they may look. But what exactly is the "woe" that speaks "go," for Adorno and Thoreau? Both Thoreau and Adorno associate modernity with a particular kind of loss. For both "life does not live" (to borrow from Adorno, who borrows from Ferdinand Kürnberger).[28] For Adorno, the loss of life and self was a literal experience under the rule of Nazism and in the concentration camps. But fascism also represented an extremely sharp illumination of already existing tendencies within modernity. For both Thoreau and Adorno, we become used to formulaic, systematic, and abstract ways of thinking that make us lose the ability to negate, to go against the grain of convention, to think critically. Without these capacities, we lack the features that define the thinking self, that allow us to really live life instead of only sleepwalking through a pale imitation. This is the modern experience that I theorize as alienation. While the word *alienation* (Ger. *Entfremdung*) does appear in Adorno's work, this is not a term that Thoreau uses to describe the loss of self and dilution of experience. Despite differences of terminology, alienation seems to be the most appropriate term to capture the condition that concerns these two thinkers because of its overtones of suffering and a palpable, painful experience of feeling bereft and in anguish; it encompasses the psychological sense of melancholy loss that figures prominently in the work of both Thoreau and Adorno.[29]

Alienation here, however, does not mean an existential despair that is an inevitable part of the human condition without regard to history. As a Marxian critical theorist, it is clear that Adorno roots this sense of loss in historically specific experiences of the social and political world. He explicitly distinguishes his own understanding of psychic anguish from Heidegger's: "Angst, that supposed '*existential*,' is the claustrophobia of a systematized society" (*Negative Dialectics*, 24). Thoreau also roots this sense of loss in historical contexts. He describes the railroad and an increasingly intense market economy as overtly alienating forces, yet he also often links the loss of self to the social and political world in more subtle ways. For example, he will refer to the plight of the factory girls at the Lowell mills ("Consider the girls in a factory—never alone, hardly in their dreams") in the middle of a critique of the superficiality of social relations.[30] Or, in a melancholy tone, he might express jealousy over the crowing of the cock—a symbol of morning and being awake, both of which are opposites of the experience of alienation for Thoreau—by noting that "Where he lives no fugitive slave laws are passed."[31]

Thoreau and Adorno root this sense of alienation in the social world, in opposition to idealist philosophies that see alienation as an existential condition. Adorno's engagement with idealism came straight from its German source: he writes about Kant, Hegel, and Heidegger. Thoreau's encounter with idealism came across the Atlantic via Emerson, who got his Kant and Hegel largely secondhand via Coleridge and Carlyle.[32] Thoreau read German very well, but it is fair to say that Emerson's study of German idealism was more sustained.[33] But despite their different relationships to it, both Thoreau and Adorno were highly influenced by, though ultimately critical of, German Transcendental

Idealism. Adorno's philosophical project is rooted in highlighting, and overcoming, the pitfalls associated with the drive to systematize, to unify, and to synthesize that he associates with Kant, Hegel, and Enlightenment rationality generally. Adorno's credentials as an opponent of idealism, then, seem secure. Thoreau's critique of idealism is less clear, and less widely known, largely because of his identification with Emerson. Emerson and Thoreau are still the two thinkers most often associated with American Transcendental idealism. But ultimately Thoreau's thought is significantly different from Emerson's. Thoreau increasingly moved away from Emersonian Transcendentalism and in doing so also became a critic of idealism. One marker of this is the way Thoreau, like Adorno but unlike Emerson, sees alienation as an historically rooted social phenomena, as opposed to a feature of the human condition as such.

Withdrawing and Distancing in the Work of Thoreau and Adorno

Traditionally, Thoreau's and Adorno's withdrawals have been seen as apathetic and apolitical. Both thinkers have been accused of being too removed and seemingly disengaged from the mainstream political issues of their days. Their lives and their works can make them appear, at first glance, elitist, misanthropic, or perhaps dangerously resistant to politics. Adorno was once imagined as a resident of the "Grand Hotel Abyss," a mandarin who lamented the dismal state of politics from a comfortably safe, though removed, position: this was Lukács's description of Adorno and other German intellectuals who were perceived as critical of, but uninvolved in, the practical politics of their day.[34] Habermas described Adorno's approach as a "strategy of hibernation."[35] In his essay "Resignation" in *The Culture Industry*, Adorno reviews the charges leveled against him:

> We older representatives of that for which the name Frankfurt School has established itself have recently had the reproach of resignation leveled against us. We had, it is stated, developed elements of a critical theory of society, but we were not prepared to draw the practical consequences from this theory. We neither designed programs for action nor did we support the actions of those who felt themselves inspired by critical theory. . . . The objection raised against us can be stated approximately in these words; a person who in the present hour doubts the possibility of radical change in society and who for that reason neither takes part in nor recommends spectacular, violent action is guilty of resignation.[36]

As Adorno writes, "Distance from praxis is disreputable in the eyes of everyone. Anyone who does not take immediate action and who is not willing to get his hands dirty is the subject of suspicion" (*Culture Industry*, 199). Adorno was seen as too unwilling to participate, a criticism loudly vocalized during the student movements of the 1960s in Germany. Critics said: "One should take part. Whoever restricts himself to thinking but does not get involved is weak, cowardly and virtually a traitor" (199).

Thoreau's distancing from mainstream politics was more literal, represented in his move away from the town of Concord, Massachusetts: he built a cabin on the shores of Walden Pond, a mile or so outside the village, where he lived by himself from July 4, 1845, to September 6, 1847. Thoreau's withdrawal prompted his contemporaries and later critics to call him a recluse, the hermit of Walden Pond. Thoreau also engaged in less dramatic minor acts of separation and distancing throughout his life: daily, he went on four-hour walks that took him into the woods or he went huckleberrying on hills outside of the town. The standard argument about Thoreau's withdrawals is that he wasted his talents and political ambitions by not acting on a more public stage, by not leading mainstream reform efforts. This was Emerson's lament at Thoreau's funeral eulogy:

> Had his genius been only contemplative, he had been fitted to his life, but with his energy and practical ability he seemed born for great enterprise and for command; and I so much regret the loss of his rare powers of action, that I cannot help counting it a fault in him that he had no ambition. Wanting this, instead of engineering for all America, he was the captain of a huckleberry party. Pounding beans is good to the end of pounding empires one of these days; but if, at the end of years, it is still only beans!³⁷

Emerson criticizes Thoreau for choosing "only" to be the captain of a huckleberry party and withdrawing into nature instead of engaging in conventional roles of political leadership and undertaking wide scale social change.

How do Thoreau and Adorno respond to these accusations? For both, the need for practices of withdrawal is tied to the alienated landscape of modernity. Both argue that to participate is to legitimate the repressive institutions of the day. Both are concerned that the thinking, critical, negating self can easily be lost in collective efforts. Both skeptically think that reforms are too often undertaken for the self-satisfaction of the activists. But their criticisms prompt them to imagine alternatives: both withdraw from conventional politics to engage in a different form of democratic politics that is not susceptive to—and works against—the problems they identify. For both, thinking against conventions and critical negation are centrally important to a truly democratic political practice. Adorno describes his alternative, "negative dialectics," as a "figuration of praxis which is more closely related to a praxis truly involved in change than in a position of mere obedience for the sake of praxis . . . thinking is actually and above all the force of resistance, alienated from resistance only with great effort" (*Culture Industry*, 202). Thoreau, on the other hand, rejects mainstream politics in favor of "living" and being a "neighbor" instead of an alienated citizen or subject. For Thoreau, living is a term richly associated with experimenting with one's life, with practicing activities such as walking, huckleberrying, and confronting the wild, which teach us to think against conventions, to see particular differences instead of perceiving abstractly and generalizing. Neighboring is also a practice that works against the impairment of the critical self that characterizes mainstream modern life.

But their democratic politics are enacted through necessary acts of withdrawal. For Adorno, to engage with the status quo is to "endorse the world's course." Theory must stand apart from the bustle or else it becomes "a piece of the politics it was supposed to lead out of."[38] He asserts that "For the intellectual, inviolable isolation is now the only way of showing some measure of solidarity. All collaboration, all the human worth of social mixing and participation, merely masks a tactic acceptance of inhumanity" (*Minima Moralia*, 26). Adorno is also critical of mass reform movements and mainstream politics: even if the cause is good, the individual thinker is easily co-opted by movements. "For the individual, life is made easier through capitulation to the collective with which he identifies . . . the ego must abrogate itself, if it is to share in the predestination of the collective. . . . The feeling of security is purchased with the sacrifice of autonomous thinking" (*Culture Industry*, 202). The ability to think is lost to the collective authority.

Thought is sacrificed to praxis and plans for reform too easily become repressive: Adorno notes "how easily the subordination of theory to praxis results in the support of renewed repression" (*Culture Industry*, 200). In a twist on Marx's eleventh thesis on Feuerbach, Adorno says "one clings to action because of the impossibility of action," which often serves to make the actors feel better rather than to effect meaningful change (199). Thinking and engaging in negative dialectics from a position of distance is the best possible defense against an alienating society. It allows us to hold onto images of alternatives: "As long as thinking is not interrupted, it has a firm grasp upon possibility" (202). Thinking itself becomes a kind of praxis because of the way it invokes a need for change and actively works against the instrumentalism and identity thinking that characterizes the "administered world" and "damaged life."[39] And further, "Open thinking points beyond itself. . . . Beyond all specialized and particular content, thinking is actually and above the all the force of resistance, alienated from resistance only with great effort" (202).

On a macro level, Adorno advocates minimal engagement with mainstream society and politics so as to preserve the individual's critical capacities against the force of the collective and to refrain from affirming the problematic status quo that he names "damaged life." But the same concerns also prompt a micro-level distancing from both other people and objects that Adorno describes in *Minima Moralia*. Adorno enacts micro-level acts of distancing that grant "preponderance to the object" and withdraw from the object so as to let it "speak." These acts of distancing are at once protests against "what is," attempts to preserve a space against "fetishized conventions," and efforts to avoid perpetrating an instrumental violence against other objects. In the aphorism titled "*Struwwelpeter*," the name of a fairy tale, Adorno notes that, in a seemingly progressive modern advance, old-fashioned manners, ornamentation, ceremony, and courtesy have been replaced by relations governed by immediacy, familiarity, directness, and transparency. And yet, paradoxically, for Adorno, this immediacy only intensifies the experience of alienation and "estrangement shows itself precisely in the elimination of distance between people":

> Every sheath interposed between men in their transactions is felt as a disturbance to the functioning of the apparatus, in which they are not only objectively incorporated but with which they proudly identify themselves. That, instead of raising their hats, they greet each other with hallos of familiar indifference, that, instead of letters, they send each other inter-office communications without address or signature, are random symptoms of a sickness of contact. *Estrangement shows itself precisely in the elimination of distance between people.* For only as long as they abstain from importuning one another with giving and taking, discussion and implementation, control and function, is there space enough between them for the delicate connecting filigree of external forms in which alone the internal can crystallize. (*Minima Moralia*, 41; italics mine)

Now people relate to each other more transparently and matter of factly and give "the other the facts full in the face." But this seemingly democratic forthrightness masks something more ominous. When people relate to each other matter-of-factly, it is partly because they assume the like-mindedness of the other. An assumption of sameness undergirds the seeming advances that Adorno describes: people can speak to others directly and without hesitations because they know that their ideas, themselves conventional, will be received without contest. The a priori power of the collective makes it possible to speak without hesitancies, concerns, or courtesies that exist when we assume that the other people might think differently from us and when we want to express respect for the other's differences. As Adorno writes, "The direct statement without divagations, hesitations or reflections, that gives the other the facts full in the face, already has the form and timbre of the command issued under Fascism by the dumb to the silent" (*Minima Moralia*, 42).

Spurred by instrumental urges and encouraged by the lack of differentiation between one and another, people treat other people as things. The words Adorno chooses to describe human relations evoke execution, implementation, order, and control. People function as if part of an apparatus, as parts of a system. We approach each other as objects available for our use. But this allows no space for that "delicate connecting filigree of external forms in which alone the internal can crystallize." The dialectical interactions that form the self, mediations between people and between the inner and the outer, have been replaced with immediacy.

Only when we grant space for the strangeness of the other can we treat him as a human instead of an object. Closeness and intimacy only deny the existence of damaged life. Immediacy assumes that the conventions of the exterior are written directly onto the interior in a way that denies a difference between these two spheres:

> Only by the recognition of distance in our neighbor is strangeness alleviated: accepted into consciousness. The presumption of undiminished nearness present from the first, however, the flat denial of strangeness, does the other supreme wrong, virtually negates him as a particular human being and therefore the humanity in him, "counts him in," incorporates him in the inventory of property. (*Minima Moralia*, 182)

In holding on to distance and a sense of strangeness, distancing our self from our "neighbor," we bear witness to the alienated conditions that Adorno calls damaged life instead of pretending with a false closeness that the problem doesn't exist. This distancing, then, is not an ideal but a necessary coping strategy. Maintaining "a distanced nearness" is the only way to contemplate the object without doing violence to it. As Adorno says in "The Robbers," "But in the long, contemplative look that fully discloses people and things, the urge toward the object is always deflected, reflected. Contemplation without violence, the source of all the joy of truth, presupposes that he who contemplates does not absorb the object into himself: a distanced nearness" (*Minima Moralia*, 89).[40]

Here, the distance between self and object is preservative and protective. The object is not absorbed into the self but is contemplated from a distance and indirectly, through deflections and reflections. Paradoxically, this mode of relation and analysis brings the object near in allowing us to better understand its truth. Minor acts of distancing are thus necessary to interact with others in a nondominating and noninstrumental way that allows a degree of unity while still preserving difference and particularity. For Adorno, knowing the object entails a necessary distance to ensure that the "not-I" is not assimilated to the "I." Thinking entails a macro-level isolation from mainstream politics, but (against instrumentalism and against positivism) it must also allow enough distance from the object so as not to violate it, to truly give preponderance to the object and let it speak.

Thoreau's most overtly political text, "Resistance to Civil Government," exemplifies his major themes of withdrawal and separation. He opposes a state that supports slavery, the war against Mexico, and atrocities such as the Fugitive Slave Law. He argues that we are not obligated to obey the unjust laws of an unjust state and are indeed bound to disobey them according to the dictates of our conscience. As Thoreau says in "Slavery in Massachusetts," "My thoughts are murder to the State, and involuntarily go plotting against her" ("Slavery," 108). But Thoreau's murderous thoughts against the state are also rooted in the way it makes men into "machines" and seems to erase their ability for independent, oppositional thought that goes against the grain of everyday conventions and conforming institutions and practices. As he says in "Resistance to Civil Government," "The mass of men serve the state thus, not as men mainly, but as machines, with their bodies. They are the standing army, and the militia, jailors, constables, *posse comitas,* &c. In most cases there is no free exercise whatever of the judgment or of the moral sense; but they put themselves on a level with wood and earth and stones; and wooden men can perhaps be manufactured that will serve the purpose as well" ("Resistance," 67).

Ironically, the rhetoric of the machine, which is damning and derogatory from Thoreau's perspective, is also a metaphor the Federalists draw from to advocate for the proposed new Constitution.[41] The Constitution would allow government to run like a self-correcting machine, fueled by factions, by the inevitable and natural self-interests of men, but churning out the common good. The Federalists use the abstract language of an "expanded," "enlarged" republic, elevated above the dangerous passions of particular interests, running smoothly of its own accord, requiring neither "enlightened statesmen" nor angelic citizens. Indeed, does such a representative government, with regulating mechanisms such as separations of power, checks and balances, bicameralism and federalism need the active engagement of people at all? Does a mechanistic government in fact create a citizenry who simply act as cogs in the machine? Thoreau seems to recognize how a machine-like government can give rise to men who are machine-like in their thinking, unwilling to contest smooth logic and conventional wisdom, unwilling to throw a wrench in the works. This is the danger of a representative government based on majority rule; peoples' voices are too mediated by the majority and by representatives, and they need not think for themselves. For Thoreau, under such a government that commits atrocities of war and slavery and also "manufactures" mechanical men who cannot think against it, the only way to escape complicity is by limiting one's ties to the State, through separation and withdrawal.

Like Adorno, Thoreau thought he would be tainted by associating with mainstream politics and with the government of his day. Thoreau asks "How does it become a man to behave toward this American government today? I answer, that he cannot but with disgrace be associated with it. I cannot for an instant recognize that political organization as *my* government which is the *slave's* government also" ("Resistance," 67). He thinks that the government's tyranny is so great as to justify a withdrawal of allegiance: "I simply wish to refuse allegiance to the State, to withdraw and stand aloof from it effectually" (84). In such a system, we only fool ourselves that mainstream political action has an effect. It is a pseudo-activity for Thoreau, as it is for Adorno. "Even voting for the right is doing nothing for it. It is only expressing to men feebly your desire that it should prevail. A wise man will not leave the right to the mercy of chance, nor wish it to prevail through the power of the majority. There is but little virtue in the action of masses of men" (69). He withdraws from mainstream politics, or as he puts it in "Life without Principle," "what is called politics" because it is "comparatively something so superficial and inhuman."⁴²

Just as mainstream politics is tainted, so are most efforts at reform. In *Walden*, Thoreau is highly critical of those devoted to "Doing-good" because their efforts seem misguided: they seem too eager to redirect attention from their own lives and avoid attending to their own affairs: "I believe that what so saddens the reformer is not his sympathy with his fellows in distress, but, though he be the holiest son of God, is his private ail" (*Walden,* 78). We join reform movements because we wish to lose ourselves in the collective; it is far harder, says Thoreau, to direct these efforts toward ourselves. It is easier to try to reform others than to really "live" ourselves.

Thoreau says, in a statement that seems to justify an apolitical withdrawal, that he has time only to live in this world, not to try to reform it: "As for adopting the ways which the state has provided for remedying the evil, I know not of such ways. They take too much time, and a man's life will be gone. I have other affairs to attend to. I came into this world, not chiefly to make this a good place to live in, but to live in it, be it good or bad" ("Resistance," 74). Here, Thoreau might be seen as egoistically saying that attending to his own self is more important that any political reforms. His criticisms of the State might be interpreted as a rejection of all government as such. Indeed, at the beginning of his essay on civil disobedience, Thoreau appears to denigrate all government: he goes beyond the motto "that government is best which governs least" to say "'That government is best which governs not at all;' and when men are prepared for it, that will be the kind of government which they will have" (63).

But by the end of the essay, Thoreau has not rejected all government *as such*. He seems to want a government that does not govern, that does not mold its citizens into shapes that meet the requirements of the State. Thoreau is hostile toward his own government because it molds men into machines. But Thoreau does not see "what is called politics" as the only possibility: "Can there not be a government in which majorities do not virtually decide right and wrong, but conscience?—in which majorities decide only those questions to which the rule of expediency is applicable? Must the citizen ever for a moment, or in the least degree, resign his conscience to the legislator?" ("Resistance," 65). Thoreau says he wants to progress beyond "democracy such as we know it" toward a form of government that has even greater respect for the individual.

Thoreau's ideal democratic state is one where citizens are not governed as machines, but are treated "with respect as a neighbor" ("Resistance," 89). Thoreau imagines a government not of citizen-machines, but of citizen-neighbors who truly "live." Thoreau says "I am as desirous of being a good neighbor as I am of being a bad subject" (84). Thus he juxtaposes two sets of concepts: on the one hand, he groups "citizens," "machines" and "subjects" and associates these with an alienated loss of self; on the other hand, he links really "living" with "neighbors." But the practices that are necessary to turn us from machine-like citizens to living neighbors can take place only in spaces removed from the town hall and the village square. Those practices of withdrawal such as walking and huckleberrying aim toward creating a new kind of democratic citizen, replacing alienated machines with neighbors who are alive and awake.

For Thoreau, as for Adorno, these acts of withdrawal work on two registers. As we will see, Thoreau's "excursionary" style where he avoids directly addressing his topics and his tendency to use what he calls an "extra-vagant" and exaggerated style of writing to convey a deeper truth, resonate with Adorno's minor acts of distancing where he grants preponderance to the object. But Thoreau also invokes the concept of the "neighbor" to describe a valuable distance from other people in a way that is similar to Adorno's "distanced nearness." Neighbors live next to each other and are connected, while also being separated and withdrawn from each other in valuable ways. Being a good neighbor is about being near without being so close as to interfere with another's critical abilities. This kind of distancing is necessary, given that conventions get in the way of true association. In his journal, Thoreau writes: "In obedience to an instinct of their nature, men have pitched their cabins within speaking distance of one another, and so formed towns and villages, but they have not associated, and society has signified only a *convention* of men." And in another journal entry: "The utmost nearness to which men approach each other amounts barely to a mechanical contact. As when you rub two stones together, though they emit an audible sound, yet they do not actually touch each other." Thoreau distances himself to avoid becoming part of a convention of machines. The forces of alienation at work in modern society require that we take these precautionary measures. These quotations are from Thoreau's journal, but he calls them "Scraps from a lecture on 'Society' written March 14, 1838. Delivered before our Lyceum, April 11th."[43]

Given these two levels of withdrawal, it is not surprising that those who seek to defend Thoreau and Adorno often feel compelled to show how they actually were politically engaged, how they were not as withdrawn as it might seem at first glance. But this requires stretching Thoreau and Adorno out of shape to fit our conventional notions of democratic politics. Instead, we should recognize the novel politics of withdrawal that comes out of the work of these thinkers. Thoreau and Adorno are both most politically engaged, paradoxically, in their moments of withdrawal. Their reconceptualizations of democracy are enacted and articulated in these acts of withdrawal.

Alternative Democratic Political Practices

Both Thoreau and Adorno propose practices that are directed toward individuals, that encourage us to pay critical attention to difference and particularity over and against abstract and conventional ways of thinking, that teach us to negate, and that are predicated on a certain amount of withdrawal and distance from mainstream society and politics. Adorno's practice of negative dialectics illuminates the theoretical significance and democratic value of Thoreau's practices of walking, huckleberrying, and confronting the wild. Adorno show us that a confrontation with the "nonidentical"—something that cannot be domesticated, categorized, or contained—can stimulate critical capacities in ways that work against the alienating loss of critical capacities. Confronting the wild, for Thoreau, yields the same critical fruit as Adorno's practice of negative dialectics.

Negative dialectics, for Adorno, is a practice of withdrawal that illuminates the nonidentical qualities of gift giving, manners, tact, small talk, running in the streets after buses, psychotherapy, neuroses, lying, positivism, and children's fairy tales, to name just a few targets of Adorno's microscopic gaze. In the aphorisms of *Minima Moralia*, Adorno grants preponderance to these objects to

highlight the damaged life of modern society. He ruptures the abstract monotony and smooth logic of a modern society under the sway of an idealist dialectic that violently reconciles and synthesizes everything unique and different.
For Adorno, the supposed harmony of society under the logic of identity and
abstract exchange is an illusion. Negative dialectics engages particular objects
to force recognition of, and widen, these cracks in the system.

Thoreau's practices of withdrawal take him outside the main streets of
town. While walking, he looks closely at wild apples and huckleberries: these
particular things prompt him to question the practices of domestication, cultivation, taming, abstract exchange, and conventional notions of politics that
characterize a modern society where men act as machines. Thoreau directs his
gaze toward the seemingly insignificant objects that "philosophically-schooled
authors" would disregard (to borrow Adorno's phrase). But for Thoreau, these
little things contain qualities that stimulate critical negation. While confronting
the wild, he thinks dissonant thoughts about Main Street and all it represents:
for example, conventional practices of buying a house, etiquette, abstract exchange, labor, furniture, and railroads. These practices of withdrawal are political for Thoreau because they recuperate the critical capacities that define what
he sees as the truly democratic citizen.

Thoreau and Adorno also *focus* their eyes in strikingly similar ways as they
undertake these critiques: how they think is deeply connected with how they
see, with their visual practices.[44] Their gazes move in a similar pattern: they look
at particular things, seemingly insignificant things, as a pathway to making
broader criticisms of more general trends in society at large. For both, little
things encapsulate something of the universal, but also contain a critique of it.
Thoreau and Adorno see particular things as containing alternative possibilities that go against the grain of convention, that hold the potential to inspire
criticism of what is and the status quo. In contrast to the abstracting idealist
gaze, both employ a microscopic gaze.[45]

Adorno can help us see the political value of Thoreau's practices of withdrawal in ways that are occluded when we read him through the lens of Emersonian Transcendental idealism. Thoreau and Adorno root their social critique
in the particular objects of the world that Emerson's abstracting gaze does not
linger on long enough. Thoreau makes broader critiques of society by looking
at those little things, at wild apples or at the tiny huckleberry; he finds rupturing
wild qualities in these little things that call into question the seemingly smooth
workings of a rapidly modernizing society. As he shows especially in the aphorisms of *Minima Moralia*, Adorno also thinks particular objects contain dissonant
nonidentical qualities that can be drawn out to highlight the illusory harmonies

of modernity. Adorno's aphorisms enact the practice of negative dialectics: he focuses his eye on seemingly insignificant things (the taboo on "talking shop," hobbies, ideals of beauty) and shows how they, like monads, contain an image of the contradictions and antagonisms of modern society. In this way, Thoreau and Adorno draw their critical practices from particular objects. Emerson also sees particular things (prisons, labor, hard-eyed husbands, and moaning women) as potentially rupturing, but rather than drawing out the dissonance they contain, he abstracts away from them and moves toward universals, horizons, and landscapes that allow him to maintain a greater sense of harmony. Thoreau and Adorno withdraw from mainstream modern society and conventional ways of thinking to engage the critical capacities that are threatened by alienating experiences of modernity by paying attention to particular objects, while Emerson employs what I call a practice of *focal distancing* that sees past these objects, toward universals (see chapter 2 in this book). Ultimately, Emerson's visual withdrawal seems to make him more sympathetic to certain modern trends that Thoreau and Adorno criticize.

Paradoxically, the critical practices performed in these spaces of withdrawal are undertaken in the name of democracy. For Adorno, the practice of critique is central to the possibility of true democracy. He writes, "Critique is essential to all democracy. Not only does democracy require the freedom to criticize and need critical impulses. Democracy is nothing less than defined by critique."[46] Yet this more true form of self-government cannot exist without a critical self: when people act like machines, democracy ceases to be practiced on an everyday level. And with such a loss come the potential dangers posed by an alienated citizenry, from Thoreau's experience of legalized slavery to the election of Hitler and popular support for the Nazi Party in Adorno's time. Without the capacity for critique, democracy becomes a meaningless name, an empty form: it is a mere categorical term that we might use to describe a government where citizens vote, but it has been drained of its true, robust, practical meaning.

Like Adorno, Thoreau is also centrally concerned with improving our practice of democracy. For Thoreau, democracy "such as we know it" and "what is called politics" are the politics of the machine, where men follow formulaic conventions without critical thought, without judgment, without acting as though they have a self. Thoreau pushes us to more truly adhere to the democratic imperative to self-govern, by engaging in practices to recuperate our critical capacities. But as we have seen, the conventions of modern society work against our ability to think independently, making it easier to say yes to the force of the collective and go along with the crowd than to throw a wrench in the machinery.

Consequently, for Thoreau and Adorno, practices of distancing and withdrawal are required to engage in the critique that defines a true democratic politics.

Working against Alienation: Enacting Theory through Style

Thoreau and Adorno both also work against modern alienation not just in what they *do,* but in what they say as well. As writers, both men make complex connections between content and style, between argument and form, between what they say and how they say it. Both were highly self-conscious prose stylists: one cannot fully understand either thinker's ideas without paying attention to their style of communication. They also use similar rhetorical and stylistic devices, often to similar ends. On the broadest level, Thoreau and Adorno write in ways that force us to engage their texts actively: neither spells out their theoretical ideas through logical argument or express themselves in reasonable, clear, simple, straightforward prose. Since both are concerned with alienation, with the loss of the self manifested as a lost ability to negate, to be critical, to think for ourselves, their style itself forces us to pay attention to each sentence, to be active instead of passive readers, and thus to be active thinkers as well. Since Thoreau and Adorno think we become trapped in conventional ways of thinking, their style of writing must evade or subvert what Thoreau calls the "common sense." They both use words as political weapons to work against an alienated modern sensibility.

One of the most striking sympathies between these two thinkers occurs at the level of individual sentences. Thoreau and Adorno both employ dialectical sentence constructions, which often take a chiastic form. A chiasmus is a grammatical construction that employs an inverted parallelism, where the second part of a grammatical construction is balanced by the first part, only in reverse order. For example, to note one famous chiasmus, "Ask not what your country can do for you, ask what you can do for your country." Thoreau and Adorno both frequently write inverted dialectical sentences that turn back on themselves and are chiastic in nature.

This rhetorical device abounds in Thoreau's work. The following chiastic constructions appear in *Walden*: "And when the farmer has got his house, he may not be the richer but the poorer for it, and it be the house that has got him" (*Walden*, 33); "We do not ride on the railroad; it rides upon us" (92); "I am wont to think that men are not so much the keepers of herds as herds are the keepers of men" (56). In "Resistance to Civil Government," the following chiasms appear: "That government is best which governs not at all" ("Resistance," 63); "Under a government which imprisons any unjustly, the true place for a just man is also a prison" (76). Elsewhere, he writes: "There is more religion in men's science, than there is science in their religion."[47] In "Slavery in Massachusetts," "The law will never make men free; it is men who have got to make the law free" ("Slavery," 98).

We see similar constructions in Adorno's writings, especially in *Minima Moralia*. E. F. N. Jephcott, the translator, tries to represent this chiastic style in the English, but it often comes across even more strongly in the German.[48] Adorno writes, "Today we should have to add: it is part of morality not to be at home in one's home" (39) ["Dem müßte man heute hinzufügen: es gehört zur Moral, nicht bei sich selber zu Hause zu sein" (43)]; "Wrong life cannot be lived rightly" (39) ["Es gibt kein richtiges Leben im falschen" (43). Literally, "There is no right life in false life."]; "The brightest rooms are the secret domain of faeces" (59) ["Wo es am hellsten ist, herrschen insgeheim die Fäkalien" (65)]. Literally, this sentence means, "There where it is brightest, feces secretly rule." Another example of Adorno's chiastic sentence structure states: "It expresses exactly what is, precisely because what is is never quite as thought expresses it" (126); here, "it" refers to thought that maintains a critical distance. ["Er spricht eben dadurch genau das aus was ist, daß es nie ganz so ist, wie er es ausspricht" (144)].[49]

A chiastic structure is reflected not only in individual sentences such as these, but also in entire aphorisms in *Minima Moralia*. Adorno will often describe a tendency that characterizes contemporary "damaged life," but then he will invert the aphorism to show how this tendency need not be, is not inevitable, and was not in existence in the same way in previous generations. Adorno uses paradox and inversion in his aphorisms to avoid reifying damaged life itself. As Gillian Rose notes in *The Melancholy Science*, "The use of chiasmus stresses the transmutation of processes into entities which is a fundamental theme of Adorno's work. He presents this theme in this way to avoid turning processes into entities himself. Sometimes he uses chiasmus directly. . . . At other times it can be seen to inform the whole structure of a piece."[50]

For both Thoreau and Adorno, in these dialectical sentence constructions, things turn into their other, signaling that there is something wrong, some kind of perversion in reality. What we anticipate and expect is inverted: we are owned by the things we are supposed to own, the brightest places are the secret domains of feces. Something is wrong in the world: ostensible movements for "freedom" become repressive, a government supposedly devoted to ensuring freedom produces unthinking machines. But if things are wrong with the world, pointing out that disorder becomes important. Both Thoreau and Adorno employ these chiastic structures to heighten our awareness of damaged life:

chiasms are used here as a way to convey truth while avoiding the pitfall of re-inscribing the problems they identify.

Both Thoreau and Adorno also employ devices that intentionally distance themselves from the object of their analysis. For Adorno, this takes the form of parallaxes or constellations, where he analyzes the object from several different perspectives or presents a set of ideas on a topic from different points of observation. For Adorno, we see things best if we do not look directly at them but instead look above, beyond, and next to them, all the while changing observation points ourselves. The object cannot speak if approached directly; objects do not go neatly into their concepts. Thus in his analyses, Adorno studies the object from different positions and groups these observations together, that we might approximate the object by taking these perspectives together. As Gillian Rose notes, Adorno sought to displace himself as an observer to try to see the object. The essay "proceeds by way of parallaxes which Adorno describes here as 'experimenting': 'For whoever seeks to criticize must necessarily experiment. He must create conditions under which an object becomes visible anew.'"[51]

Thoreau employs a different kind of parallax view. He writes in an "excursionary" style, where he walks around the topic he is writing about instead of addressing it head-on and directly. The essay "Walking" exemplifies this intertwining of form and content. Thoreau writes about freedom by writing about nature, the wild, and the practice of walking. Thoreau walks around his main topic, addressing it by indirection. He explores his topic by experimenting with his own position as a critic, walking to create conditions within himself that will allow him to see his topic in a new and uncommon way.

Thoreau and Adorno also both employ exaggeration, hyperbole, and irony in an effort to get at a deeper truth that undercuts the common sense of words or ideas and surface appearances. Both take words and concepts out of their common usage and employ them in ironic or exaggerated ways, to overcome the ways they have been dulled in everyday exchange. For example, in *Minima Moralia,* Adorno inverts the common meanings of several ideas: "Underlying the prevalent health is death" (*Minima Moralia,* 59); "Life does not live" (19). Health is death? Life does not live? These statements negate the conventional meanings of the ideas of health and life. Adorno presents us with the extreme inversion of the notions of health and life as a way of accessing a deeper truth: "The dialectic advances by way of extremes, driving thoughts with the utmost consequentiality to the point where they turn back on themselves, instead of qualifying them" (86*).* In these extreme inversions, Adorno forces the reader to confront a disjointed social reality. Adorno is widening the gap, sharpening the contradiction, enhancing the disharmony.

Gillian Rose writes, "Adorno thus had to find an alternative way of using concepts, and the relation of a thought or a concept to what it is intended to cover, its object, is problematic. It follows from this that standard modes of communication are also inadequate, since they depend on the ordinary use of concepts. The question of communicating his ideas becomes the question of what the reader should experience when confronting the text, and Adorno insists that expressing the relation of the thought to its object should be prior to any concern with ease of communicating that thought."[52] Adorno writes specifically to unsettle the reader, to force the reader to think against conventional ideas. To do this, he takes words and ideas out of their common circulation. In so doing, he hopes to show how the truth of concepts such as "life" and "health" is not being fulfilled.

Thoreau speaks of his own tendency toward exaggeration and hyperbole as a way of working against conventional truths to approximate something more real and raw.[53] He sees conventional expressions as too dull and common. To unsettle the reader, he exaggerates and uses what he calls "extra-vagant" expressions: "I fear chiefly lest my expression may not be *extra-vagant* enough, may not wander far enough beyond the narrow limits of my daily experience, so as to be adequate to the truth of which I have been convinced. Extravagance! It depends on how you are yarded. . . . I desire to speak somewhere *without* bounds; like a man in a waking moment, to men in their waking moments; for I am convinced that I cannot exaggerate enough even to lay the foundation of a true expression" (*Walden*, 324). As Joseph J. Moldenhauer writes in his essay "The Extra-Vagant Maneuver: Paradox in *Walden*": "Habitually aware of the 'common sense,' the dulled perception that desperate life produces, he [Thoreau] could turn the world of his audience upside down by rhetorical means. . . . With all the features of his characteristic extravagance—hyperbole, wordplay, paradox, mock-heroics, loaded questions, and the ironic manipulation of cliché, proverb and allusion—Thoreau urges new perspectives upon his reader. These rhetorical distortions or dislocations . . . are Thoreau's means of waking his neighbors up. They exasperate, provoke, tease, and cajole; they are the chanticleer's call to intellectual morning."[54]

We see this attempt to take concepts out of their common circulation in Thoreau's famous story of how he lost a hound, bay horse, and a turtledove. In *Walden*, Thoreau says "I long ago lost a hound, a bay horse and a turtle-dove and am still on their trail. Many are the travelers I have spoken to concerning them, describing their tracks and what calls they answered to. I have met one or two who had heard the hound, and the tramp of the horse, and even seen the dove disappear behind a cloud, and they seemed as anxious to recover them as if they had lost them themselves" (*Walden,* 17). This paragraph comes as a non sequitur and seems to have no relationship to the paragraphs coming before or after. But it is especially mystifying because Thoreau never owned any of these animals and consequently, was not in a position to lose them. He is trying to convey some truth about his experience of loss that requires him to exaggerate about having lost these animals. But Thoreau's own explanation of why he chose these metaphors is especially revealing. When an admirer wrote Thoreau a letter to ask what these symbols represented, Thoreau artfully dodges the question. He says "How shall we account for our pursuits if they are original? We get the language with which to describe our various lives out of a common mint. If others have their losses, which they are busy repairing, so I have *mine* & their hound & horse may *perhaps* be the symbols of some use to them. But also I have lost, or am in danger of losing, a far finer and, more ethereal treasure, which commonly no loss of which they are conscious will symbolize—this I answer hastily and with some hesitation, according as I now understand my words."[55]

Language, as Thoreau notes, comes out of a "common mint," but this circulation eviscerates that which is particular and unique. To convey his truth, Thoreau has to invent his own symbols to describe his loss and alienation. And he cannot explain these symbols for us without doing violence to their descriptive power.[56] He must use language to subvert convention. Thoreau has to invent his own inexplicable symbols to describe his loss. What is the "finer and more ethereal treasure" that he is in danger of losing, that no one else can be conscious of? It seems like it may be his own power to express his particularity in words, in powerful language that has not been faded by its use in that common mint. In his *Journal,* we see a similar idea. Thoreau says "There are times when thought elbows her way through the underwood of words to the clear blue beyond . . . but let her don her cumbersome working-day garment and each sparkling dew-drop will seem 'a slough of despond.'"[57] The "working day" or everyday meanings of words cannot fully capture the thoughts Thoreau wants to express. He must use language in unconventional ways to elbow his way though common sense meanings. Thoreau's style is part and parcel of his project to awaken us from our alienated sensibility.

While it is generally recognized that Adorno self-consciously uses his prose style as a tool to work against the logic of identity, the politics behind Thoreau's style has historically been misunderstood.[58] Many scholars have seen Thoreau's paradoxical and contradictory style as a reflection of a troubled mind, or at the very least, as an expression of his ornery contrariness.[59] Later generations of scholars have, instead, delighted in Thoreau's complex style as an example of his "literariness" without associating his writing with any particular political project. Walter Benn Michaels's essay "*Walden*'s False Bottoms" (see chapter 5 in this book) is an exception in that he shows how Thoreau's style enacts a principle of uncertainty that tries to unsettle stable foundations. But whereas Adorno himself wrote extensively on the connections between his style and his politics, Thoreau is silent on this topic. But Adorno can help us understand the way Thoreau's use of paradox, contradiction, exaggeration, and other devices link to his project of working against an alienated sensibility. Their styles attempt to penetrate the tendency for our thinking to be dominated by common sense, for Thoreau, or the logic of identity, for Adorno.

The Organization of the Book

This book is divided into two parts. Part 1 contains a chapter on Adorno and a chapter on Emerson, both of which lay the groundwork for the focus on Thoreau that comprises part 2. The first chapter in part 1 analyzes Adorno's critique of idealism and the way negative dialectics works against modern experiences of alienation. But the chapter is primarily devoted to reading the aphorisms of *Minima Moralia* as engagements of the particular object that enact the practice of negative dialectics in democratically valuable ways. I select aphorisms that explore certain themes, which recur in my readings of Thoreau.

The next chapter explores Emerson's thoughts on the experience of alienation that conditions our existence and the visual practices he enacts to try to work against it. Without losing sight of Emerson's influence on Thoreau, this chapter primarily works as a corrective against the tendency to read Thoreau through the lens of Emersonian Transcendentalism. Because of their very different attitudes toward modernity and toward alienation, reading Thoreau primarily through Emerson's eyes can be misleading: their eyes see in very different ways, with different implications for their politics.

Part 2 contains three chapters on Thoreau. The first chapter shows how Thoreau's thought responds to the intensity of nascent modernization in the Northeast generally and in Concord specifically. We see how Thoreau's dark and frustrated depictions of the experience of alienation and the loss of critical capacities in modern society share important features with Adorno's thought. Chapter 4 theorizes Thoreau's practices of withdrawal as his attempt to articulate a politics that will work against the loss of critical capacities, which he associates with modernization and which leads to the creation of citizens who are really unthinking machines. Adorno's practice of negative dialectics gives us a richer understanding of the theoretical and political importance of Thoreau's excursions.

This part's final chapter shows how Thoreau associates the concept of "home" with an uncritical complacency, a sense of comfort, familiarity, and thoughtlessness that can be dangerous for democracy. Thoreau travels away from this ideological space of home and cultivates a border life that he sees as democratically valuable, even though his "homelessness" places him in spaces of withdrawal that are removed from the conventional places of politics.

The concluding chapter considers how these two iconoclastic thinkers expand our understanding of what kinds of practices can be valuable in a democracy, giving us a language to speak of the democratic value of withdrawal itself. Thoreau and Adorno caution us against uncritically accepting the participatory imperatives of contemporary democratic theory and deliberative democracy in particular. In addition, these thinkers can help revitalize the study of alienation: I offer some reasons to explain the crowding out of social theories of alienation and explain how Thoreau's and Adorno's unique approaches to this problem may help overcome the limitations of previous approaches in ways that can stimulate a method of social theorizing that seems to have recently fallen out of favor in recent decades.

❖

PART I

Two Interlocutors
for Thoreau:
Adorno and Emerson

❖

1

Damaged Life, the Microscopic Gaze, and Adorno's Practice of Negative Dialectics

So, not only is negative dialectic not totalizing, an attempt to arrive at absolute knowing or the absolute idea, and not only is dialectic negative because it is moved by the negative experiences of pain and suffering, and not only is dialectic negative because it lives through a continual awareness of contradiction, but dialectic is negative because its condition of possibility is the negative or wrong state of things.

J. M. Bernstein

In *Negative Dialectics,* Adorno tells us to let our thought yield to the object, to focus our attention on the object, not on its category.[1] If we would focus on particular objects and try to hear their dissonant speech, they would help us develop a critique of the illusory harmonies of the logics of modern capitalist society. If we could see in this way, new critical possibilities would open up and "the very objects would start talking under the lingering eye."[2] This is the practice Adorno enacts as "negative dialectics." In *Minima Moralia,* Adorno trains his gaze on these objects, looking closely at technology, at the designs of our homes, at how people tell lies, how they chase after buses, at manners and notions of tact, small talk, sleepless nights, gift giving, customer service, love, marriage, or divorce. Paying attention to these particular things, he highlights aspects that refuse to be synthesized, unified, or reconciled, illuminating what he calls the "nonidentical." Adorno dialectically engages these particular things in ways that avoid both projecting the self onto them or approaching them as facts, as given or self-explanatory: the thinker actively and creatively, but noninstrumentally and without anxiety, engages the object to draw out an image of its rupturing, critical, contradictory potential. Approached in this way, the nonidentical qualities of particular things allow us to see how the identifying and abstracting logics of modernity mask violence, damage life, and turn us into unthinking, conforming, alienated, machinelike creatures.

For Adorno, we can truly engage in the practice of negative dialectics only when we pay attention to particular objects and listen to their discordant speech. This form of critical thinking is potentially a shared human form of praxis, though by no means easily accessible or immediately available to all. But, since the qualities that can stimulate this kind of thinking are contained within the antagonistic features of objects, it exists at least as a universal *possibility* for those who can learn to see, listen to, and engage particular objects. Given this potential praxis, under the unthinking, mechanical conditions of "damaged life," we are not only alienated from the objects of the world but also from a collective human endeavor. In addition to deadening experience, this alienated sensibility also has dire consequences for politics: Adorno associates the abandonment to a collective authority with fascism, whereas the possibility for democracy exists in the practice of thinking against, in negative dialectics.

Modern society, however, has developed powerful obstacles that work against these critical practices, blinding us to all that is unharmonious, rupturing, and negative. For Adorno, the idealist dialectic and the logic of abstract exchange represent conventional ways of thinking that work to maintain harmony, stability, and the status quo. When we conform to these dominant ways of thinking, we tend to see in abstract and identifying ways and let the authority of the collective rule. This life that "does not live," as Adorno says, describing the personal, psychological, and social effects of modernity characterized by the urge to identify, to classify and categorize that which is other, particular, unique, different, and nonidentical. For Adorno, this damaged life or "vanished life" is alienated life: a dull, lifeless, monotonous, and formulaic mode of experience. As J. M. Bernstein notes in the quotation that introduces this chapter, Adorno's thought is moved by the experiences of pain and suffering that accompany the violence of the logic of identity. Adorno makes us first feel this loss and then, through the aphorisms of *Minima Moralia*, models how to work against it. But the specific conditions of modernity necessitate that we engage in negative dialectics through practices of withdrawal and distancing from mainstream society. Paradoxically, to engage in the (potentially collective) praxis of thinking, we must withdraw from mainstream society.

This chapter begins building the scaffolding for my readings of Thoreau. Here, my analysis of Adorno is not exhaustive but focuses most deeply on the areas of his thought that will help illuminate Thoreau's work. Later chapters pick up on these same themes as they appear in Thoreau's writings. Toward this end, I discuss Adorno's critique of the logic of identity and idealism. His criticisms of the harmonizing tendencies of abstraction and identification become important for understanding the political stakes of the differences between Emerson and Thoreau (discussed more in the next chapter). Adorno's practice of negative dialectics will help us better understand the theoretical and political significance of Thoreau's seemingly insignificant excursions into nature (explored in chapters 4 and 5). Adorno's critique of the increasingly mechanized view of subjectivity that characterizes modernity parallels Thoreau's depiction of the modern citizen as a machine (discussed in chapter 3). Looking at specific practices of withdrawal in Adorno's thought, especially in *Minima Moralia,* we will later be able to see (in chapter 4) how Thoreau finds it necessary to engage in a similar kind of distancing for similar reasons. Analyzing Adorno's thoughts on the dangers of being comfortably "at home" and the value he found, paradoxically, in his forced exile and displacement helps us understand the theoretical importance of the value Thoreau places on "traveling" and "homelessness" (themes I explore in chapter 5.) Finally, Adorno's lecture "The Meaning of Working Through the Past" serves to illustrate how the problem of alienation affects the possibility of democracy, a central concern throughout my discussion of Thoreau's writings. The themes that I explore with respect to Adorno all have bearing on, and reappear in different ways in, Thoreau's work. By highlighting these sympathies between Thoreau and Adorno, I hope we can see Thoreau in a new way, to better understand the theoretical underpinnings and implications of his thought.

The Idealist Gaze and Adorno's Practice of Negative Dialectics

Adorno's thought works against systems, against logics that seek to resolve all contradictions and reconcile all differences. On a theoretical level, his arguments are directed toward the idealist dialectic. For Adorno, "The name of dialectics says no more, to begin with, than that objects do not go into their concepts without leaving a remainder" (*Negative Dialectics,* 5). But under an identifying dialectic, this remainder (the nonidentical) is lost and its unique qualities are violated in the rush toward reconciliation. Hegel's idealist dialectic is a primary target for Adorno: he critiques Hegel's notion of an absolute subject, but his primary problem is that this dialectic represents "a totality to which nothing remains extraneous" (24). Every difference, every particularity is violated by being immediately designated as something problematically divergent that must be absorbed into an all-consuming system that demands totality.

In everyday modern capitalist society, the logics of identity and abstract exchange are the most pervasive representations of the idealist dialectic. Under capitalism, one thing can be replaced for another different and unique thing as long as they have equivalent monetary value. The logic of abstract exchange does violence to specific objects in the interest of promoting fungibility between disparate things, reducing everything to its monetary value: everything is then interchangeable in these terms. Adorno states that "The barter principle, the reduction of human labor to the abstract universal concept of average working hours, is fundamentally akin to the principle of identification. Barter is the social model of the principle, and without the principle there would be no barter; it is through barter that nonidentical individuals and performances become commensurable and identical. The spread of the principle imposes on the whole world an obligation to become identical, to become total. . . . From olden times, the main characteristic of the exchange of equivalents has been that unequal things would be exchanged in its name" (*Negative Dialectics*, 146).[3] The exchange principle also turns subjects into objects, transforming the subject's labor into a calculation of hourly wages. The principle of identity is conservative: it smoothes over the chasms between disparate things that characterize capitalist society. This way of thinking would have us believe that the subject's labor and the wage he is paid truly are fungible and equivalent things, giving the appearance that the whole system is stable, unified, and harmonious.

For Adorno, the logic of identity reflects a rage against what is different, other, and seems irreconcilable: the "not I." In a section titled "Idealism as Rage," he likens the urge to identify to the rage the predator must feel to dare to attack his prey in the interest of self-preservation:

> The system in which the sovereign mind imagined itself transfigured, has its primal history in the pre-mental, the animal life of the species. Predators get hungry, but pouncing on their prey is difficult and often dangerous; additional impulses may be needed for the beast to dare it. These impulses and the unpleasantness of hunger fuse into rage at the victim, a rage whose expression in turn serves the end of frightening and paralyzing the victim. . . . The animal to be devoured must be evil. . . . Idealism . . . gives unconscious sway to the ideology that the not-I, *l'autrui*, and finally all that reminds us of nature is inferior, so the unity of the self-preserving thought may devour it without misgivings. . . .

The system is the belly turned mind, and rage is the mark of each and every idealism. (*Negative Dialectics*, 22)

Even in this intentionally hyperbolic and evocative example, the logic behind the exchange principle and the identity principle resonates: the object is treated instrumentally and only as a means to an end. Identity, here represented as idealist dialectics, does violence to the object.

But there is hope, because the harmony and reconciliation that the system strives for is illusory and ultimately impossible to maintain. Concepts can never fully cover their objects: "Experience forbids the resolution in the consciousness of whatever appears contradictory. For instance, a contradiction like the one between the definition which an individual knows as his own and his 'role,' the definition forced upon him by society when he would make his living—such a contradiction cannot be brought under any unity without manipulation, without the insertion of some wretched cover concepts that will make the crucial differences vanish" (*Negative Dialectics*, 152). It is in the interest of power to try to smooth over any potential conflict between the individual's own life ambitions and society's need to manipulate individuals into certain modes of living, but this effort is not completely successful. The deceptions necessary to try to overcome these contradictions leave scars. These nonidentical remainders are what idealism "rages" at, but they also open up the possibility for Adorno's practice of negative dialectics.

Something inevitably "slips past the unifying net" and "contradictions testify to antagonisms in reality."[4] Objective reality highlights the inevitability of the nonidentical: in other words, "Non-reconciliatory thinking was compelled by objective conditions."[5] Adorno's negative dialectics is an "anti-system" that shines light on what has hitherto been neglected by traditional philosophy and idealist dialectics, dismissed by Hegel and Plato alike as "transitory and insignificant"—the nonidentical and the particular—that eludes general concepts and cannot be subsumed (*Negative Dialectics*, 8). Negative dialectics describes a continual process of upsetting "what is," highlighting its contingency and instability: "Adorno himself names his critique one of 'dissonance.' It is the dissonance between thought and actuality, concept and object, identity and nonidentity, that must be revealed. The task of the critic is to illuminate those cracks in the totality, those fissures in the social net, those moments of disharmony and discrepancy, through which the untruth of the whole is revealed and glimmers of another life become visible."[6] We can, however, get to this critical point only by paying attention to the difference, particularity, and uniqueness of objects.

To prioritize the object would be to avoid instrumentally seeing the "not-I" only in terms of the needs of the "I." Adorno speaks of the need to "disenchant" and "demythologize" the notion of an absolute, supreme, unifying, reconciling subject. This is part of his critique of Hegel. Adorno prioritizes the object, not to leave the subject out of the equation entirely, but to limit its status as absolute, primary, and unconditioned. Adorno wants to be able to understand not only how the subject is mediated by the object but also how the object is mediated by the subject. To achieve both aims we must first grant "preponderance to the object" to dispel the subject's claim to supremacy. The primacy of the object also means that the subject is object—"everything that is in the subject can be attributed to the object."[7] This is how something like the feeling of alienation can have objective roots: "The general assurance that innervations, insights, cognitions are 'only subjective' no longer helps as soon as subjectivity is seen though as a form of object" ("On Subject and Object," 251). Thus, thinking is a capacity that stems from the particular and nonidentical qualities of objects themselves. The mistake that idealism makes is in positing the transcendental subject as absolute, in not recognizing the ways it is shaped by the objects of the world.[8]

To work against these instrumental, identifying, abstracting, and alienating modern ways of thinking, Adorno tries to see with a "microscopic gaze," a visual practice deeply influenced by Walter Benjamin.[9] Adorno is interested in the very kinds of particular phenomena that Hegel dismissed as "foul existence."[10] Adorno sees the particular as a monad that contains an image of the whole, yet cannot be subsumed by the whole: herein lies its potential to yield a critique of bourgeois society.[11] Particular objects contain a truth about the illusions of modern society that could be released through the interpretation of the thinker. But the particular also contains "truth" in a second sense: in their resistance to the whole, in their nonidentity, in their contradictions, particular things testify to an alternative possibility to the bourgeois "false" life. There is "a utopian dimension" to the particular—as Susan Buck-Morss notes, "The transitoriness of particulars was the promise of a different future, while their small size, their elusiveness to categorization implied a defiance of the very social structure they expressed."[12]

Negative dialectics is a practice of thinking that contains the possibility of change, but Adorno's thought is not revolutionary in the sense that change comes from new beginnings. Hope for change exists, modestly, found through excavating the nonidentical qualities of particular objects, through a recuperation of the possibility that exists within and alongside the elements of bourgeois society that Adorno criticizes. These possibilities exist in the form of contradictions that may be opened more widely to critique the illusory harmonies of conventions, to work against the false manipulations of the identity principle, to disrupt the logic that upholds "what is" as inevitable. But, in many of the aphorisms of *Minima Moralia*, Adorno also travels back in time to the previous generation, to find moments of possibility, of "vanished life," that existed but were unfilled. He is not indulging in nostalgic reminiscences about the "good old days" by any means: instead, he is mining the past to look for alternative possibilities that existed even within the generation that gave rise to Fascism, to illuminate the nonidentical moments that show how another path might have been taken. "That would not be much," writes J. M. Bernstein, "but pointing to a possible exit when one thought there was none is something."[13]

Adorno's practice of negative dialectics sometimes takes this form of excavation in the realm of memory, as he sifts through the detritus of the past to salvage moments that point toward an alternative future. A similar dialectical pattern characterizes many of the aphorisms in *Minima Moralia*. In "Promise me this, my child," Adorno writes that there was even something valuable (since lost) in the act of lying. Lying, for Adorno, is not "immoral" because it offends "sacrosanct truth" because if "the whole is the false," then what is the point of preserving minor truths? As he says, "It ill befits universal untruth to insist on a particular truth, while immediately converting it into its opposite" (*Minima Moralia*, 30). Lying is valuable because it highlights an uncomfortable contradiction: "A man who lies is ashamed, for each lie teaches him the degradation of a world which, forcing him to lie in order to live, promptly sings the praises of loyalty and truthfulness" (30). But for Adorno, the lie contained a moment of possibility because of the very fact that it made us face up to a disjunction between the realities of everyday existence and our society's abstract values of truthfulness. Today, in contrast with the previous "liberal era," lying has ceased to become uncomfortable, shameful: today, "the lie has long since lost its honest function of misrepresenting reality" (30). People do not value truthfulness and loyalty: "Nobody believes anybody, everyone is in the know" (30). Lies are no longer told to shield other people's feelings. We tell lies to other people who know we are lying to show them we do not need them nor do we care about their opinion. The lie used to be a way of trying to protect people. But "The lie, once a liberal means of communication, has today become one of the techniques of insolence enabling each individual to spread around him the glacial atmosphere in whose shelter he can survive" (30).

In another aphorism, "More Haste, Less Speed," Adorno contrasts the present, where men run in the streets, chasing after buses, with the previous era of the stroll, the promenade, the bourgeois form of walking. As Adorno says,

"Running in the streets conveys an impression of terror. The victim's fall is already mimed in this attempt to escape it. The position of the head, trying to hold itself up, is that of a drowned man, and the straining face grimaces as if under torture" (*Minima Moralia*, 162). Adorno associates this terror with a "truth" that "something is amiss with security." Running in the streets is an expression of the underlying panic and terror that people enact with their bodily motions but do not consciously realize. In the previous bourgeois era, walking was itself problematic for Adorno: walking, strolling, promenading was "the bourgeois form of locomotion: physical demythologization, free of the spell of hieratic pacing, roofless wandering, breathless flight" (162).[14] To stroll in this manner was to give the illusion that one had all the time in the world, was at home in world, in control of the world, master of the domain. Adorno is critical of this element of the past era, but he finds one positive possibility among the rubbish: "Human dignity insisted on the right to walk, a rhythm not extorted from the body by command or terror" (162).

In these examples, Adorno enacts the practice of negative dialectics to shine a spotlight on the nonidentical moments that highlight the contingency of the status quo of "damaged life" and evokes the possibility of change. As Tom Huhn writes, "Thought and other dead things might be taken to be object lessons for life because they exhibit the stasis wherein life, for whatever reason, neglected to continue, except in a damaged and damaging fashion. And this means that life might be something more than whatever it is that blossomed and withered in the coming to be of other objects, including especially that premier object, the subject."[15] Appreciating the recuperative nature of Adorno's practice of critique will help us better understand how Thoreau also tries to recover possibilities for change in natural spaces that have been deeply scarred by the instrumental tendencies of modernization. Adorno's practice of negative dialectics finds possibility even in damaged life, while Thoreau's political practices take place in burned-over hillsides, in woods where trees have been cut down, in swamps that have been drained for timber. Thoreau, like Adorno, focuses on seemingly insignificant things to disrupt the abstract logics of modernity. While walking and in his writings on "Wild Apples" and "Huckleberries," Thoreau employs a microscopic gaze that is similar to Adorno's, drawing out the wild qualities of little things like huckleberries or wild apples to make broader critiques of the domesticating and taming tendencies of modern society. In his nature writings, through engaging particular things, Thoreau enacts a dissonant critique of modern society. But while Adorno's ways of working against modern alienation are largely cognitive, taking place through mental activities, through thinking, Thoreau's critical practices of recuperation take place in space and through corporeal activities. Adorno travels to places in his memory, to times past, to the previous bourgeois generation, to excavate the unfulfilled possibilities that could highlight a path out of damaged life. Thoreau's recoveries, however, occur in specific physical locations: in the huckleberry fields, in the woods, in the swamps. These differences in part reflect their different life contexts, their different experiences of alienation in modernity.

"Damaged Life": Adorno on Alienation

Adorno's theory of modern alienation comes through his depiction of "damaged life." His critique of the logics of identity and idealism are not purely philosophical discussions: we also feel the costs of these ways of thinking in our everyday lives. The logic of identity deadens experience in imposing sameness on the world.[16] As Adorno writes, "Unquestionably, one who submits to the dialectical discipline has to pay dearly in the qualitative variety of experience. Still, in the administered world the impoverishment of experience by dialectics, which outrages healthy opinion, proves appropriate to the abstract monotony of that world. Its agony is the world's agony raised to a concept" (*Negative Dialectics*, 6).[17] Adorno prefaces *Minima Moralia: Reflections from Damaged Life* with the quotation "Life does not live."[18] He tells us that we need to withdraw and detach from modern society if we are to try to live at all, yet this is not an act of "superior choice" but an undesirable coping strategy, forced on us by capitalist society, that is never assured of success anyway: "While he gropingly forms his own life in the frail image of a true existence, he should never forget its frailty, nor how little the image is a substitute for true life" (*Minima Moralia*, 26). Adorno laments "the subjugation of life to the process of production" (27). In the fragmentary aphorisms of *Minima Moralia*, Adorno shows how "our perspective of life has passed into an ideology which conceals the fact that there is life no longer" (15). This alienated state is the felt experience of "damaged life" under the identifying logic of idealism. But, as we saw in several examples above, at the same time that Adorno gives us "reflections from damaged life," he is also working against it, drawing out the nonidentical in the practice of negative dialectics.

In an aphorism on tact, Adorno helps us see how the logic of identity is not only expressed through the idealist dialectic but also characterizes modern "systematized society." Applied to individuals, this logic forces humans into mechanical conformity with conventions and fits behavior into social norms and categories. Society is organized in ways that leave no room for the impulsive, the extraneous. Individual behavior is coerced into forms that elide the possibility for negation or for going against convention. As Adorno says, manners and notions of tact and etiquette were created to protect against deviant, awkward, or rude behavior, to normalize individual behavior, to smooth out the rough edges of personalities. This was bad enough, but then the situation got even worse. Today, individual behavior is organized by social conventions that have lost their original meanings; people abide by prescriptions of tact today unthinkingly and out of rote habit. We simply go through the motions. As Adorno notes, "The precondition of tact is convention no longer intact yet still present. Now fallen into irreparable ruin, it lives on only in the parody of forms, an arbitrarily devised or recollected etiquette for the ignorant, of the kind preached by unsolicited advisers in newspapers, while the basic agreement that carried those conventions in their human hour has given way to the blind conformity of car-owners and radio-listeners" (*Minima Moralia*, 36).

The blindly tactful life is the life that does not live, for Adorno. The evisceration of the individual's capacity to escape conventional formulas makes experience dull and monotonous. Life exists in nonidentity; in actions that elude expected patterns of behavior and reflect something unique to the individual. He longs for these authentic expressions of "vanished life," yet there are increasingly few expressions of it: "Scarcely ever does an unhappily furrowed brow, bearing witness to terrible and long-forgotten exertions, or a moment of pathic stupidity disrupting smooth logic, or an awkward gesture, embarrassingly preserve a trace of vanished life" (*Minima Moralia*, 59). Enacting negative dialectics, Adorno focuses on the nonidentical qualities of the seemingly insignificant precepts of tact.

Alienation for Adorno is also reflected in the seeming health of conventional behavior and conventional ways of life. Those who are most alienated are the apparently "healthy" people who are ultimately more repressed and better at masking their loss: "the regular guy, the popular girl have to repress not only their desires and insights but even symptoms that in bourgeois times resulted from repression" (*Minima Moralia*, 58). But again, this seemingly harmonious picture of prevalent health contains rupturing contradictions that Adorno draws out: "exuberant health is always, as such, sickness also. Its antidote is a sickness aware of what it is, a 'curbing of life itself'" (77). He focuses on the "sickness of the healthy"; he thinks we should study "the inferno in which were forged the deformations that later emerge to daylight as cheerfulness, openness, sociability, successful adaptation to the inevitable, an equable, practical frame of mind" (59).

In these examples, "damaged life" is represented through an image of man as a machine, made up of smoothly working parts that move without the jarring interruption of thought. In different ways, both Thoreau and Adorno draw upon the machine as a metaphor for the alienated modern man. Thoreau sees modern citizens as cogs in a machine, as "wooden men" manufactured by the State. Adorno describes the conventional, well-mannered, tactful individual (the "regular guy" and the "popular girl") in mechanistic terms. But Adorno also shows how our very understanding of the construction of the subject is modeled on the machine and a mode of production organized around the division of labor. Biology, psychology, and anthropology increasingly portray the individual as an apparatus composed of different parts, different instincts, psychological mechanisms, biological impulses, and inherited traits and characteristics. From the ground up, the modern individual itself acts and is imagined, is treated, like a kind of machine comprised of standardized parts.

Psychology, and psychoanalysis in particular, dissect humans into separate faculties, mechanisms, and instincts in a way that is "inseparable from the interest in deploying them and manipulating them to greater advantage" (*Minima Moralia*, 63–64).[19] The ego takes on the role of "business manager," deploying certain traits and characteristics at will to fit different social situations (230). Thus the individual's traits, characteristics, mechanisms, and instincts are confronted as external objects to be manipulated. But the management of the self is not left up to the individual; rather, it is controlled by the collective authority of society. This division of labor within the self establishes "the person as a measuring instrument deployed and calibrated by a central authority" (231). There is no mediation between the individual and collective authority: collective authority determines the deployment of these traits, mechanisms, and impulses. Individual behavior is programmed and "mechanical": "quick reactions," "push-button behavior patterns," and "prompt, unresistant reflexes" characterize behavior.

Psychoanalysis was supposed to work against alienation by making us more self-aware and critical, by highlighting the repressive nature of social norms. But psychoanalysis has also become geared toward helping individuals to adapt, to fit in, without questioning the status quo, thus intensifying this mechanistic quality of modern man. Psychoanalysis, "the last grandly conceived theorem of bourgeois self-criticism," has become "a means of making bourgeois self-alienation absolute" (*Minima Moralia*, 65). Adorno writes that analysis instills in people an "empty, mechanized quality," a "pattern of reflex-dominated, follow-my-leader behavior" that is "to be entered to the account not only of their illness but also of their cure" (61). This modern subject-as-machine reflects Adorno's notion of alienation as an unthinking state where we do not negate: convention and collective authority act as the operators pushing the buttons, and we respond immediately. Although his notion of it is less holistic (reflecting the less complete state of modernization in the nineteenth century), Thoreau's practices are directed toward disrupting a similar kind of mechanized subject.

Mechanization, normality, and exuberant health are symptoms of an alienation that is not even sensed, while angst and psychic suffering become valuable for Adorno in that they at least indicate some shadow part of the self that is conscious of and struggling against its own liquidation. Sickness, neuroses, and psychic uneasiness represent the nonidentical, for Adorno. These submerged particularities are more generally silenced and masked in the interest of maintaining the harmonious picture of health, but when we focus on these minor phenomena, they testify to the truth of society and illuminate "wrong life." But unless we let "thought yield to the object," we cannot draw out its nonidentity. And we cannot truly think unless we can linger with particularity in this way. If we stay on the level of conventions and categories and focus on harmonious reconciliations and synthesis, we do not engage in the practice of thinking, but sanction the status quo and accept what we are told is self-evident. The culture of modernity has "broken thought of the habit to ask what all this may be, and to what end" (*Negative Dialectics*, 85). Mainstream society has enfeebled the "genuinely critical need" to resist "what is"; instead of questioning the status quo, we yield to the "cultural bustle" (85). In contrast, to truly think is to negate: "The effort implied in the concept of thought itself, as the counterpart of passive contemplation, is negative already—a revolt against being importuned to bow to every immediate thing" (19). This loss of the ability to think captures the alienated sensibility, for Adorno. The ego is liquidated so that it has no interior.[20] The authority of the collective extends into the self. We cannot see alternatives to conventions and are lulled into acquiesce by the illusory harmonies of things that appear to be inevitable. We do not see the particular object or listen to its dissonant speech, but close our eyes and stop our ears.

In such a situation, the alienated can barely even register their loss. Angst and suffering at least indicate some level of rage against what is, a consciousness that all is not right. But this is more and more rare. For Thoreau, on the other hand, alienation is still primarily registered as a sense of loss, as "discontent," as "incessant anxiety." He speaks to "the mass of men" who "lead lives of quiet desperation" (*Walden*, 8). But at least there *is* a felt desperation. Thoreau's practices (walking, huckleberrying, confronting the wild), like Adorno's practice of negative dialectics, are directed toward increasing our awareness of our alienation. But in late modern society, we are scarcely even aware of our discontent: Adorno gives us images, not of desperate individuals but of healthy, normal, tactful, conventional, well-mannered, if wholly mechanical, individuals.

Adorno and the Dangers of "Home"

Because the spatial location of Concord was such a significant influence on Thoreau's thought, it seems important to spend a moment thinking about the very different biographical features of Adorno's life, especially as we turn to the concept of home. Adorno, as a German Jew who was exiled during the Nazi era, was without a permanent home and country for nearly twenty years. He emigrated to England in 1934, to New York in 1938, then California in 1941. He was only able to permanently return to his hometown of Frankfurt in 1953. Displaced in this way, Adorno works against damaged life through a kind of remembrance of things past that nevertheless avoids any nostalgia for the prior era, itself flawed. *Minima Moralia* contains aphorisms that both chart the experience of exile and enact Adorno's own practices of working against the loss of both self and home. Stefan Müller-Doohm writes in his book *Adorno: A Biography*, "Taken together, the texts of *Minima Moralia* express the melancholy and despair that their author attributed to his own experience of homelessness. It was not for nothing that he took as his motto for Part I of the volume a sentence from the novel *Der Amerika—Müde* (*Tired of America*) by the Austrian writer Ferdinand Kürnberger: 'Life does not live.'"[21] Here I study Adorno's relentless cautioning against the dangerous ways of thinking that we may fall into when we ensconce ourselves in domesticity, when we come to feel "at home." Adorno identifies a valuable critical distance in the experience of exile, just as Thoreau seeks to think like the "traveler" and the "walker" and explores different experiments in self-imposed homelessness, all while never leaving Concord, Massachusetts.

In one aphorism in *Minima Moralia*, Adorno gives advice to the writer on his craft. His helpful hints are practical on one level (don't be afraid to delete, avoid cliché), but each editorial guideline also encapsulates an element of Adorno's larger philosophy. For example, he says "one should never begrudge deletions" because "Nothing should be thought worthy to exist simply because it exists, has been written down" (*Minima Moralia*, 85). Adorno is telling us that the present conditions are neither inevitable nor natural, but contingent—there are alternatives to "what is." Later, when Adorno says to "avoid cliché," he also means we should avoid "drab common sense" in our thinking as well. Adorno also cautions against excessive restraint, limitation, and reserve in our writing: too much prudence is "an agent of social control" that we acquiesce to out of "stupefication." These modest ways of writing cannot express the dialectic: "Rather, the dialectic advances by way of extremes, driving thoughts with the utmost consequentiality to the point where they turn back on themselves, instead of qualifying them" (86). Adorno's practice of negative dialectics also grants preponderance to the object, not by addressing the object head on but by arranging thoughts around the object in constellations. Adorno says that thought "proves its relation to the object as soon as other objects crystallize around it. In the light that it casts on its chosen substance, others begin to glow" (87).

Adorno tells writers that their words should reflect their philosophy "in every text, every piece, every paragraph"; the writer should "check whether the central motif stands out clearly enough" (*Minima Moralia*, 85). If "properly written," texts "are like spiders' webs: tight, concentric, transparent, well-spun and firm" (87). But then Adorno seems to shift gears and tells us that "In his text, the writer sets up house" (87). Suddenly, we seem no longer to be talking about writing but about exile. Adorno says "For a man who no longer has a homeland, writing becomes a place to live." To add another layer to the puzzle, the aphorism is titled *Hinter den Spiegel*. This phrase alludes to a German idiom with several meanings, all of which Adorno seems to draw upon. The full idiomatic expression would be *sich etwas hinter den Spiegel stecken*.[22] Literally translated, it means to put something (for oneself) behind the mirror. But the idiom's real meaning is figurative: it means to set something aside to look at it, to take note of it daily, as a reminder, like a keepsake. For example, one might slide an invitation, photograph, or a calling card—something meaningful and close to one's heart—behind a mirror hanging on the wall, so that it is both partially hidden while also in sight as a remembrance. Indeed, the title is translated as "Memento" in the English version. Mementos or keepsakes are things from the past that we bring into the present. Adorno is also likely alluding to Lewis Carroll's story of Alice in Wonderland, *Through the Looking-Glass,* or *Durch den Spiegel* in German.[23] In *Minima Moralia*, Adorno frequently alludes to children's fairy-tales; he uses them as another way of drawing out the possibilities of the past (here, childhood) for the present.

But then, just as we have become happier, more comfortable, envisioning Adorno the exile in the new home created by his writing, surrounded by keepsakes and mementos, he pulls the rug out from under us. The aphorism ends with a thought that turns back on itself: "In the end, the writer is not even allowed to live in his writing" (*Minima Moralia*, 87). Here, the second valence of that German idiom becomes clear; this expression also means more generally to have something impressed upon you, especially something that makes you uncomfortable or is unwelcome and embarrassing (*Unangenehmes*). Adorno ends the aphorism by implying that even in the home we create in our writing, we can experience a dangerous level of comfortable complacency. Here "home" is associated with "a slackening of intellectual tension," with "drifting along idly," with a "warm atmosphere" (87). It is a danger to be either too comfortable in our self-created home or too self-pitying about the lack of a home. This is why Adorno concludes by emphasizing the critical value of homelessness itself. Homelessness demands "that one harden oneself against self-pity" and maintain "the utmost alertness," but ultimately the uncomfortable position of homelessness seems to yield the possibility of an important critical distance (87).

As we might expect, Adorno takes his own advice and uses this piece, ostensibly on writing, to say something about the larger central motif of his philosophy. This aphorism, in miniature, enacts Adorno's practice of negative dialectics. On the broadest level Adorno's text forces the reader to engage the text, to put the puzzle pieces together, to think about the connections between seemingly disparate pieces, to figure out how the parts work as a whole. The text compels the reader to be an active instead of a passive reader, to think for one's self. The logic is not spelled out for us; we must follow the hints Adorno gives us. Adorno compels the reader to resist easy explanations and critically confront the text.

Within the aphorism, we have a constellation composed of thoughts on writing, on exile and homelessness, and on memory and bringing the past into the present. The practice of negative dialectics, as Adorno models it, is about thinking against conventional "drab common sense," granting preponderance to the object through thinking in constellations, calling into question "what is," and occupying an uncomfortable, negative position instead of a harmonious affirmative reconciliation. Negative dialectics is not about regaining a comfortable home but instead about the difficult practice of maintaining a critical distance from comfortable and familiar places. As an emigrant in exile, Adorno's practices of working against alienation are necessarily carried out in the realm of time and memory, and on the page instead of more topographical locations.

Adorno did not choose his status as an exile, but he did find something valuable within this situation. Stefan Müller-Doohm observes that, "As someone who had been marginalized, Adorno made the acquaintance of the intermediary position of those social critics who both live in society and are yet not quite of it. This state of uncertainty between inside and outside was the ideal observation post from his point of view."[24] Adorno in fact *intensifies* the experience of exile by refusing to soften the blow. In the aphorism called "Refuge for the Homeless" (*Asyl für Obdachlose*), Adorno states "The best mode of conduct, in face of all this [enforced migration] still seems an uncommitted, suspended one: to lead a private life, as far as the social order and one's own needs will tolerate nothing else, but not to attach weight to it as to something still socially substantial and individually appropriate. 'It is even part of my good fortune not to be a house-owner,' Nietzsche already wrote in *The Gay Science.* Today we should have to add: it is part of morality not to be at home in one's home" (*Minima Moralia,* 39).

Adorno discusses the dangers of comfortable familiarity and the value of the uncanny further in his posthumously compiled book of lectures titled *Kant's Critique of Pure Reason.* The uncanny comes up as part of his lecture on Kant's two worlds—the noumenal realm (the realm of the things-in-themselves), and the phenomenal realm (the only world we can really know, given the way the categories of time, space, and causality condition our experience). Adorno argues that Kant's "duplication of the world" expresses a paradox whereby "familiarity with our own world is purchased at the price of metaphysical despair."[25] Adorno means that bourgeois perception *makes the world familiar* by creating the world in its own image and forming the world from the categories of the mind. To establish security, stability, and certainty, to feel at-home, we "strip the world of its uncanny aspect" and make the world our "property," our "product" (*Kant's Critique,* 110). But the more we project ourselves onto the world in search for certainty, stability, and a feeling of at-homeness, the more alienated we are from the other, from objects, from the world itself.[26] Or as Max Horkheimer and Adorno say in their *Dialectic of Enlightenment*: "men pay for the increase of their power with alienation from that over which they exercise their power."[27] The more we identify, the more we are alienated.

But even as we *try* to establish certainty and stability by making the world in our own image, we can never fully vanquish the specter of moments of anxiety and dislocation represented by the uncanny and the nonidentical. Even Kant, who for Adorno represents the exemplar of bourgeois thinkers, is ultimately uprooted by the nonidentical. Kant's philosophy is an identity philosophy because of the way it unifies everything as a system rooted in the subject's categories of experience: Kant "attempts to ground being in the subject" (*Kant's Critique,* 66). But despite his desire for "system, unity, reason," even Kant could not ignore the fact of the nonidentical: Adorno argues that Kant's own contradictions indicate the inevitability of a nonidentical that is "more than just mind or reason" (67).[28] Our feelings of uneasiness are themselves the flashes of nonidentity that call the unity of the whole system into question. There is *not* harmony in the whole, in unity and in reason. We can sustain this illusion only through instrumental rationality, by building the world in our own image. This is how we stave off feelings of the uncanny and makes ourselves feel "at home." But if these motivations for security and certainty result in alienation and reification, it becomes clear why a feeling of the uncanny has such positive value for Adorno. Uncertainty, instability, and a sense of dislocation indicate that all is indeed not right with the world. When we recognize the way we have built the world in our own image through instrumental rationality, we feel ill at ease; yet, for Adorno, this discomfort is productive.

The image of home is perhaps most starkly at work in Adorno's reading of Kierkegaard. Adorno creates an image of the bourgeois *intérieur* of the nineteenth-century flat to capture and illuminate the "unintended truth" of Kierkegaard's despair and melancholy, to highlight the historically situated roots of his supposedly existential situation. Adorno shows that the *intérieur* is "polemically the equivalent of Kierkegaard's 'subjective thinker.'"[29] Kierkegaard's withdrawal into the bourgeois flat captures the objectless inwardness of his existential thought, the receding into subjectivity, into the spiritual *intérieur* of the self.[30] Adorno's book on Kierkegaard was his first published work, so it predates his more mature philosophy.[31] Nevertheless, his image of the bourgeois flat engages in a nascent practice of negative dialectics. Here, Adorno uses seemingly insignificant details and passing references in Kierkegaard's work to construct an image of life that is concrete, historical, and works against abstract concepts. He pays attention to small things like furniture and the design of the flat itself, minor details that (as Adorno notes) "philosophically-schooled authors have not yet given any attention to" (*Kierkegaard*, 41). Adorno, like Thoreau, trains his microscopic gaze on little things, particularity, to think against abstractions: "It is the bourgeois *intérieur* of the nineteenth century, before which all talk of subject, object, indifferentiation, and situation pales to an abstract metaphor" (41). Adorno illuminates how the material evidence in Kierkegaard's own writings has a nonidentical quality that contradicts his existentialism and shows the historical basis for his thought.

For Adorno, Kierkegaard's very "objectlessness," the way he "omits the world," testifies to a retreat from a historically specific experience of reification and alienation: "Fleeing precisely from reification, he withdraws into 'inwardness'" (*Kierkegaard*, 50). But because the nineteenth-century flat is more obviously a historical phenomenon, it allows us to see how history is also implicated in Kierkegaard's melancholy, despairing inwardness. The place of Kierkegaard's thought, the site of his existential despair is a historically specific type of dwelling, the home of the petit-bourgeois *rentier* dependent on "borrowed capital, not required to sell his labor power" (48). Kierkegaard's thinker is the man of independent means, who is distanced from the means of production. He is "isolated," "the private person, solitary, inactive, and separated from the economic process of production (42). He is surrounded by furnishings that bear the marks of a reified capitalist mode of production: the tables and chairs confront him as alien beings that he tries to make less strange by arranging and rearranging, to "draw meaning out of them" (44). Domesticity and being what we might today call "house-proud" becomes a way to fight against a melancholy that we do not recognize as a historical experience of alienation.

Just as Adorno thinks Kierkegaard tries to create a world inside the mind as an (unrecognized) response to modern capitalism, so he also tries to create a world inside the house. In one fascinating passage, Adorno draws from an instance in Kierkegaard's early writings where he describes adventures with his father, where they went walking and exploring—all without ever leaving the house. They created a world inside the house in their "promenades in the parlor." Kierkegaard describes the adventures of Johannes Climacus, his pseudonymous self. Here, Adorno describes Kierkegaard's adventures:

> When Johannes on occasion asked for permission to go out, he was most often denied; as an alternative, the father occasionally offered his hand for a walk up and down the hall. At first this was a meager ersatz, and yet . . . something totally out of the ordinary was hidden in it. The suggestion would be accepted, and it would be left entirely up to Johannes where they would go. Then they went out the front door to a nearby garden or house, or to the beach, just as Johannes desired; for the father was capable of everything. And now they went up and down the hall, the father pointed out everything they saw; they greeted others passing by, cars noisily crossed their way, drowning out the father's voice; the cakes in the bakery window were more inviting than ever. (*Kierkegaard*, 41)

Because of the state of affairs that Adorno will later characterize as damaged life, Johannes cannot have anything but reified relations with the objects of the world. The actual world outside may be random, mean, and meaningless; an intimacy with objects has been lost and we approach them as alien things, so inside we try to recapture what has been lost in the gardens, beaches, and bakeries outside. Johannes's adventures in the house signal a "mourning" for and an attempt to re-create in an inward space, the lost immediacy of this world. "Home" is figured as a space of retreat from the alienation and reification of the process of abstract exchange.

Adorno's image finds sympathy with the critiques of traditional homes (and the kinds of thinking that these spaces engender) that we will see in Thoreau's writings. Thoreau will describe houses filled with comfortable luxurious things, which are really dead things that burden us and prevent us from truly living. Thoreau associates thinking "inside," in houses, with the domestication, taming, and instrumentalization of particular objects. (Instead, he favors the ways of thinking associated with those who travel away from home with the traveler, the walker, and the huckleberryer). But what is wrong with thinking "at home"?

Both Thoreau and Adorno seem to identify a dangerous quality in the idea of a space where we try to insulate ourselves from the problems of modernity. In his aphorism "Memento," Adorno describes the feeling of being at home, of being ensconced in a warm atmosphere of domesticity, as something to be avoided at all costs. In such a space, we try to insulate ourselves from the painful world, and our thoughts become complacent or complementary to the instrumental and violent tendencies of modern society, instead of relentlessly trying to disrupt these patterns. Similarly, Thoreau associates the traditional idea of "home" with a movement away from jarring and disruptive confrontations with the wild particular objects of the world.

This kind of retreat is dangerous because such engagements with particularity are critically valuable. Walking, like negative dialectics, works against becoming settled in a home space that allows us to relax from working against alienation, that is a space removed both from the wild and the nonidentical. For Thoreau and Adorno, we recuperate critical capacities by engaging particular objects in the outside world, thus they both are more wary of the recesses of the bourgeois *intérieur* or the act of building a home in our minds. When we are at home in this way, we think abstractly and may violate objects by acting masterfully and instrumentally. Like negative dialectics, Thoreau's practices of withdrawal (traveling, walking, huckleberrying) relentlessly confront particular objects to work against these relaxed, familiar, comfortable, domestic ways of thinking.

Adorno's discussions of home also help mark another distinction between Thoreau and Emerson. Emerson also abstracts away from particular objects of the world while drawing on images of home. He exhorts us to "build, therefore, your own world" in our mind, implying this can be a house protected from the "disagreeable" objects of the external world that he finds disruptive and unharmonious.[32] Emerson is far more chastened, less optimistic, and more sensitive to the costs of this kind of inward creation by the time he writes "Experience." But still, there remains in his thought a flight away from particular objects: he seeks a space that is removed from the objects of the world that disrupt his efforts to find harmony. Thoreau and Adorno also withdraw from modern society but never to retreat from particular objects: both explicitly refuse any place that seems like a comfortable space away from the particular objects that highlight our alienation, where we might tend to forget our deadened condition of damaged life.

Alienation, Critique, and Democracy

It nearly goes without saying that the image of alienation we have seen so far has dire consequences for politics. Adorno sees negative dialectics as an important political practice, but in several essays he ties the problems of alienation and the practice of negative dialectics more directly to the possibility of democracy. In his valuable book *Adorno and the Political*, Espen Hammer undertakes an extensive analysis of the political dimensions of Adorno's work. Hammer shows how theory itself became praxis for Adorno and characterizes critique as a "placeholder politics," given the problems associated with conventional political action. But Hammer does not make the stronger case that I will advance here, to show how Adorno reconfigures and redefines democratic politics itself in terms of the practice of negative dialectics. Ultimately, Adorno does not see critique as only a "placeholder" for politics but as the essence and foundation of democratic politics as such.[33]

In the autumn of 1959, Adorno delivered a lecture at a conference of the Council for Christian-Jewish Cooperation devoted to "The Meaning of Working Through the Past."[34] In the lecture, published as an essay of the same name and later presented as a radio address, Adorno's intended audience seems to be the German public, not necessarily theorists or intellectuals. He is clearly aiming to speak more accessibly than is usual in his writing. The first published version of the essay even included a formal discussion between Adorno and students, who had pressed him to clarify parts of his lecture even more explicitly.[35]

The topic of "The Meaning of Working Through the Past" is Germany's fascist past: Adorno describes the ways of thinking that characterized the Nazi era, shows how they have continued to characterize the post-Nazi era despite the advent of German parliamentary democracy, and discusses what might be done to create a more truly democratic Germany.[36] Adorno argues that for Nazism to be truly consigned to the past, people must become subjects capable of thinking for themselves, instead of authoritarian subjects with weak egos who seek the safety of the collective. There are changes in the objective economic order that must be made if such subjects are to be created: a democracy based on self-determination cannot exist in an economic structure that makes people feel powerless and dependent. But Adorno spends most of his time discussing the conformist ways of thinking that characterized life under the authoritarian regime and shows how they persist under German parliamentary democracy. His major point is that a democracy is not created only by instituting a new form of political rule. For a state to be truly democratic, it must have politically mature, autonomous, thinking citizens. It must have subjects whose sense of self is strong enough for them to speak against the existent conditions, for them to think against the collective. Without such constituents, a state is a democracy in name only. Adorno implies that Germany, with alienated subjects who possess only weak critical capacities, is still strongly in the shadow of Nazism.

Many of the theoretical elements discussed in this chapter have applied to a specific historical context. For Adorno, the Nazi era exemplified, in horrific form, the problematic tendencies of modernity more generally. His theory developed and was shaped by the experience of fascism under the National Socialist regime. In "The Meaning of Working Through the Past," then, Adorno comes full circle, to discuss how Germany can resign Nazism to the past. Adorno discusses the problem of alienation and the political dangers posed by a loss of self. We see the dangers of the collective and the importance of withdrawing and distancing the individual from the collective, especially in a democracy. Adorno highlights the dangers of immersion in an unthinking collective. And we see how alienation fits into the problem. In other words, how a weak capacity for critical thinking motivates this kind of comfortable participation in collective conventions. He describes how alienation is specifically a problem for democracy and also implies (without going into great detail) that people can engage in practices to change their ways of thinking, to become democratic subjects instead of subjects of an authoritarian state. Not surprisingly, the changes Adorno describes reflect the practice of negative dialectics. Democracy depends on the cultivation of a stronger subject, which Adorno implies can be created by employing the thought practices of negative dialectics.

Adorno begins the essay by trying to show how the authoritarian personality, which seeks comfort in collectives, persists even under a democratic political system: "It must be defined in terms of character traits such as a thinking oriented along the dimensions of power and powerlessness, a rigidity and an inability to react, conventionality, the lack of self-reflection, and ultimately an overall inability to experience. Authoritarian personalities identify themselves with real-existing power per se, prior to any particular contents. Basically, they possess weak egos and therefore require the compensation of identifying themselves with, and finding security in, great collectives" ("Working Through the Past," 94). In the years after World War II, the authoritarian personality has manifested itself in the denials, refusals, qualifications, and forgettings of the atrocities of the Nazi era. There exists what Adorno, borrowing Franz Böhm's term, calls "non-public opinion," which attempts to downplay and minimize the German people's complicity in Nazism. There is comfort in going along with this collective delusion: these impulses "are rational in the sense that they rely on societal tendencies and that anyone who so reacts knows he is in accord with the spirit of the times. . . . Whoever doesn't entertain any idle thoughts doesn't throw any wrenches into the machinery" (92).[37] Those with "weakened memories" feel powerful and base their own self-worth on the glory of the Nazi era and are unwilling to detach themselves from this "collective fantasy of power."

To move beyond Nazism, individuals must reject the comforts of this collective delusion and think for themselves, to engage in individual critical self-reflection. But the economic system stands in the way of cultivating strong subjects who are able to assert themselves in this way. Fascism will live on as long as there is an economic order that makes people passive and dependent:

> The economic order, and to a great extent also the economic organization modeled upon it, now as then renders the majority of people dependent upon conditions beyond their control and thus maintains them in a state of political immaturity. If they want to live, then no other avenue remains but to adapt, submit themselves to the given conditions; they must negate precisely that autonomous subjectivity to which the idea of democracy appeals; they can preserve themselves only if they renounce their self. To see through the nexus of deception, they would need to make precisely that painful intellectual effort that the organization of everyday life, and not least of all the culture industry inflated to the point of totality, prevents. The necessity of such adaptation, of identification with the given, the status quo, with power as such, creates the potential for totalitarianism. Because reality does not deliver the autonomy, or ultimately, the potential happiness that the concept of democracy actually promises, people remain indifferent to democracy, if they do not in fact secretly detest it. . . . Those whose real powerlessness shows no sign of ceasing cannot tolerate even the semblance of what would be better; they would prefer to get rid of the obligation of autonomy, which they suspect cannot be a model for their lives, and prefer to throw themselves into the melting pot of the collective ego. ("Working Through the Past," 98–99)

At one point, Adorno says "Using the language of philosophy, one could indeed say that the people's alienation from democracy reflects the self-alienation of society" (93). In the later formal question-and-answer session regarding this essay, Adorno is asked about this comment regarding "the self-alienation of society." He says by this he meant that "because of the preponderance of innumerable societal processes over the particular individuals, people in their societal role are not identical with what they are as immediate, living people. Democracy, according to its very idea, promises people that they themselves would make decisions about their world" ("Discussion to Lecture," 296). But if people are alienated in this way, they cannot be said to be deciding for themselves, speaking for themselves, because they are *not* themselves. Without the possibility of critique, then, there can be no democracy. In an essay titled "Critique," Adorno describes the central role that critique plays in democracy: "Critique is essential to all democracy. Not only does democracy require the freedom to criticize and need critical impulses. Democracy is nothing less than defined by critique." The second "prerequisite of democracy" and of critique is "political maturity," which is "demonstrated in the power to resist established opinions and, one and the same, also to resist existing institutions, to resist everything that is merely posited, that justifies itself with its existence."[38] Adorno says that the politically mature person thinks and speaks for himself; without such maturity, neither critique nor democracy is possible.

But how can this capacity for critique be created? Adorno recognizes that something needs to happen before people are prepared for democracy, something needs to prepare them to think critically. It is not enough to simply tell people they should think for themselves. When asked how this kind of self-examination can succeed if it "already assumes abilities the majority of people doesn't have?" Adorno responds: "This is of course correct. And here you define precisely the problem, that is, it would be wholly wrong if we were to preach self-examination and then expect that because of this sermon people will examine themselves. That is illusory" ("Discussion to Lecture," 300). It is not enough to point out the nature of the problem because people must be given the tools to work against an alienated sensibility. Adorno again answers the earlier question: "What we can do is give people contents, give them categories, give them forms of consciousness, by means of which they can approach self-reflection" (300). We can, in other words, model the practice of negative dialectics.

Adorno describes the critical consciousness that is rooted in the realization that things might be otherwise, that existing conditions are not necessary, that we might think against the status quo. He is concerned with people's willingness to follow the lead of others, to conform to conventional opinion, to bend to the will of seemingly immutable historical forces. But once people realize that "we are not only spectators looking upon this predominance of the institutional and the objective that confronts us" but can also influence the shape of society, they may be less willing to simply unthinkingly bow to the existing conditions ("Discussion to Lecture," 298). And further, "morality has transformed itself nowadays into the resistance against this blind force, against this predominance against the merely existent, under which in fact we all must suffer today" (297). People should not just see themselves as pawns of history, but as subjects. They must, essentially, become subjects. Adorno is describing a process where people reclaim a self, to work against the modern loss of the thinking self. Adorno says that "A working through of the past understood as enlightenment is especially such a turn toward the subject, the reinforcement of a person's self-consciousness and hence also of his self" ("Working Through the Past," 102).

Thus, negative dialectics is a practice of thinking that strengthens the subject's critical consciousness. It highlights the comfortable dangers of conforming to non-public opinion and conventional thought. It is about the exercise of that capacity to think against the existent, to critique. Negative dialectics, as Adorno sees it and practices it, describes a disruptive, rupturing, and unharmonious way of thinking that teaches us to think for ourselves against convention. Indeed, "The Meaning of Working Through the Past" is itself an enactment of this practice: it is jarring, intended to make people uncomfortable and even uses exaggeration as a tool to highlight the holes in the logic that people yearn to ignore. Adorno says "I have exaggerated the somber side, following the maxim that only exaggeration per se today can be the medium of truth. . . . My intention was to delineate a tendency concealed behind the smooth façade of everyday life" ("Working Through the Past," 99). This very kind of "enlightened education" can work to strengthen subjectivity so as to better prepare German citizens for democracy. Adorno advocates "enlightened instruction against the non-public opinion" (100). We can see that Adorno saw himself as participating in this process, but he also says that teachers and psychologists have an important role to play in the collective process of subjective enlightenment that is necessary if Germany is to be more truly democratic.

Adorno's "The Meaning of Working Through the Past" was not a theoretical piece, and this is what makes it illuminating. He shows that negative dialectics is not just a philosophical theory but a practice that can be useful in cultivating citizens who can think for themselves in creating the kinds of citizens a democracy cannot do without. Democracy depends upon changing the way people think, and negative dialectics is a practice that can help make these changes. Adorno's tools often require withdrawal and distancing on the part of the subject, but they also work toward creating subjects who can engage in the critique that defines democracy.

Conclusion

Adorno's diagnosis of the problem of alienation in modern society, his views on the threats it poses to democracy as well as his ways of working against it, all helpfully inform our understanding of Thoreau. Thoreau too will describe an alienated modern landscape that resembles Adorno's depiction, in nascent form. Thoreau will paint an image of a modern man whose actions and thought reflect contemporary modes of production—man comes to resemble a machine, with dire effects for the possibility of a true democracy. This is the state of subjectivity that Thoreau's practices of withdrawal are designed to counteract. Thoreau will withdraw from mainstream society to engage in practices that, like

Adorno's negative dialectics, pay attention to particularity, to what he calls "little things," in ways that work specifically to counteract the alienating effects of modernity. As part of his project to sharpen our critical capacities, Thoreau (like Adorno) will also place value on "traveling" as opposed to feeling comfortably "at home." Thoreau's excursionary practices try to unsettle the familiar, complacent, conventional, and indeed dangerous identity that he links with the concept of home. Like Adorno, Thoreau will see these critical practices as articulating a more truly democratic politics, though they are predicated on a withdrawal and distancing.

The next chapter looks to Emerson as another interlocutor to help us understand Thoreau's theoretical position. Emerson comes from a very different perspective than Adorno. But these two thinkers, taken together, will prepare us to more deeply understand the theoretical and political significance of my readings of Thoreau in part 2.

2

Alienated Existence,
Focal Distancing, and Emerson's
Transcendental Idealism

There comes—, for instance; to see him's rare sport / Tread in Emerson's tracks with legs painfully short; / How he jumps, how he strains, and gets red in the face, / To keep step with the mystagogue's natural pace! / He follows as close as a stick to a rocket, / His fingers exploring the prophet's each pocket. / Fie, for shame, brother bard; with good fruits of your own, / Can't you let neighbor Emerson's orchards alone?

James Russell Lowell

Most Emerson–Thoreau criticism in our time has tended to follow Mark Van Doren in his statements, made in 1916, that "Thoreau is a specific Emerson" and that Thoreau's philosophical position was "almost identical with Emerson's."

Joel Porte

The passages above portray Thoreau as a somewhat annoying younger brother, struggling in vain to keep up with Emerson, fingers probing into the older "mystagogue's" pockets to steal his ideas.[1] Thoreau has often been interpreted as a poor imitation of his older, more worldly Concord neighbor: younger, more outdoorsy, perhaps, but cut from the same basic mold. Thoreau's writings are usually read through the lens of Emersonian Transcendentalism, which reifies his image as a "specific Emerson," while rendering less visible the many tensions between these thinkers. Emerson and Thoreau have different views on the experience of alienation and on modernity, but perhaps most importantly, they *see* the world differently and engage in different visual practices. Emerson's idealist way of seeing might well be called "transcendental," but this movement cannot capture Thoreau's microscopic gaze. Because this chapter emphasizes the contrasts between these two men of Concord, however, I begin by recalling their affinities. After all, in the quotation cited earlier, Adorno called *both* Thoreau and Emerson like-minded critics of "Americanism." Indeed, all three of the thinkers in this study—Adorno, Emerson, and Thoreau—share important common ground.

Like Thoreau and like Adorno, Emerson enacts practices that work against conformity, against people's tendency to depend, unthinkingly, on external authorities. Emerson laments that we do not trust in ourselves. For him, "imitation is suicide."[2] Self-reliance is the life practice he advocates to get us to think against conventional wisdom, as a way of working against our readiness to simply play follow-the-leader instead of leading ourselves. He sees self-reliance as democratically valuable in that it represents a new "constitution," it founds a new state.[3] Stanley Cavell tells us that Emerson's choice of these words, which recur in his writing, is deliberate: he enacts the creation of a more robust individual who can think against convention, and in doing so represents a new model of the democratic citizen; he participates in the creation of a new America. Reading Emerson, Cavell says, "I am already participating in that transformation of myself of which the transformed city, the good city, is the expression."[4] Like negative dialectics, walking, or huckleberrying, self-reliance works to sharpen our critical capacities against an unthinking conformism in democratically valuable ways.

Style also puts theory into practice in deeply important ways for all three of these thinkers. Like Thoreau and Adorno, Emerson employs paradox, contradiction, and exaggeration in his writing style, to unsettle us, to upset conventional ways of thinking. The meaning behind his writing is not immediately obtainable; his style is difficult, textured, layered, and labyrinthine. His prose fights our desire for easy accessibility: he is trying to frustrate our need for familiarity and comfort. His writing is not linear, another commonality with Thoreau and Adorno. Each sentence represents nearly the whole in miniature (itself an enactment of his philosophy). In short, he practices his philosophy through his writing style, which is part and parcel of his content.

Emerson also does not explain or argue. His writing is conscious of the limits of rationalism and eschews traditional forms of logic; he conveys meaning by evoking emotions, appealing to our sensibilities, to our affect. To the extent that Thoreau is shaped by Idealism or Transcendentalism, he seems most influenced by the Romantic tendencies in these theories. Both Emerson and Thoreau reject the cold rationality of the Enlightenment in favor of the imaginative, the emotional, and the inspirational.

To note a final similarity between these two Concordians, Emerson also engages in a kind of withdrawal. He employs a practice of "focal distancing" to better see reality. But the effects of Emerson's way of seeing, perhaps against his intentions, seem to complement rather than negate the conventional ways of thinking in modernity. While Thoreau and Adorno withdraw to see better the truth of particular objects, to grant preponderance to the object, Emerson's focal distancing looks for reality *beyond* the very objects Thoreau and Adorno seem most interested in. Emerson distances himself to get a better sense of the underlying harmony of the universe while Thoreau and Adorno distance themselves to disrupt, toward a critique of apparent equilibrium.

Despite important sympathies and despite the conventional wisdom that Thoreau "is a specific Emerson," scholars today are typically more sensitive to the differences between these two thinkers.[5] In particular, Emerson's belief that reality is fundamentally ideal in nature and that the soul is a microcosm containing the world seems difficult to reconcile with Thoreau's view of humans as shaped (in alienating ways) by the contingent historical features of modern life. In this way, viewing Thoreau solely through the lens of Emersonian transcendentalism can serve to depoliticize his work and cause us to miss his challenges to Emerson's worldview. But even when we recognize that the paths of Thoreau and Emerson diverge, we may not fully reckon the implications of their departures from one another. Bringing Adorno into the picture helps clarify the stakes of these differences, politically and theoretically: the sympathies that exist between Thoreau and the Adorno, and the tensions that exist between Emerson and Adorno, help us weigh and measure these differences to more clearly characterize the relationship between these two famous men of Concord.

Emerson was influenced by Kantian transcendental idealism, and Adorno was deeply critical of this way of thinking. Instead of relying on these labels, however, we can differentiate these thinkers by exploring their visual practices: in contrast to Emerson's idealist gaze, Thoreau and Adorno employ a microscopic gaze. Adorno helps us see how Emerson enacts a modern dilemma in his struggles to hold onto a sense of equilibrium and harmony against the disrupting influence of particular objects that are sometimes natural and sometimes products of modernization. Spiders, hard-eyed husbands, moaning women, politics, prisons, labor: these "disagreeable" objects are all things that Emerson wishes to look beyond, to distance himself from. Unwittingly corroborating Adorno, Emerson seems to find it hard to maintain his theory of compensation and harmony if he looks too closely at these objects. He struggles against a sense of uneasiness unleashed by these things. Yet as he hastens away from disagreeable particularity toward more affirmative universals, he engages in practices that Thoreau and Adorno would see as deepening our experience of alienation.

For Adorno, the more we abstract and identify, the more alienated we are: bourgeois perception makes the world more familiar and more comfortable by projecting the subject's own image onto the world. Emerson echoes this urge when he exhorts us to "build, therefore, your own world" in the mind, whereupon disagreeable appearances will vanish.[6] Thoreau and Adorno both are wary of such movements toward creating harmony and equilibrium. In contrast to Emerson, Thoreau and Adorno work against alienation by trying to exacerbate our sense of uneasiness and dislocation. They want to harness the rupturing quality of things like those hard-eyed husbands, those prisons, and labor toward a critique of society's illusory harmonies. Emerson's writings illustrate some important ways that idealism can, perhaps unwittingly, uphold and work in conjunction with a modern market society based on the logic of abstract exchange rather than providing a way to critique and negate it. Ultimately, Emerson's way of seeing the world around him does not let him make the kinds of critiques of modernity that Thoreau (and Adorno) will make.

Emersonian Transcendental Idealism

Emerson was first exposed to Kant through reading Coleridge. Robert Richardson (a scholar who has written excellent intellectual biographies of both Emerson and Thoreau) notes that Emerson adopted from Coleridge the idea that "the highest, most trustworthy knowledge consists of intuitive graspings, moments of direct perception, free mental acts of cognition and recognition." From Thomas Carlyle's "The State of German Literature," Emerson was introduced to the idealist notion of the essential unity of all things, the underlying identity that exists beneath more superficial differences.[7] Identity was to become a key concept for Emerson, but Richardson argues that these readings in German idealism really came together for Emerson when he read an article by Frederic Hedge, a friend, on Kant, Fichte, and Schelling.[8] Having mastered these idealist philosophers in the original German, Hedge felt that Coleridge's reading of Kant was inadequate. So Hedge explained Kantianism to his largely American audience in a deep and systematic way; thus Emerson came to know his Kant and to identify as a Transcendental Idealist.[9] Indeed, Richardson calls

Emerson's *Nature* the "American version of Kant."[10] Emerson himself says, "It is well known to most of my audience that the Idealism of the present day acquired the name of Transcendental from the use of that term by Immanuel Kant, of Königsberg . . . showing that there was a very important class of ideas or imperative forms, which did not come by experience, but through which experience was acquired; that there were intuitions of the mind itself; and he denominated them *Transcendental* forms."[11]

Emerson's essay "The Transcendentalist" propounds that the idealist believes the external world cannot be relied upon; all that we can be sure of is our own perception of that world: "Mind is the only reality, of which all men and all other natures are better or worse reflectors" ("The Transcendentalist," 203). For Emerson, the external world is unreal and unknowable in comparison to the mind and consciousness. Man is the center of the world and the world exists for us. And he says, evocatively, "I—this thought which is called I,—is the mould into which the world is poured like melted wax" (204). The world is *in us*; we are not in the world. If the world exists within us and for us, it is also ours to shape: "You think me the child of my circumstances: I make my circumstance" (204). This ability to act purposefully and not be shaped by context is what separates the Idealists from the Materialists, according to Emerson. He defines Materialists as those who believe men are molded by "facts," "history," and "the force of circumstance" (201). The Idealist insists instead "on the power of Thought and of Will, on inspiration, on miracle, on individual culture" (201). As Emerson says, "In the order of thought, the materialist takes his departure from the external world, and esteems man as one product of that. The idealist takes his departure from his consciousness, and reckons the world as appearance. The materialist respects sensible masses, Society, Government, social art, and luxury, every establishment, every mass, whether majority of numbers, or extent of space, or amount of objects, every social action" (203).

Society itself does not shape us; rather, the world appears as we see it because of the faculties of the mind itself: "Man and woman and their social life, poverty, labor, sleep, fear, fortune, are known to you. Learn that none of these things is superficial, but that each phenomenon hath its roots in the faculties and affections of the mind" (*Nature*, 44). But Emerson's sense of the unreality of the concrete objects of the world around him is not just an *effect* of his idealism, but is itself a motivation for his theory that the universal mind is the ultimate reality.

"Optical Illusions": Emerson's View of Alienated Existence

For Emerson, existence is a state of being lost in a hazy realm where we cannot see clearly. He continually uses vision as a metaphor: things in the world around us appear illusory, unreal, fleeting, shadowy, and spectral. We feel like visitors from another planet in our own world: "We are as much strangers in nature as we are aliens from God. We do not understand the notes of birds. The fox and the deer run away from us; the bear and the tiger rend us. We do not know the uses of more than a few plants, as corn and the apple, the potato and the vine" (*Nature*, 39). Nature appears inhospitable, incomprehensible, "opaque," and "the world lacks unity and lies broken and in heaps" (43).

Not only are we mired in a shadowy realm of appearances, but we are also lost to ourselves. "What we commonly call man, the eating, drinking, planting, counting man, does not, as we know him, represent himself, but misrepresents himself."[12] In our ordinary human activities and everyday lives, we are not our true selves. Emerson again states "We know better than we do. We do not yet possess ourselves, and we know at the same time that we are much more" ("Oversoul," 165). In "The Poet," Emerson describes a life of dislocation and detachment. Life is a realm of decay and "disagreeable facts."[13] He writes "The fate of the poor shepherd, who, blinded and lost in the snowstorm, perishes in a drift within a few feet of his cottage door, is an emblem of the state of man. On the brink of the waters of life and truth, we are miserably dying" ("The Poet," 19). We seem to be on the threshold of a reality that is unclear to us; this true reality is life but we are surrounded by death, by shifting things that change and are unstable.

In Emerson's famous essay "Experience," we read his most haunting and evocative description of this sense of loss and estrangement. Here Emerson does not express a self-assured optimism in our world-building capacities that we see in earlier writings. This essay was written two years after the death of Emerson's young son, Waldo, and fairly vibrates with grief. Yet grief also prompts Emerson to analyze this experience of living in a world of phenomenal appearances in the most searching and illuminating terms. He begins the essay with a description of our feeling of being in the middle of a journey without a map: "Where do we find ourselves? In a series, of which we do not know the extremes, and believe that it has none. We wake and find ourselves on a stair: there are stairs below us, which we seem to have ascended; there are stairs above us, many a one, which go upward and out of sight."[14] Again, Emerson uses the trope of vision to describe this estranged state: "Sleep lingers all our lifetime about our eyes. . . . All things swim and glimmer. Our life is not so much threatened as our perception" ("Experience," 27). The things we see around us are not real: "There is an optical illusion about every person we meet" (31).

Our vision swims when we look at the world around us, but objects themselves are also illusory and slip away from us when we try to hold onto them. "I take this evanescence and lubricity of all objects, which lets them slip through our fingers then when we clutch hardest, to be the most unhandsome part of our condition" ("Experience," 29).[15] Even sons turn out to be evanescent, like a skin that the snake sheds: "In the death of my son, now more than two years ago, I seem to have lost a beautiful estate,—no more. I cannot get it nearer to me . . . this calamity; it does not touch me: something which I fancied was a part of me, which could not be torn away without tearing me, nor enlarged without enriching me, falls off from me, and leaves no scar. It was caduceus. I grieve that grief can teach me nothing, nor carry me one step into real nature" (29).

Rather shockingly, the loss of his son ultimately seems to only intensify Emerson's experience of the shallow, superficial, phenomenal world around him. Instead of touching the "reality, sharp peaks and edges of truth," he finds only "scene-painting and counterfeit" ("Experience," 29). "The only thing grief has taught me, is to know how shallow it is. That, like all the rest, plays about the surface, and never introduces me into the reality, for contact with which we would even pay the costly price of sons and lovers" (29).[16] Then, "Grief too will make us idealists" (29), for idealism offers solace and is a way of coping with this experience of alienation. But, for Emerson, both the problem and the solution are internal; he continually tells us the problem of our grief and loss and feelings of estrangement are rooted inside us, in problems of vision.

Emerson describes his "uneasiness" at "the thought of our helplessness in the chain of causes" but also recognizes that this comes from a flaw in our perception, and "results from looking too much at one condition of nature, namely, Motion."[17] He describes how we must train the eye to abstract, to identify, and to see nature as a medium that exists for us. Once we learn to see with the correct perspective, we will recognize a level of stability, equilibrium, compensation, harmony, and affirmation in the world around us that we would not previously have thought possible. After all, "The ruin or blank, that we see when we look at nature, is in our own eye. . . . The reason why the world lacks unity, and lies broken and in heaps, is, because man is disunited with himself" (*Nature*, 43). Changing the way we perceive is fundamental to understanding the central role the practice of self-reliance plays in Emerson's thought.

"Focal Distance," Abstraction, and Identity

In "Experience," Emerson asks "Of what use is genius, if the organ is too convex or too concave, and cannot find a focal distance within the actual horizon of human life?" ("Experience," 30). Of what use is genius if it cannot help us overcome the optical illusion that impairs our vision and tricks our perception into thinking that reality is found in the objects around us? For Emerson, genius is about being able to find the proper focal distance at which our eyes adjust, the blurry shadows and illusions pass away, and the true reality comes into focus.[18] Paradoxically, we see things more clearly from a distance: the eye seeks out abstractions, universals, horizons, stars and moons, landscapes, and rooflines. The words *universe* or *universal* appear eleven times in "Experience," while the word *horizon* appears five times. Emerson says "The health of the eye seems to demand a horizon. We are never tired so long as we can see far enough" (*Nature*, 13). But we have to develop and cultivate the correct focal distance; it is not our innate way of viewing the world. We have to train our eyes to focus beyond the ephemeral phenomena of particular things around us, to see truth and reality itself. When we see properly, without illusions, we perceive that reality is composed of Spirit, that everything flows from the Universal Mind, that we ourselves are part of this Universal.

In *Nature,* Emerson famously recounts his own experience of sight, of revelation, where he became "a transparent eye-ball":

> Crossing a bare common, in snow puddles, at twilight, under a clouded sky, without having in my thoughts any occurance of special good fortune, I have enjoyed a perfect exhilaration. . . . In the woods, we return to faith and reason. There I feel that nothing can befal me in life,—no disgrace, no calamity (leaving my eyes,) which nature cannot repair. Standing on the bare ground,—my head bathed by blithe air, and uplifted into infinite space,—all mean egotism vanishes. I become a transparent eye-ball. I am nothing. I see all. The currents of Universal Being circulate through me. . . . In the tranquil landscape and especially in the distant line of the horizon, man beholds somewhat as beautiful as his own nature." (*Nature*, 10)

When we have cultivated this form of vision, we see past all particular things, with their innumerable differences: "Nature is an endless combination and repetition of a very few laws. She hums the old well known airs through innumerable variations."[19] With the proper focal distance, we can see the "guiding identity" that "runs through all the surprises and contrasts" of particular natural objects ("Nature," 106). Particular objects move, change, and are unstable. But, beyond this surface, there is a deeper "Rest or Identity" that exists in the unchanging, eternal, Universal Spirit (112). We are "always engaged with particulars, and often enslaved to them," yet "we bring with us to every experiment the innate universal laws" that "exist in the mind as ideas" (113). Seeing the universal brings us "sanity to expose and cure the insanity of men. Our servitude to particulars betrays us into a hundred foolish expectations" (113). There is something healing and sane about abstractions and something insane, ugly, painful, and frightening about particulars: "Every roof is agreeable to the eye, until it is lifted; then we find tragedy and moaning women, and hard-eyed husbands, and deluges of lethe" ("Experience," 28).

With the proper focal distance, we can perceive an underlying identity in people as well, not just particular objects. The Universal mind is protean and takes different shapes, but because it courses through us all, Jesus, Moses, Socrates, even Prometheus are kindred spirits: "Tantalus is but a name for you and me" ("History," 18). Here Emerson writes that "There is one mind common to all individual men. Every man is an inlet to the same and to all of the same. . . . What Plato has thought, he may think; what a saint has felt, he may feel" (3). Because of this common circulation of the universal mind, we can be self-reliant through self-abandonment. Again, the Emersonian paradox: on the one hand, he speaks of abandonment and emphasizes the importance of letting go of our desires to rationalize, to think, to deliberate, giving ourselves over to more subterranean instincts, intuitions, and emotions. Indeed, Emerson frequently praises children because they are ruled by instincts and not bogged down by rationality: "Their mind being whole, their eye is as yet unconquered, and when we look in their faces, we are disconcerted. Infancy conforms to nobody."[20] He praises whimsy over rational explanation: "I would write on the lintels of the door-post, *Whim*. I hope it is somewhat better than whim at last, but we cannot spend the day in explanation" ("Self-Reliance," 30). He states that every man "knows that to his involuntary perceptions a perfect faith is due . . . the idlest reverie, the faintest native emotion, command my curiosity and respect" (37).

But on the other hand, in contrast to self-abandonment, Emerson also encourages us to exert our force of will, to become self-reliant, to be heroic, to be true individuals. He is concerned with conformity and with people's dependence on external authority; he wants us to think for ourselves, to be great, to be independent, to exert our own will: "Trust thyself: every heart vibrates to that iron string" ("Self-Reliance," 28). He says "Your conformity explains nothing. Act singly, and what you have already done singly, will justify you now. Greatness appeals to the future" (34). In his essay "Heroism," he conjures an image of the fife and calls heroism a "military attitude of the soul": "Its rudest form is the contempt for safety and ease, which makes the attractiveness of war."[21] Heroism is the assertion of the "secret impulse of an individual's character" that "works in contradiction to the voice of mankind, and in contradiction, for a time, to the voice of the great and good" ("Heroism," 149).

Understanding how Emerson can, at once, stress both self-reliance and self-abandonment is an important key to his thought. Though he would not lose sleep over paradox or contradiction ("A foolish consistency is the hobgoblin of little minds") it happens that this particular paradox does have a resolution.[22] When we abandon the self to our *intuitions*, we abandon ourselves to the common mind, the universal soul. When we abandon our *rationality*, we allow the universal to enter into the self. This is why we can trust our intuitions, our emotions, and our instincts. By letting go in this way, we become self-reliant: the individual is not predictable when open to the universal, but nonconforming, unique, and idiosyncratic. Paradoxically, Emerson overcomes the problem of conformity through a belief in a deeper identity, the identity between the self and the universal mind, the idea that the universal works through the self, that the self is identical, in its soul, with the universal. This is the path to greatness, to being a true individual. Heroic "representative men" are those truly great individuals who tap into the universal. "Great men" have always "confided themselves childlike to the genius of their age" ("Self-Reliance," 28). And for Emerson, abandoning the self to the universal is also the only way of confronting what is real, overcoming the sense of being lost among ephemeral appearances.

Ultimately, we cannot practice self-reliance through rationality, deliberation, or explanation. Self-Reliance is a life practice oriented toward attuning us to the pull of universal currents manifested in our intuitions and instincts. "Heroism feels and never reasons, and therefore is always right" ("Heroism," 148). Self-trust and self-reliance are based on giving ourselves over to the "aboriginal Self on which a universal reliance may be grounded": the source of this "genius," "virtue," and "life" is in "Spontaneity or Instinct," also called "Intuition" ("Self-Reliance," 37).

Once again, Emerson finds affirmation and reassurance in this concept of the universal mind. He is ambivalent about whether the universal mind is a stable foundation on which we may "ground" ourselves, as the quotation above implies, or whether the universal itself is constantly in flux, in a progressive process of becoming. This is the more Nietzschean interpretation of Emerson that we see in George Kateb's and Stanley Cavell's readings.[23] But whether we see the universal as a foundation or not, Emerson identifies an affirmative, harmonizing quality in it. He has faith that the universal will pull us in the right direction, if only we abandon ourselves to it. If we abstract and identify in this way, "So shall we come to look at the world with new eyes" and recognize that "Nature is not fixed but fluid. Spirit alters, moulds, makes it. . . . Every spirit builds itself a house; and beyond its house, a world; and beyond its world, a heaven" (*Nature*, 44). Emerson famously wrote "Build, therefore, your own world. As fast as you conform your life to the pure idea in your mind, that will unfold its greatest proportions. A correspondent revolution in things will attend the influx of the spirit. So fast will disagreeable appearances, swine, spiders, snakes, pests, mad-houses, prisons, enemies, vanish; they are temporary and shall be no more seen" (45).

In *Essays: Second Series*, Emerson speaks similar words in a more tired, world-weary, and chastened tone. The bravado of the above quotation has fallen away. In "Experience," Emerson write "I know the world I converse with in the city and in the farms, is not the world I *think*. I observe that difference, and shall observe it" ("Experience," 48). "But," he says, and we hear an unfamiliar note of defeat in his voice, "I have not found that much was gained by manipular attempts to realize the world of thought. Many eager persons successively make an experiment in this way, and make themselves ridiculous" (48). Given the death of his son Waldo, which colors the essay "Experience," he is indeed battle-scarred.[24] He seems to realize that something is lost when we attempt to instrumentally project our own world outward; he questions the violence his idealism might exact on the world of particular objects.[25]

But, after a pause, after some doubts, he pushes on, despite uncertainty, despite the possibility of ridicule: "I say polemically, or in reply to the inquiry, why not realize your world? . . . Patience and patience, we shall win at the last" ("Experience," 48). "Never mind the ridicule," he writes, "never mind the defeat: up again, old heart!—it seems to say,—there is victory yet for all justice; and the true romance which the world exists to realize, will be the transformation of genius into practical power" (49). These are the final words of the essay. In the end, he has not completely abandoned the hope that we can quell our feelings of loss and of being lost by abandoning ourselves to the universal: up again, old heart, patience, patience, we shall win at last. Emerson still believes in the existence of an affirmative, harmonizing universal where objects do not slip away from us: "I am ready to die out of nature, and be born again into this new yet unapproachable America I have found in the West" (41).[26] Thus, "America" becomes a future ideal, a metaphor for the universal. This "region of life," this America is described as the "inland mountains, with the tranquil, eternal meadows at their base, whereon flocks graze, and shepherds pipe and dance," this "sunbright Mecca of the desert." But this ideal is both within our reach and just out of our grasp. "I do not make it; I arrive there, and behold what was there already. I make! Oh, no!" (41). Emerson's wonderful prose enacts his dilemma: he seems certain that this eternal realm exists, but he is far less sure that we can access it, whereas he once seemed to have no doubts that we could "make," that we could build our own world. The "First cause," the "ineffable cause," the universal "Being" now, for Emerson, lies within our sight but we are not assured of reaching it: we think we can make, we think we can make it, but can we?

We could read "Experience" as looking forward to the experience of the universal, the eternal in death, or looking for this experience in a new America that we might still build in our minds, with patience, in the here and now. But either way, Emerson's eye engages in the same movement, the same focal distancing. However we read it, Emerson's America describes a pastoral ideal that echoes the tropes we see throughout his writings. Grief will make us idealists: grief and pain make us dream of a reality that exists up and away: his line of sight continually moves away from particulars, toward rooflines, landscapes, mountains, horizons, and universes.

Cavell's Emerson and the Practice of Emersonian Perfectionism

Stanley Cavell sees Emerson as constantly struggling between two opposing urges, one "handsome," the other "unhandsome." He takes the metaphor of the hand seriously: "unhandsome" moments come when we try to access reality by instrumentally grasping and clutching evanescent objects, while in our more "handsome" moments, we are passive, receptive, abandoned, and let the universal flow through the self.

> See how this works itself out in an astounding, obviously key passage from "Experience": "I take this evanescence and lubricity of all objects, which lets them slip through our fingers then when we clutch hardest, to be the most unhandsome part of our condition." Look first as the connection between the hand in "unhandsome" and the impotently clutching fingers. What is unhandsome is, I think, not that objects for us, to which we seek attachment, are, as it were, in themselves evanescent and lubricious; the unhandsome is rather what happens when we seek to deny the standoffishness of objects by clutching at them, which is to say, when we conceive thinking, say the application of concepts in judgments, as grasping something, say synthesizing."[27]

Cavell links Emerson's statement about handsome and unhandsome conditions to Heidegger's "Thinking is a handicraft" where Heidegger depicts the hand as a uniquely human tool, a unique "grasping organ" different from "paws, claws, fangs:" "Emerson's image of clutching and Heidegger's of grasping, emblematize their interpretation of Western conceptualization as a kind of sublimized violence. . . . The overcoming of this conceptualizing will require the achievement of a form of knowledge both Emerson and Heidegger call reception, alluding to the Kantian idea that knowledge is active, and sensuous reception alone passive or receptive."[28]

For Emerson and for Cavell, this unhandsomeness is part of our human condition. We are constantly struggling against our urges to conceptualize, to synthesize, trying instead to handsomely and passively receive reality as a circulation of Being. We see this instrumental tendency throughout Emerson's writings, though it appears most unequivocally and unapologetically in his early writings. In *Nature*, Emerson describes all the ways that everything outside of our own soul exists to "minister" to us, to "nourish" us. Emerson's feelings of despair, of being incomplete, lost, and alone seem assuaged by realizing man's place at the center of everything, by realizing that everything ministers to man and exists for man. In the section on Discipline, Emerson describes nature as man's tool and instrument: "Nature is thoroughly mediate. It is made to serve. . . . It offers all its kingdoms to man as the raw material which he may mould into what is useful. Man is never weary of working it up. . . . One after another his victorious thought comes up with and reduces all things, until the world becomes at last only a realized will—the double of man" (*Nature*, 25).

But we see how Emerson's thought affirms the instrumental tendencies of a modernizing market society most clearly in the "Commodity" section of *Nature*. Here, Emerson describes all of nature as a potential commodity, lying in wait to be used by man. He defines commodities as all the advantages—natural and man-made—which man finds useful: "Nature, in its ministry to man, is not only the material, but is also the process and the result. All the parts incessantly work into each other's hands for the profit of man" (*Nature*, 11). Nature itself ministers to man, as his potential tool, and man-made tools and "the useful arts" "are but reproductions or new combinations by the wit of man, of the same natural benefactors" (11). Emerson praises the steam engine, the railroad carting merchandise throughout the country, the cities, ships, canals, post offices, and bookshops (11).[29]

But is Emerson saying that our instincts to clutch are unhandsome, as in Cavell's reading, or is he lamenting the slipperiness of objects that prevents us from getting a hold on them? Here, what is unhandsome also seems to be the very fact that objects elude us: the unhandsome quality is in the objects, not in us. Emerson *wants* to clutch the objects but cannot. The ambivalence of this passage is deepened when we recall Emerson's more enthusiastic attitude toward instrumentalism in *Nature*, for example. But we need not resolve the ambivalence that Emerson himself seems to maintain. His prose seems to, perhaps intentionally, support both readings.

When Emerson turns away from the immediacy of "what is," he hopes to be moving toward a more intimate relationship with reality: we cannot create this intimacy by clutching and grasping, but only by abandoning the self to what is next, which is hopefully a recovery and recuperation of intimacy with reality and truth. There are only endless circlings toward the next. We are always trying to come in contact with the reality that already is, but out of reach, with the self that already is, but is also out of reach. Cavell describes Emersonian perfectionism as a continual process of transformation of both the self and the world whereby we, in circling spirals that never end, continually project the world we *think,* the world we imagine and dream of, as the possibility for the world we live in now, as the possible next. This process of aversive circling begins with a sense of pain, mourning, and loss where we register our disgust with the self as it is, the world as it is, our state as it is. "A text such as Emerson's 'Self-Reliance' is virtually a study of shame, and perceives what we now call human society as one in which the moral law is nowhere (or almost nowhere) in existence. His perception presents itself to him as a vision of us as 'bugs, spawn,' as a 'mob.' . . . It is a violent perception of a circumstance of violence. How do we, as Emerson puts it, 'come out' of that? How do we become self-reliant? . . . We must become averse to this conformity, which means convert from it, which means transform our conformity, as if we are to be born (again)."[30]

It is significant that men in their alienated state are described as natural creatures, as "bugs," for Emerson, whereas Thoreau continually uses the non-naturalistic trope of the machine to describe this state. For Thoreau, men are machines due to contingent social factors instead of natural, inevitable, human conditions. But for Emerson, we turn away from being bugs and become human by abandoning ourselves to the better state that is always present, but not immediate. The better self, the self-reliant self is presented as "always having been attained" and "always having to be attained." Emerson's notion of this sense of self is about having "the courage to be what you are": as Cavell notes, this is like the army slogan "Be all that you can be" and resonates with one of Nietzsche's *Ecce Homo* subtitles: *How One Becomes What One Is.*[31]

For Cavell, who sees Emerson and Thoreau as underwriting the ordinary language philosophy of J. L. Austin and the later Wittgenstein, returning words to their everyday use, using words in a different and unconventional context, is a way of realizing this ideal self, this next world, this philosopher's city of words, of acting it out, living it, enacting it. Returning words to their ordinary meaning parallels the return of the self and of the world to something that is at once new but also familiar, already present but also unattained. Using "constitution" to mean at once, bodily constitution, and the constitution of government, using "representative" as Emerson uses it, prefigures this return of the self and of the world to something already present yet unattained. For Cavell, words parallel the self, which parallels the world. Things as they stand (the world, our selves) are always partial and incomplete: we wait for what is next. Emerson enacts the practice of philosophy as mourning for an (inevitable) loss of reality, but philosophy is about knowing how to go on. Philosophy is about withstanding present misery and affirming what will come next, affirming the transformation, affirming the misery because it *will* change. Cavell calls the practice of philosophy "lasting" and describes "thinking as knowing how to go on, being on the way, onward and onward."[32] This notion of continual (re)turn and (re)formation of the self is part of what makes Emerson such an interesting and provocative thinker.

But these ideas also have costs that Emerson does not always appreciate, apart from a momentary doubt in "Experience," and that Cavell also seems to miss. Reading Emerson with Adorno in mind, however, we become far more sensitive to the costs entailed in Emerson's circlings. In the notion of the unhandsome, we see resonances of Adorno's notion of the instrumentalizing, identifying, synthesizing (idealist) way of thinking that does violence to the object. For Adorno, however, this condition is not part of an inevitable human condition but a way of thinking associated with idealism and reflective of modern tendencies toward abstraction.

From Adorno's perspective, Emerson enacts a violence on the objects of the world *even* in his more passive, receptive, handsome moments, because even in the act of abandonment, the self is constantly and immediately turning away from this world of particular things, in what Cavell calls an "aversive" circling to what is "next," the next self, the next world. Emerson never spends enough time with the particular objects of the world. Emerson's idea that self and society are both in a stage of progress gives him a tendency to immediately look beyond present miseries to the ways they will be worked out in the next circle, the next incarnation of society. Throughout his writings, he accumulates a list of those objects that are denigrated as appearances and quickly looked past: society, government, social art and luxury, "every establishment," "every mass," men and women and their social life, and the like.

But these are exactly the kinds of objects that Thoreau and Adorno make visible, toward a critique of a society that only *appears* harmonious if seen with an abstracting gaze. Thoreau and Adorno focus on the misery that is here, now, in the immediate line of our sight. For Adorno and Thoreau, change can come about only through seeing the damaged objects around us: for Thoreau, the suicidal shopkeepers, the machinelike citizens, the superficial newspapers, the alienating market, the invasive influence of manners and etiquette . . . the list goes on. These are all objects that Thoreau grants "preponderance" to, to borrow Adorno's term. Thoreau pays attention to these particular objects in the way Adorno enacts the practice of negative dialectics by giving us images, in the aphorisms of *Minima Moralia,* of the ways that particular objects such as gift-giving, tact, and psychoanalysis all cast a supposedly harmonious society into a more truthful, if damaged, light. But for both men, the valuable practice is in lingering *with* the objects and illuminating the critical potential that lies in their flaws, disharmony, and ugliness, in all the things that cause Emerson to avert his eye toward the horizon.

Furthermore, Adorno shows us that reality and truth are not only accessible by, on the one hand, "unhandsomely" synthesizing, violently conceptualizing, or instrumentalizing, or on the other hand, passively abandoning oneself to the currents of universal Being. In fact, we might understand negative dialectics as Adorno's enactment of how one avoids both clutching and grasping at the object *and* avoids (or flies past) the ugliness of immediate objects of the here and now for the possibility of what comes next. In negative dialectics, Adorno shows us another way of thinking that illuminates the truth of objects without doing violence to them or by looking past them.

Emerson's Paradoxical "Home": Unsettling to Sit in the Flow of Universal Spirit

The idea of continual circlings indicates that there is value in becoming "unsettled" from the seemingly firm foundations that ground our thoughts. In "Circles," Emerson seems to attach a much more positive valence to the conditions he describes elsewhere as indicative of the alienated nature of existence: being constantly in a series, in a circling progression, where things seem to be constantly moving and not fixed.[33] Given that things "look" and "appear" stable and permanent, Emerson's job is to upset those seemingly firm foundations. He says "I unsettle all things. No facts are to me sacred; none are profane" ("Circles," 188). People find such dislocation uncomfortable, it seems. Emerson says "People wish to be settled" but "only as far as they are unsettled, is there any hope for them" (189). Cavell's reading seems primarily drawn from this Emerson.[34]

But these sentiments seem very different from Emerson's tone in other essays, where he denigrates the world of disagreeable appearances and instead yearns for "reality," for something more eternal, more affirmative, more harmonious. What are we to make, then, of the value attached to being unsettled in "Circles"? Emerson says "I unsettle all things," but for what purpose? Emerson upsets our vision, our ways of seeing the everyday world around us, but toward what end? Just as we are "safe," so to speak, when we abandon ourselves to intuition because of the affirmative and harmonious nature of the universal spirit, so we are also "unsettled" from the world of appearances to rest in the flow of a deeper reality of Being.[35] Spirit or the universal seems to be the paradoxical basis that we can rest upon, when we have been unsettled from our typical ways of seeing the world.

We can be self-reliant when we open ourselves to the universal. Emerson states in "The American Scholar" that we need not look to Europe for our geniuses but can find them on our native soil: the universal spirit also circulates through Americans. Emerson implies that once we recognize this universality of mind and spirit, we can "sit" at home: "We need not go far afield to find heroism; it exists in Concord, even: "Why should these words, Athenian, Roman, Asia, and England, so tingle in the ear? Where the heart is, there the muses, there the gods sojourn, and not in any geography of fame. Massachusetts, Connecticut River, Boston Bay, you think paltry places, and the ear loves names of foreign and classic topography. But here we are; and, if we tarry a little, we may come to learn that here is best . . . and the Supreme Being, shall not be absent from the chamber where thou sittest" ("Heroism," 152).

Once we see with the proper focal distance, we need not go looking elsewhere for genius but can let it rise up through us. In "Self-Reliance," Emerson says "Thus all concentrates; let us not rove; let us sit at home with the cause" ("Self-Reliance," 41). We need not travel to other places, for the same is within us: "So let us always sit. . . . All men have my blood, and I have all men's" (41). We feel the need to travel only to the extent that we fail to recognize how all we need is "at home," within us. When we are truly self-reliant, we can stay at home and open ourselves up to the currents of the universal mind. Emerson says "Travelling is a fool's paradise": "It is for want of self-culture that the superstition of Travelling, whose idols are Italy, England, Egypt, retains its fascination for all educated Americans. . . . The soul is no traveler; the wise man stays at home, and when his necessities, his duties, on any occasion call him from his house, or into foreign lands, he is at home still" (46). Here, Emerson is criticizing a trend in nineteenth-century America, where the nouveau riche look for culture in the Grand Tour abroad. He sees such superficial traveling as an escape from self-culture and a foolhardy search for culture in the Roman ruins.[36]

But Emerson's critique of traveling also resonates with another imperative: in *Nature* he is calling on us to build our own "house," our own "world." There is the implication that when we allow "the influx" of spirit into the self, we are on more assured and affirming terrain: once we build our own world, "A correspondent revolution in things will attend the influx of the spirit." The temporary, disagreeable objects that Emerson envisions "shall be seen no more" (*Nature*, 45). This "house" lacks a firm foundation and is grounded only in the universal; *but* there is something secure and harmonious about this basis, spirit though it is.

Given that Emerson, as we have seen, consistently describes particular objects as things to be looked past, the harmony of the house we build in spirit seems related to its removal from those jarring things.

To take both of these two passages together, Emerson implies that can "sit at home with the cause" when we "build our house" in the essentially affirmative, harmonious, and compensatory spirit. Emerson is not singing the praises of a lazy complacency, but he is seeking to assure us of our own (potential) genius, to assure us we can rely on our self. Emerson's injunctive to rest at home aims to decrease our conformist dependence on others and increase our independence. He sees weakness and insecurity around him and wants to encourage and to comfort us to trust in ourselves, to feel truly "at home."

Ultimately, Emerson, Thoreau, and Adorno all draw on images of home as a comfortable place removed from the alienating objects of the world. But their attitudes toward it are very different: unlike Emerson, Thoreau and Adorno are more attuned to the dangers of such a refuge. Thoreau and Adorno see people as too unthinkingly self-assured, too much "at home" in the world, so to speak. Both seem more receptive to the dangers of settling in the self because they do not share Emerson's affirmative and harmonious view of the universal. Thoreau and Adorno travel away from places of self-assurance and comfort. As we have seen, for Adorno, "home" connotes images of thoughtlessness, of a slackening of critical capacities, a tendency toward instrumentalism. It can also represent a retreat where we insulate ourselves from the alienating world: Kierkegaard's subject withdraws into the *intérieur*, away from reified objects.

Thoreau also idealizes the abstract home where one is clearly not "at home" in the sense of feeling comfortable and assured: he idealizes building a house in a "dismal" and "quaking" swamp and at other times idealizes places, such as inns, that lodge "travelers." The traveler, like Thoreau's neighbor, walker, or huckleberryer, is figured as someone questing to borderlands, seeking jarring, disruptive confrontations with the wild to recuperate the critical capacities lost to Main Street, to the village. Thoreau and Adorno court engagements with the objects Emerson's eye flies past; they draw out the rupturing qualities of particular things, such as Thoreau's wild apples, or Adorno's bourgeois *intérieurs*, children's fairytales or how we greet one another. Adorno and Thoreau are both travelers in that they identify a critical value in continually frustrating feelings of self-assurance, harmony and affirmation: neither let us rest "at home." These different attitudes reflect the different views toward modernization that Emerson, Thoreau, and Adorno hold. Emerson is optimistic, with his eye trained on this unfolding, circling process of realization and maturity. But Thoreau and

Adorno see no such harmonious horizon and always have their microscopic gaze directed on particular objects that highlight the costs and violence of modernization.

Equilibrium, Compensation, Harmony

For Emerson, modernity and culture, are processes whereby man becomes increasingly self-confident, recognizing his position at the center of the world, perceiving nature as phenomenon, and appreciating nature as his instrument. Emerson believes that people initially resist the notion that nature is mere phenomenon, but that culture and education can eventually correct this "unrenewed understanding": "culture" can eventually teach us the truth: "To the senses and the unrenewed understanding, belongs a sort of instinctual belief in the absolute existence of nature. . . . Things are ultimates and they never look beyond their sphere. The presence of Reason mars this faith. The first effort of thought tends to relax this despotism of the senses which binds us to nature as if we were a part of it, and shows us nature aloof and as it were afloat. . . . If the Reason be stimulated to more earnest vision, outlines and surfaces become transparent, and are no longer sees; causes and spirits are seen through them. The best moments of life are these delicious awakenings of the higher powers" (*Nature*, 30).

On the other hand, Thoreau seems to associate modernizing tendencies with such derogatory words as "domestication" and "taming." But Emerson can place this optimistic value on modernity because of his underlying belief in compensation, in the idea that all things eventually find equilibrium and work out for the best. The universal mind allows an underlying harmony, even when we cannot appreciate it with our surface-vision. Even in "Experience," even after the death of a son, despite momentary doubts, Emerson's faith in this equilibrium is ultimately reassured. He says that life is chance, yet "Underneath the inharmonious and trivial particulars, is a musical perfection, the Ideal journeying always within us, the heaven without rent or seam" ("Experience," 41).

Emerson expresses these sentiments most clearly in his essay "Compensation."[37] He begins the essay with a response to a preacher who says "that the wicked are successful; that the good are miserable; and then urged from reason and Scripture a compensation to be made to both parties in the next life" ("Compensation," 55). No, Emerson says, instead, all things are balanced out, compensated for, equilibrated, in the here and now. But we arrive at this recognition, not through rationality or dusty books, but through intuition of the wholeness and harmony of the universal Soul at work in this world. He says that the daily life of men testify to the truth of compensation, over and against the dogma of religion (56).

Emerson's world is one of oppositions: "All things are double, one against another.—Tit for tat; an eye for an eye" ("Compensation," 64). He says "If the south attracts, the north repels. To empty here, you must condense there. An inevitable dualism bisects nature, so that each thing is a half, and suggests another thing to make it whole; as spirit, matter; man, woman; odd, even; subjective, objective; in, out; upper, under; motion, rest; yea, nay" (57). But in Emerson's dialectic, all of these oppositions are reconciled and synthesized, and the end result is harmonious: "The world looks like a multiplication table or a mathematical equation, which, turn it how you will, balances itself" (60). This harmony prevails even in social relations: "There is always some leveling circumstance that puts down the overbearing, the strong, the rich, the fortunate, substantially on the same ground with all others" (58).

Here, Emerson presents the kind of dialectical reconciliation that Adorno criticizes. Whereas Adorno and Thoreau will both emphasize negation in place of illusory reconciliations and emphasize disjuncture over false harmonies, Emerson has a more affirmative outlook. He reaches this conclusion, again, because he believes that beneath surface appearances lies the balancing force of the universal: "Being is the vast affirmative, excluding negation, self-balanced, and swallowing up all relations, parts and times, within itself" ("Compensation," 70). Adorno and Thoreau take exception to this notion of affirmative balance and seek to cast a spotlight instead on the particularities this "smooth logic" (to use Adorno's phrase) masks, covers over, and leaves out. But Emerson also unwittingly testifies to Adorno's illumination of the disruptive qualities of particular objects. As we have seen, Emerson seems to look past his disagreeable particulars *because* they threaten his affirmative narrative of compensation. In this way, Emerson enacts the modern struggle that Adorno identifies.[38]

· Emerson's thought is also more compatible with the logic of abstract exchange. Emerson's emphasis on the ultimate identity of all things means that nothing is lost or elided if, for example, we exchange a pint of huckleberries for something else of equal value, say a pound of flour. Thoreau will say that the essence of the huckleberry cannot survive the market, but Emerson's thought cannot speak to such a loss, cannot see it. For Adorno, the logic of abstract exchange is fundamentally related to the logic of identity: objects lose their uniqueness, their particularity. For Thoreau, this means that huckleberries as they are sold on the market do not carry with them the activity of huckleberrying: the meadow, the huckleberry field, the experience of picking the berries does not survive the market. But Emerson's thought is blind to the violence of abstract exchange. He cannot see the deadening of experience that Adorno and Thoreau associate with the logic of abstract exchange. Thus, Adorno's critiques of idealism help us better understand the scope and terrain of Thoreau's critical departures from Emerson.

Emerson and Thoreau:
Different Visual Practices

The central difference between Emerson and Thoreau concerns the difference between an eye that abstracts away from particulars and an eye that particularizes the abstract. Emerson tends to project his eye up and away, transcending the objects of the world around him. Thoreau, on the other hand, is a highly observant student of "little things"; he lingers within nature, with all its tiny, unique, particularities. He knew all the varieties of huckleberry bushes and could tell you exactly on which day of they year they ripened. He knew how thick the ice was on Walden Pond. He knew how wild apples tasted when they had been frozen through by frost. He was familiar with every wildflower in Concord. Neither an abstract nor a generalizing thinker, he observes the world through eyes that look at little things closely, whereas Emerson writes often about universes and horizons, and tends to look away from the constitutive parts that make up a beautiful landscape.

For Emerson, landscapes in their abstract entirety are reassuring, whereas particular things seem strange to him and seem to make him feel separated from his world, from his context in a way that evoke a sense of loss and alienation. When this sense of estrangement occurs, when "the contrast between us and our house is more evident," Emerson's eye moves upward from these particulars to remind himself that, after all, nature exists for us and all the world ministers to man (*Nature*, 39). Emerson says: "It is not so pertinent to man to know all the individuals of the animal kingdom" (39). He laments the urge that "evermore separate and classifies things": he wants us to be able to simple see unity amid multitude and understand where that unity comes from (40). And further, "All the endless variety of things makes an identical impression. . . . A leaf, a drop, a crystal, a moment of time, is related to the whole, and partakes of the perfection of the whole. Each particle is a microcosm and faithfully renders the likeness of the world" (27). Emerson is interested in unity, but Thoreau would probably have been more captivated by the endless variety of those particular leafs, drops of water, and crystals. In a journal entry Thoreau writes "Nature will bear the closest inspection. She invites us to lay our eye level with her smallest leaf and take an insect view of its plain."[39]

But to really appreciate their differences, let us look at two passages where Thoreau and Emerson use similar sounding language toward very different ends. Recall again the quotation from *Nature* where Emerson tell us to build our own world in our minds and says that a corresponding revolution in things will occur, making disagreeable appearances vanish. Interestingly, Thoreau writes a passage in *Walden* that is strikingly similar to Emerson's quote, yet importantly different in illuminating ways. It is worth quoting at length:

> By closing the eye and slumbering, and consenting to be deceived by shows, men establish and confirm their daily life of routine and habit everywhere, which is still built on purely illusory foundations. . . . I perceive that we inhabitants of New England live this mean life that we do because our vision does not penetrate the surface of things. We think that *is* which *appears* to be. If a man should walk through this town and see only the reality, where think you, would the 'Mill-dam' go to? If he should give us an account of the realities he beheld there, we should not recognize the place in his description. Look at a meeting-house, or a court-house, or a jail, or a shop, or a dwelling-house, and say what that thing really is before a true gaze, and they would all go to pieces in your account of them. Men esteem truth remote, in the outskirts of the system, behind the farthest star, before Adam and after the last man. In eternity there is indeed something true and sublime. But all these times and places and occasions are now and here. God himself culminates in the present moment, and will never be more divine in the lapse of all the ages. And we are enabled to apprehend all what is sublime and noble only by the perpetual instilment and drenching of the reality that surrounds us. . . . Let us settle ourselves, and work and wedge our feet downward through the mud and slush of opinion, and prejudice, and tradition, and delusion, and appearance, that alluvion which covers the globe, through Paris and London, through New York and Boston and Concord, through Church and State, through poetry and philosophy and religion, till we come to a hard bottom and rocks in place, which we can call *reality and say, This is, and no mistake;* . . . If you stand right fronting and face to face to a fact, you will see the sun glimmer on both its surfaces, as if it were a cimeter, and feel its sweet edge dividing you through heart and marrow, and so you would happily conclude your mortal career. Be it life or death, we crave only reality. (*Walden*, 96–98)

Thoreau's statement about craving reality, be it life or death, echoes Emerson's "Experience." Here too, Thoreau describes a revolutionary change in our relation to the world of objects that occurs when we awaken from slumber and see reality for what it is, just as Emerson does in his similar quotation. Thoreau uses the metaphors of sleep and of vision, as does Emerson. But there are important differences in their worldviews that come to light when we compare these passages, even if they use language that *sounds* similar.

Thoreau, elsewhere in his writings, draws parallels between "slumbering" and the "common sense," which is the unthinking, conformist sensibility of the machines who populate modern society.[40] In our daily lives, we do not see reality but are deceived by "appearances"; for Thoreau, the world around us is not *fundamentally* phenomenal and unreal (as it is for Emerson), but contingent, the product of habit and routine. Similarly, our ways of seeing are also conventional rather than existential. For Thoreau, men "consent to slumber": it is prejudice that can be cast off, not an inevitable fact of human existence, of life, as it is for Emerson. In "Experience," in contrast, Emerson says "Life itself is a bubble and a skepticism, and a sleep within a sleep" ("Experience," 38). There is a vast difference between saying that men "consent" to slumber and saying that life "itself" is a sleep.

But in the next few sentences, Thoreau goes even further in illustrating the nature of his departure from Emerson on the question of alienation. In a sentence that nearly perfectly parallels Emerson's phrase from *Nature*, Thoreau says that if we would only look and see true "reality," all the things that we *think* we know (the mill-dam, the meeting-house, the shops, etc.) would "go to pieces" in our account of them. Whereas Emerson speaks of reality as "unfolding proportions," as reality as a "pure idea" that expands and unfolds, becoming more whole, for Thoreau when we truly see, things "go to pieces." Thoreau's way of seeing breaks apart wholes and causes abstractions to fall apart. For Thoreau, places like the meeting-house and the courthouse are spaces we associate with conventional politics as they are public spaces of debate, of collective deliberation, and we associate them with the kinds of activities that define democracy as it is commonly understood. When we take apart the abstract idea, these are not places where people come together to engage in truly democratic practices nor where citizens congregate to think critically, to disagree, to dissent, to question conventions. In such conventional spaces of politics, men only act like "machines" and the individual is lost among the moving parts of the collective. For Thoreau, the huckleberry field is a more truly democratic space.

But we can only see the reality of the meeting-house if we move away from abstractions: Thoreau thinks we need to "wedge our feet downward through the mud and slush of opinion, prejudice and tradition and delusion . . . till we come to a hard bottom." We need to be guided downward by our feet, instead of moving, as Emerson does, upward into our minds, letting our eye gaze outward toward the horizon. We need to move down to fact, to real experience that cuts us like a sword until we "feel its sweet edge." Thoreau courts particular visceral experiences that bring us face to face with untamed, undomesticated, and undiluted experiences so that we can form our own opinions instead of relying on comfortable common sense. His contact with reality is more sensory and involves touching or even tasting.

In speaking of being led toward reality by our "feet" in a passage that so closely parallels Emerson's statement, Thoreau makes a sharp contrast with Emerson's emphasis on the reality of the universal and on the abstract focal distance of the eye. But Thoreau even goes further: he seems to critique Emerson again when he says that "men esteem truth remote, in the outskirts of the system" and esteem eternity as "true and sublime." These notions of remote and abstract truths and timelessness evoke Emersonian values. But Thoreau seems to move away from those ideals to the here and now, calling for us to experience the sublime by "drenching" ourselves in real experiences in the present. In this passage Thoreau implies we can counteract alienated common sense by moving downward to become more attuned to the particularities of experience, of the objects around us. By paying attention to particularity in this way, we become adept at seeing for ourselves instead of relying on established ideas.

Ultimately, both Thoreau and Emerson are concerned with the problem of conformity. For both, in different ways, man is lost to himself in his everyday life, his everyday ways of seeing and experiencing the world around him. But the ways Emerson works against a sense of loss are the kinds of moves that work to increase Thoreau's sense of alienation. For Thoreau and Adorno, particularity opens up a pathway for critical thinking and critique. Emerson also emphasizes the need to see and think for ourselves, but to get to this point he advocates a different route, a path of moving away from particular experiences toward the universal.

❖

PART 2

Thoreau's Democratic Withdrawal

❖

3

Man as Machine

Thoreau and Modern Alienation

The mass of men lead lives of quiet desperation.
Henry David Thoreau

The mass of men serve the state thus, not as men mainly, but as machines.
Henry David Thoreau

When Emerson and Thoreau are compared, Emerson is typically described as a pillar of society who took an active part in the political and social issues of his era while Thoreau is most remembered for his solitary sojourn in a cabin on the shores of Walden Pond. In his own time and even today, Thoreau has been criticized for not being worldly enough, sociable enough, or politically engaged enough. While Emerson was looked up to in Concord and was truly a leader of his town and country, Thoreau was the hermit who criticized the superficiality of society and had only scorn for the politics of his day.

But the picture is considerably more complicated when we move from comparing Emerson and Thoreau as people to comparing their ideas. Theoretically, Emerson's way of seeing the world seems to remove and disengage him from his historical context. In contrast, Thoreau's withdrawal from mainstream society and politics paradoxically works to highlight the deeply situated nature of his critical dialogue with the processes of modernization that characterized his own time. If for Emerson, "grief too will make us idealists" and motivates us to abstract away from the objects around us, for Thoreau suffering inspires political practices of withdrawal that engage particular objects to critique modern conditions of alienation in the world around us.[1] Thoreau does not dismiss the objects of the world as disagreeable appearances and hasten toward a more harmonious and affirmative universal, as does Emerson. Instead, Thoreau pays the greatest attention to objects in the world and describes them in concrete terms.

He takes seriously how nineteenth-century modernity was negatively shaping subjectivity: through the market and consumerism, through mainstream politics, and through social conventions such as manners and etiquette. These forces prompt him to withdraw from society to go walking and huckleberrying, practices which recuperate the same critical capacities that are threatened by modern society. Looking at Thoreau's depiction of the alienated nature of experience in Concord, Massachusetts, we can trace his common ground with Adorno. Here, I lay out the problem that motivates Thoreau to go walking, to go huckleberrying, to confront the wild, and that, a century later, will stimulate Adorno's practice of negative dialectics.

Understanding Alienation in Historical Context: Thoreau's Concord

The specific setting for Thoreau's writings is a town located eighteen miles inland from Boston, Massachusetts, where the Sudbury joins the Assabet to form the Concord River. Concord provided the context for every aspect of Thoreau's life. He "used to say that he had been born in just the right place at just the right time," according to Mary Hosmer Brown, the granddaughter of Edmund Hosmer, a Concord farmer and intellectual who was a friend of Thoreau's.[2] Thoreau was born and died in Concord. After college at Harvard, he was almost never away from his native town, except for a few brief excursions elsewhere in the United States and in Canada. But Thoreau is not just tied to Concord because he spent a lot of time there. His work cannot easily be abstracted away from Concord to apply to anyplace or anytime. Thoreau's writing itself is situated, concrete, and specific. Concord was the setting for his thought and action: as he said, "The old coat that I wear is Concord: it is my morning robe and study gown, my working dress and suit of ceremony, and my nightgown after all."[3] On the surface, then, Thoreau's statement that he had been born in just the right place and time seems to reaffirm his love of his hometown. But this isn't a completely satisfying reading. While it is true that

Thoreau loved the landscape and nature around Concord, his writings about the town and his fellow townsmen tend to be very critical and come from a place of frustration. Thoreau is highly critical of the trappings of modernity as he understands them: the instrumentalization of nature, an increasing preoccupation with business and commerce, cultural refinement, superficial manners, and rules of etiquette.[4] He was also born in just the right time and place to witness the ill effects of the process of modernization. Thoreau's statement might signal his own recognition that he was in a perfect position to observe the birth of a nascent form of modernity in Massachusetts specifically and in the United States generally. Born in 1817 and died in 1862, he lived during the era recognized by historians as an important turning point in America's mid-nineteenth century.

Unless we recognize how perfectly his lifespan corresponds to these dramatic years of urbanization and modernization in Massachusetts specifically, it becomes too easy to dismiss Thoreau as a misanthropic, overly critical, ill-humored, humbug instead of seeing him as a very real social critic responding to a new experience of modernity.[5] And it is too easy to romanticize Thoreau's era as bucolic, emblematic of the good and simple life. We read Thoreau's critiques of the obsession with "getting ahead," the incessant busy-ness of trips to the post office and gossipy newspapers, and his wonder at the ways people burden their lives and ruin their health with luxury and material wealth. If we are inclined to romanticize life during his era, Thoreau ends up looking a bit crazy. After all, what could Thoreau possibly have had to complain about in pretty little pastoral Concord? If we can dispel our tendencies to create an overly romantic notion of Thoreau's time as rustic, bucolic, and simple, we can the recognize the ways that Thoreau's lifetime corresponds almost exactly to a period of intense and dramatic transformation in New England, and we are able to appreciate his social criticism of burgeoning modernity as prescient and insightful. It may not have been *our* modernity but it was certainly *a* modernity with some importantly similar features.

The first half of the nineteenth century was an era of intense transition throughout the country. The population increased and there was a general shift away from rural ways of life to more urban lifestyles, with concomitant changes in the organization of everyday life. The historian Richard Brown notes in his *Massachusetts: A Concise History,* "after 1780 and especially in the decades after 1820, the population grew swiftly, at rates comparable to the most dynamic periods of colonial settlement. . . . The population density has risen from 33 persons per square mile in 1780 to 153 persons per square mile in 1860. Massachusetts became the most thickly settled state in the union, save only for tiny Rhode

Island."[6] Within Concord itself, the population was growing steadily as well. In 1765, the census marked the population at 1,569 people. By 1830, it was 2,017. But the biggest jump in any ten-year period occurred between 1840 and 1850, during the very period when Thoreau chronicled his experiences at Walden Pond. In 1840, the population was counted as 1,784, but by 1850 it measured 2,240.[7]

With the population boom and lowered transportation costs, farmers moved away from family-based subsistence agriculture and began to grow surplus that could then supply the nearby markets of Boston. The railroads were a major factor in opening up these new markets for farmers. But while new markets were created for profit-oriented farmers, overall agriculture declined and more people moved toward manufacturing. The years from about 1790 to 1860 saw a shift from household or workshop production of consumer goods to factory-based production. Brown calls this trend the "urbanization of Massachusetts" and notes that "the more people turned to market production, even on this small scale, the more thoroughly they became enmeshed in the world of commerce."[8]

Concord was only about fifteen miles away from Lowell, Massachusetts, where the textile boom was in full swing. The first mill at Lowell was built in 1826, and the "urbanization based on industry" was "far more rapid and intense than in other towns," but it was only a difference in degree, not of kind: "the direction was the same almost everywhere in Massachusetts during the first half of the 19th century." Brown writes further, "Between 1820 and the Civil War, Massachusetts turned toward industry and away from agriculture. From a labor force where 60 percent of workers were in agriculture, by 1865 only 13 percent were on farms. . . . Now workers were largely employees, no longer owning property or small businesses. The demand for skilled artisans declined and self-employment became unusual. Workers had become dependent on others for employment."[9]

With urbanization and industrialization came changes in people's values, ideals, choices, and habits that reshaped everyday lifestyles. New possibilities were introduced; a higher degree of refinement and luxury was available to a broader population. The "range of such industries was almost endless: buttons and bedsteads, cigars and spectacles, stove polish and perfume, candy and combs. Virtually anything money could buy was being produced in the state where two centuries before, sumptuary laws had required frugality." Now, a more bourgeois class of people began to develop in Massachusetts. By looking at what items then became popular on the market, we can see the shift in people's material desires and aspirations to greater refinement and gentility:

"The production of consumer goods—items like clothing, home furnishings, musical instruments and books—reflected the radical changes in American ways of life between 1800 and 1860. These were the years when semi-subsistence farming all but disappeared and the ideals of bourgeois comfort and amenities characteristic of the Victorian age supplanted the rustic simplicity that religious beliefs and economic realities had forced on the majority of people from Winthrop's day to John Hancock's."[10]

Were these massive changes reflected in the town of Concord as well? By looking at the advertisements in the newspaper Thoreau would likely have read, the *Concord Freeman*, we can get a sense of the goods available to Concordians.[11] This newspaper came out every Friday and was about thirteen inches wide and eighteen inches long, with six columns of text. Issues were typically three pages long, but about one-third of each issue (the entire back page) was taken up with advertisements. Readers of the July 4, 1844, issue (exactly one year before Thoreau's move to Walden Pond) would have seen advertisements for the Fitchburg Railroad's special fares and timetables to take people to see the fireworks at Charlestown.[12] The Cheap Cash Store at the Mill-Dam (the name for an area of downtown Concord) advertised newly received French Doe Skins, Fancy Tweeds, Cassimeres, Gambroons, Linen Drills and French Muslins cheap. Another store advertises Dress Goods, printed lawns, Cambric Muslins for Whites Dresses, and Splendid Organdies. French and Italian silks are sold. A clothing store sells "Goods Cheap," specializing in men's calf pegged boots. Another store says it recently received a shipment of four hundred pairs of Ladies Kid slippers. There are announcements for parasols, fancy dress materials of various prints, and the spring fashions in bonnets and dresses. Gentlemen's summer garments can be had for the right price, as well as damask tablecloths.

At the grocery store, many varieties of tea could be purchased: Old Hyson, Young Hyson, Pouchong, Ningyong Caper, Souchong. Another store announces that it recently hired "a superior artist (from London)" to paint "transparent window curtains." Old paintings can also be repaired and a variety of "fancy paintings" on wood can be done for a low price. Books are also advertised, as are medicines (Sherry Wine Bitters for Health and Strength).

But the advertisements for "Rich Fancy Goods" and "Fancy Goods" in clothing make up the vast majority of the space on the back page of the *Concord Freeman*. The sellers emphasize the ways their clothes are patterned after European styles. In general, the advertisers betray the prejudices of their intended consumers, who seem to desire things that are indeed fancy, for clothing designed for "ladies and gentlemen," and that are modeled after the fashions of England and France.

There is a wealth of local history recounting what modernization looked like in Concord during Thoreau's time, many of which were written by his near-contemporaries.[13] But one work in particular stands out: Edward Jarvis's *Traditions and Reminiscences of Concord, 1779–1878*.[14] Jarvis was a contemporary of Thoreau and nearly an exact contemporary of Thoreau's friend and neighbor, Emerson. Both were born in 1803; Emerson died in 1882 while Jarvis died in 1884. But whereas Thoreau was criticizing many elements of the new modernization, Jarvis was a booster for the new trends toward urbanization, independence, self-sufficiency, refinement, and gentility. Jarvis was a leader of a general townwide move to "civilize" and gentrify Concord. He shows a culture reshaping itself along European models, leaning toward more Victorian styles of manner and affect. Jarvis is at pains to show how many Concordians traveled abroad, how many were educated at Harvard, how many people attended dancing schools, and how families of "high culture" influenced the town for the better. Amid these efforts at remaking the town, class was becoming an increasingly divisive issue in Concord.[15] These concerns with gentility, refinement, "civilization," and class all come to a controversial climax in Jarvis's history of the Concord Centennial celebration. He himself suggested this celebration, scheduled for September 1835, but the town was at that point divided over how to organize it. Some wanted to have a more folksy, popular, simple celebration that drew in all the citizens of the town and featured "oration, singing and religious exercise in the meetinghouse and a dinner in a tent large enough to accommodate great multitudes and so simple and plain that none should be kept away on account of cost." Others, including Jarvis, one suspects, "desired this to be a grand celebration to draw men of high degree from other towns and sites and to give Concord a name and fame abroad. They wanted an orator of the greatest eloquence and renown whose speech should impress the world and carry the name of Concord with it. They wanted a magnificent dinner that would speak well for the town and speeches from noted men whose words would give honor and dignity to the occasion in other lands and in after times."[16]

Those favoring gentility and promoting Concord abroad won out, but the exclusive fancy dinner was not without mishap. Not surprisingly, "it was represented that this feast was for the aristocracy, the cultivated, the favored, to which the less-favored might be admitted to look on and admire and perhaps to receive some of the bounties as gifts from the superiors to the inferiors." This understandably irritated townspeople who were "less-favored." Another problem arose because the ladies could not possibly pour their own coffee and so retained a young woman from the town to make coffee and fill the ladies' cups. The young woman from town was at first honored to be chosen, but then someone told her that this was "a menial service, a humiliation that she ought not to submit to" and she refused to serve the ladies who were then forced, amid great outrage, to pour their own coffee! A similar clash took place in 1825 when the Marquis de Lafayette visited Concord and the town "reformers" (likely including Jarvis) tried to put their "best" citizens forward during his visit and unceremoniously hide the less refined and genteel of their town.[17]

Robert A. Gross, a social historian of Thoreau and Concord, writes in his introduction to Jarvis's volume,

> This process of economic change—the expansion of markets, the spread of money, the growth of specialized roles—was tied, in Jarvis's view, to the advance of civilization. . . . Hence Jarvis's emphasis upon the proliferation of books, newspapers, and periodicals; the number of college graduates in town; the ever-greater immersion of Concord in a wider world of travel and communications; and the softening of manners and advances of culture in school and home, as evidenced by the many pianos in the town's parlors. To Jarvis . . . the key to this process was the influence of a cultivated elite. [Jarvis writes that] "The presence of families of high culture, the refinement of their social influence, the sympathy of the favored classes with the other—all these wrought a good work in the town and Concord gradually became what it now is, one of the most cultivated towns in New England."[18]

Gross calls this concern with refinement and gentility "a defining feature of the middle-class culture that Jarvis and his contemporaries created. . . . Gentility meant politeness, delicacy, and taste. It involved cultivation of the mind, acquisition of bodily grace, and sensitivity to the feelings of others. In practice, aspiring gentlemen like Edward Jarvis learned to talk and dance in the best company with dignity and ease. And they judged others clearly by this standard."[19]

In addition to this concern with refinement and gentility, Jarvis acts as a booster for the new independence that was beginning to characterize the town. Like other historians who wrote about Concord retrospectively, Jarvis appreciated, during his own lifetime, that people were shifting away from cooperative and more communal methods of living and toward more independent and self-sufficient ways of life. Speaking about his childhood, before urbanizing and modernizing influences had gained much of a foothold in Concord, Jarvis writes of the ways that social concerns took greater precedence in the formation of the self: "We were led to take an interest in all the past traditionary history of the town and the living scenes and movements that were about us. We noticed them with a lively intensity, and they were fixed in our minds almost as parts [of] our own being. We were made social in our feelings, conversations and habits. We lived not alone. The whole society, neighborhood, and town were almost a part of ourselves or at least intimately interwoven with the web of our existence."[20]

But this cooperative way of life, despite the lovely descriptions he gives of it, was ultimately disagreeable to Jarvis and to others who pushed for greater individualism and independence (which they associated with being "modern") in the town. Jarvis praises the town for becoming increasingly self-sustaining as the nineteenth century progressed: "The people of Concord are no less kind, sympathetic, and generous then their fathers, but they are stronger in leading and in heart. They are more self-sustaining, and it is better that each should do his own work, with his own hands or by such aid as he can compensate in the ordinary way. Those burdens that in the past required the cooperation of friends and neighbors are now but ordinary affairs and are met by the ordinary means and their own exertions."[21]

The people of Concord, in other words, are becoming more modern. Thoreau was no booster for modernization, as Jarvis was. Thoreau criticizes modernization not only because of the negative effects of an increasingly market-based society and industrialization, but because of the unpalatable fruits of the new concerns with fashion, style, manners, etiquette, and refinement. Thoreau and Jarvis tell a similar story about the changes taking place in Concord but with dramatically different attitudes. The very aspects of modernization that Jarvis applauds and encourages motivate Thoreau's most scathing criticisms.

Modernization and the Deadening of Individual Experience

There are two different facets to Thoreau's discussion of alienation. Thoreau describes a more generalized deadening of individual experience that he associates with modernization. But then there are several specific instances where modern alienation strikes close to home for Thoreau, and he seems to be personally gripped by a dark depression and melancholy. In these cases, we may be tempted to simply attribute these moments to his own wounded psyche, but they point toward a more objective source: in each case Thoreau subtly links his experiences of loss with specific social and political conditions.

As society became more "modern," people's lives were organized in ways that systematized behavior, in greater coordination with the market. As communication and transportation technologies advance, routines are created. The activity of weeks and months took on greater regularity and predictability, following the schedules of the railroads, the demands for goods in Boston, and the schedules of employers. More people became employees, with subsequent rigid codes of conduct governing their behavior. As the population increased, people began living in closer proximity to other people and were able to compare and model their own lifestyles on the lifestyles of others. Style and fashion became more meaningful in people's everyday lives.

But, in Thoreau's measure (as in Adorno's), these changes entailed a loss, a watering down of experience that can best be described as a sense of alienation. Everyday life was tamed and domesticated. People were cultivated, just as nature was increasingly becoming the material for consumption and industry. Lives took on predictable shapes and activity conformed to expected patterns. Thoreau constantly urges himself and his readers to bite more deeply into life, to experience in unconventional ways, and move past expected and formulaic ways of thinking and acting. "Life," for Thoreau, is a unique and unexpected surplus that exceeds common expectations. He sees people's lives passing them by, because the individual does not experiment for himself or herself: "Here is life, an experiment to a great extent untried by me."[22] Real life and real experience are defined in opposition to regularized codes of conduct, habits, and manners. As he says in the "Where I Lived and What I Lived For" chapter, "I went to the woods because I wished to live deliberately, to front only the essential facts of life, and see if I could not learn what it had to teach, and not, when I came to die, discover that I had not lived. I did not wish to live what was not life . . . I wanted to live deep and suck out all the marrow of life" (*Walden*, 90).

Thoreau contrasts *really* living as a kind of experimentation that flies in the face of modern ways of simply "getting a living" where we conform to the market and to conventional ways of making money: "There is no more fatal blunderer than he who consumes the greater part of his life getting his living."[23] In "Life Without Principle," he asks us to "consider the way in which we spend our lives," punning that we literally buy our way out of real life ("Life," 156). Thoreau opposes the market and consumerism with "life" and really living.

Thoreau does not use the word *alienation* explicitly but expresses this experience by using the term *common sense*, which evokes images of the self-evident, the obvious, ideas that are immediately understandable to an everyday, mainstream sensibility. But common sense is problematic for Thoreau in that it is a way of thinking that follows conventional patterns. To be alienated is to think and say exactly what we are expected to think and say, what everyone else thinks and says, to say "yes" to conventions. But on the other hand, Thoreau places the greatest value on the part of us that can say "no," and think against the grain of common thought. Thoreau wants to "transcend" this common sensibility by awakening an ability to negate familiar modes of perception for something more wild, idiosyncratic, unexpected, and unpredictable.

And here, Thoreau is trying to address a modern problem of alienation. Adorno also says modern life "does not live." Similarly, Thoreau links the evisceration of life and our ability to truly and fully live to the modernization taking place around him. Routines, habits, patterns of conduct, and formulas for how we should behave do indeed work, seductively, to tame and domesticate the self so that we can scarcely negate convention at all. In the opening passages of *Walden* he says "I have traveled a good deal in Concord [a major understatement]; and everywhere, in shops and offices, and fields, the inhabitants have appeared to me to be doing penance in a thousand remarkable ways" (*Walden*, 4). Their penance takes the form of having "inherited" farms where they have no choice in how to order their lives but have their destinies mapped out before them. It is not the activity of farming itself that Thoreau objects to, but the lack of choice involved in most people's livelihood: their lives follow a pattern that they have not themselves created. But in losing the ability to negate, to choose, to experiment outside of convention, "the better part of the man is soon plowed into the soil for compost" (5). The laboring man "has no time to be anything but a machine" (6). Thoreau argues that we are slaves to the conventions that have come to rest within ourselves, to public opinions that have become privatized. We have, so to speak, internalized external authority so that we do not even recognize that we haven't chosen how to order our lives: we *believe* we have freely chosen.[24] Thoreau says "it is hard to have a Southern overseer; it is worse to have a Northern one; but worst of all when you are the slave driver of yourself. . . . Public opinion is a weak tyrant compared with our own private opinion" (7). Seemingly, men are not aware of their lack of choice: "it appears as if men had deliberately chosen the common mode of living because they preferred it to any other. Yet they honestly think there is no choice left" (8).

But, as for Adorno, modernization does not take place without leaving a scar, a remainder, which Thoreau measures as a deep discontent: "the mass of men lead lives of quiet desperation" (*Walden*, 8). Thoreau notices that "the incessant anxiety and strain of some is a well-nigh incurable form of disease" (11). Yet we deny that change is possible: "So thoroughly and sincerely are we compelled to live, reverencing our life and denying the possibility of change. This is the only way, we say; but there are as many ways as there can be drawn radii from one center" (11). In his essay "Walking," Thoreau again draws our attention to the dire effects of the ways our lives have become routinized by modernization: "When sometimes I am reminded that the mechanics and shopkeepers stay in their shops not only all the forenoon, but all the afternoon too, sitting with crossed legs . . . I think that they deserve some credit for not having all committed suicide long ago" ("Walking," 227). These men are not "living" in the way Thoreau understands the term: by staying in their shops all day, every day, they are conforming to the patterns of the market, they are very nearly dead already. Thoreau is primarily concerned with the way the patterns of economic modernization seem to deny the possibility of alternative choices, action, and experimentation.

But, writing in mid-nineteenth century, something else might also have been in the air, lurking in the back of the minds of the men of Thoreau's generation, especially those who lived in Concord. After all, he is part of one of the first generations who inherited the established republic but was not alive during the Revolution. During Thoreau and Emerson's time, there were still those who were eyewitnesses to the Revolution. But as those spectators died out, that era increasingly became a memory, something memorialized and enshrined. Reminders of the Revolution would have surrounded men of Thoreau's generation, however. Concord had played a central role in the war. The North Bridge ("the rude bridge that arched the flood") over the Concord River, not very far from the center of town, was the site of the first organized armed resistance against British soldiers. Years later, at the dedication of a memorial at this bridge, Emerson would read his poem "Concord Hymn," which describes the "shot heard round the world." Emerson's father is said to have watched the battle at North Bridge from the upstairs window of the Emerson family home, the "Old Manse" (now a museum open to the public).[25]

By the mid-nineteenth century, the possibility of creating something new, of choosing, of acting, of what Hannah Arendt calls "natality," had given way to coping with something already in existence.[26] Possibilities seemed more limited, the status quo more constraining. This capacity for free action that creates something new (instead of reacting to a "historical necessity") is what Hannah Arendt refers to as the "lost treasure" of the "revolution."[27] Arendt laments that the republic, after the American Revolution, became immediately concerned with securing longevity and stability in ways that did not safeguard a space for free, creative, public action. Instead, true freedom to act and create was restricted to the founding generation. We might imagine that the sense of this lost freedom also was felt in the air during Thoreau's time. Indeed, in the beginning of "Resistance to Civil Government," Thoreau refers to "this American Government" as a "tradition, though a recent one," already indicating its sedimented, authoritative, enshrined nature ("Resistance," 63). Compared with the possibilities of the Revolutionary era, Thoreau's generation might well have seemed filled with constraints and constrictions, an important background condition. But in the foreground, Thoreau identifies this loss of possibilities with the process of economic modernization.

The Railroad and Sleeping Men

The introduction of the railroad in Concord was, for Thoreau, a major factor in the increasingly routine and formulaic ways of ordering the day. In the "Sounds" chapter of *Walden*, Thoreau describes how the regular whistles of the trains coming back and forth from Boston became markers of time and dictators of action: "I watch the passage of the morning cars with the same feeling that I do the rising of the sun, which is hardly more regular. . . . If the enterprise were as innocent as it is early! . . . If the enterprise were as heroic and commanding as it is protracted and unwearied! . . . The startings and arrivals of the cars are now the epochs in the village day. They come and go with such regularity and precision, and their whistle can be heard so far, that the farmers set their clocks by them, and thus one well-conducted institutions regulates a whole country. . . . We have constructed a fate, an *Atropos,* that never turns aside. . . . Every path but your own is the path of fate. Keep on your own track, then" (*Walden,* 116).

The movements of people and railroads are thus synchronized with the market. The farmers in the country send raw materials, cotton and wool, to Boston. The factories and the merchants send back the finished products of woven cloth. "The whistle of the locomotive penetrates my woods summer and winter, sounding like the scream of a hawk sailing over some farmer's yard, informing me that in any restless city merchants are arriving within the circle of the town, or adventurous country traders from the other side. Here come your groceries, country: your rations, countrymen! Nor is there any man so independent on his farm that he can say them nay. And here's your pay for them! screams the countryman's whistle. . . . Up comes the cotton, down goes the woven cloth; up comes the silk, down goes the woolen; up come the books, but down goes the wit that writes them" (*Walden,* 115). Activity is coordinated on increasingly large scales: the railroads indeed "regulate a whole country" and we obey the whistle as if it were fate. The railroad coordinates activity to make certain artificial patterns of action look natural, as regular and inevitable as the rising and setting of the sun.

This routinization works against our ability to "experiment," which Thoreau associates with life and living. In a striking passage, Thoreau explicitly ties the railroad to not living, to death, to slumbering and sleeping (whereas, for Thoreau, "morning" and being "awake" always symbolize really living life in unalienated ways):

> We do not ride upon the railroad, it rides upon us. Did you ever think what those sleepers are that underlie the railroad? Each one is a man, an Irishman, or

a Yankee man. The rails are laid on them, and they are covered with sand, and the cars run smoothly over them. They are sound sleepers, I assure you. And every few years a new lot is laid down and run over; so that, if some have the pleasure of riding on a rail, others have the misfortune to be ridden upon. And when they run over a man that is walking in his sleep, a supernumerary sleeper in the wrong position, and wake him up, they suddenly stop the cars, and make a hue and cry about it, as if this were an exception. I am glad to know that it takes a gang of men for every five miles to keep the sleepers down and level in their beds as it is, for this is a sign that they may sometime get up again." (*Walden*, 92)

"Sleepers" here functions as a pun that refers to the wooden railroad ties that line the tracks and also to those men who have worked to lay them down. Here, Thoreau seems at once critical of a class society where some ride the rails and others are run over by the trains, but also insensitive to those who laid the rails. For Thoreau to call these men "sleepers" implies that they are not awake, that they are not thinking for themselves or experimenting with their own lives. They are not acting like real men, even though Thoreau reminds us that "each one is a man." But to call these men "sleepers" seems, at first glance, insensitive to the lack of choice and free agency that confronted them. Thoreau is criticizing them for "sleeping" through life by working on the railroad, yet did they have a choice? Their employment on the railroad probably felt more like coerced labor that had to be undertaken in light of a dearth of alternatives. Thoreau certainly seems as if he is high-handedly preaching to the ignorant masses who cannot see, or do not care to see, that they are choosing death over life. We see this attitude expressed elsewhere in his work as well. In "Life Without Principle," he haughtily intones that "The ways by which you may get money almost without exception lead downward. To have done anything by which you earned money *merely* is to have been truly idle or worse. . . . Those services which the community will most readily pay for, it is most disagreeable to render. You are paid for being something less than a man" ("Life," 158). Again in "Life Without Principle," Thoreau argues that "The ways in which most men get their living, that is, live are mere makeshifts and a shirking of the real business of life — *chiefly because they do not know but partly because they do not mean, any better*" (162; italics mine). In passages such as these, Thoreau shows an unsettling lack of sympathy to the ways the market might operate as a system to preclude men from choosing how they get their living.

Yet this is not the whole story of why people do not really "live life." It is not simply ignorance and a matter of choosing poorly. Thoreau also writes that we are *all* being taken for a ride by the railroad. "We," not just "them" are all being ridden upon by the railroad: "We do not ride on the railroad; it rides upon us." Here there is no choice: we are being ridden over rough-shod by rails, whether we like it or not. In another passage from *Walden,* Thoreau writes that we are "compelled" to live in certain ways: "So thoroughly and sincerely are we compelled to live, reverencing our life, and denying the possibility of change. This is the only way, we say" (*Walden,* 11). But that men fail to really live seems less a matter of choice and more an honest feeling that there are no alternatives. Thoreau calls this force "a seeming fate, commonly called necessity, they are employed, as it says in an old book, laying up treasures which moth and rust will corrupt and thieves break through and steal" (5).[28] Thoreau's diagnosis of the state of the mass of men is starkly at odds with the American republic's self-image as a place where individual freedom is the preeminent value, but the ideal does not match the reality of experience. In modern society, the "better part of the man" is lost because our capacity to think against common modes of living and experiment with life is overpowered by the power of convention and collective authority.

This force has its locus: it is centered in the town, on Main Street, in the village, in the courthouse, in mainstream politics, and in places where refined society exists. But these places do not penetrate all spaces. "From many a hill I can see civilization and the abodes of man from afar. The farmers and their works are scarcely more obvious than woodchucks and their burrows. Man and his affairs, church and state and school, trade and commerce, and manufactures and agriculture, even politics, the most alarming of all,—I am pleased to see how little space they occupy in the landscape. Politics is but a narrow field. . . . If you would go to the political world, follow the great road—follow that market-man, keep his dust in your eyes, and it will lead you straight to it; for it, too, has its place merely, and does not occupy all space" ("Walking," 230).

With respect to such a politics, Thoreau says two things in the passage quoted above. First, he implies a connection between mainstream politics and the market: to get to politics, follow the market-man. Thoreau seems to imply that the market, a sphere increasingly dominated by industrialization and machinery, is itself the path to a machinelike politics. The path of the market leads us also to a certain *kind* of politics—the existence of a nascent system where the economic world increasingly shapes other social institutions and conventions. Mainstream politics is a realm where "the mass of men serve the state thus, not as men mainly, but as machines, with their bodies" ("Resistance," 66). The trope of the machine, for Thoreau, connotes a state where we do not think for ourselves, do not negate or dissent, but simply follow convention, to simply become a machine. But, as Thoreau writes, this "alarming" form of politics is "comparatively something so superficial and inhuman, that practically I have never fairly recognized that it concerns me at all" ("Life," 177).

Second, Thoreau carefully describes the limits of this system. The market, politics, church, state, school, trade, commerce, manufactures, and agriculture are all places that Thoreau can walk beyond. Modernization, like politics, is as yet "a narrow field" that is not fully pervasive in Thoreau's life. Modernization increasingly regulates individual behavior to follow certain preset patterns; the new shapes of the economy and of the market also mold politics in certain alienated ways; men increasingly do not really live and often act as machines instead of men. But despite these alienating tendencies, modernity is not (yet) an all encompassing system.

We can walk beyond the forces of convention and leave the "alarming" form of machinelike politics behind, but this does not necessarily mean we leave politics as it might alternatively be imagined. Thoreau withdraws from the tainted world of conventional politics to engage in a different kind of political practice, articulated through walking, huckleberrying, and confronting the wild. Thoreau seems concerned to expand our notion of the political by showing how these practices help us recuperate the critical capacities that are necessary for democratic citizens, yet starkly absent in contemporary politics. But these practices importantly take place in liminal spaces in nature, away from Main Street and all it represents.

Abstract Exchange

The patterns of modern market society have a deadening effect on us that is just as strong as its effect on a wild huckleberry. In "The Ponds" chapter of *Walden*, Thoreau writes that huckleberries cannot be sold on the market without suffering a complete loss of essence:

> The fruits do not yield their true flavor to the purchaser of them, not to him who raises them for the market. There is but one way to obtain it, yet few take that way. If you would know the true flavor of huckleberries, ask the cow-boy or the partridge. It is a vulgar error to suppose that you had tasted huckleberries who never plucked them. A huckleberry never reaches Boston; they have not been known there since they grew on her three hills. The ambrosial and essential part of the fruit is lost with the bloom which is rubbed off in the market-cart, and they become mere provender. As long as Eternal Justice remains, not one innocent huckleberry can be transported thither from the country hills. (*Walden*, 173)

Thoreau is speaking in both practical and metaphorical terms here. Practically speaking, wild berries, such as the huckleberry, have historically been difficult to ship and have not enjoyed a wide circulation. First of all, this fruit fades quickly: it is best when picked and eaten immediately. Before modern flash freezing methods where the berries can be frozen, packaged, and shipped the day they are picked, huckleberries were hard to enjoy unless you picked them yourself. Then, these berries are also resistant to cultivation: they are naturally wild and hard to domesticate. Both of these reasons are clues as to why Thoreau wrote an essay on the huckleberry (and wrote about other similar wild fruits like the wild apple) and why he refers to them so often in his work. But metaphorically, Thoreau is saying that something is lost through engagement with the market. The essential part of the fruit, it's wildness, is lost in the market basket. For Thoreau, the most attractive feature of the huckleberry *is* its uncultivated nature, its unmarketability. This is the "ambrosial" quality that is violated when we try to sell such wild fruits. And just as the essence of the huckleberry is lost on the market, so the defining feature of the self for Thoreau (the ability to negate and to resist conforming, regularizing activities) seems increasingly threatened by the seductive patterns of a modernizing society.

In "Wild Apples," Thoreau describes a similarly violent process of abstract exchange.[29] He says that the most important qualities of wild apples are lost when they are "vulgarized" by being bought and sold. The objects that end up on the market are not apples at all:

> There is thus about all natural products a certain volatile and ethereal quality which represents their highest value, and which cannot be vulgarized, or bought or sold. . . . When I see a particularly mean man carrying a load of fair and fragrant early apples to market, I seem to see a contest going on between him and his horse, on the one side, and the apples on the other and, to my mind, the apples always gain it. . . . Our driver begins to lose his load the moment he tries to transport them to where they do not belong. . . . Though he gets out from time to time, and feels of them, and thinks they are all there, I see the stream of their evanescent and celestial qualities going to heaven from his cart, while the pulp and skin and core only are going to market. They are not apples but pomace. ("Wild Apples," 448)

One of the qualities that Thoreau identifies as "the highest value" of the apples is their volatility, that quality which resists the market and cannot be bought or sold. But when it *is* sold, it is not an apple at all but mere "pomace." (Pomace is the pulpy material that remains after the juice has been extracted from a fruit or vegetable.) Thoreau says that the evisceration of the important qualities of objects is an effect of the market. He describes watching a farmer during apple harvest time, "between the fifth and twentieth of October," who is "selecting some choice barrels to fulfil an order. He turns a specked one over many times before he leaves it out. If I were to tell what is passing in my mind, I should say that every one was specked one over many times which he had handled; for he rubs off all the bloom, and those fugacious ethereal qualities leave it" ("Wild Apples," 449).

In *American Romanticism and the Marketplace,* Michael Gilmore studies the effects of the modern market on nineteenth-century writers, including Hawthorne, Emerson, Melville, and Thoreau. Gilmore is a literary critic who is interested in the ways the demands and restraints of the market influenced the major literary works of these writers. Gilmore's chapter titled *"Walden* and 'The Curse of Trade'" specifically analyzes how trade and the market shaped Thoreau's most important text

> [Thoreau's] quarrel with the marketplace is in large measure ontological. He sees the exchange process as emptying the world of its concrete reality and not only converting objects into dollars but causing their "it-ness" or being to disappear. . . . Thoreau believes that along with the degradation of the physical object in exchange there occurs a shriveling of the individual. Men in the marketplace do not relate as persons but as something less than human; they commit violence against their persons by their incessant anxiety to induce others to buy their products. . . . The laborer's self, his authentic being has as little chance to survive the exchange process. . . . To satisfy his employer, he has to suppress his individuality and become a mechanical thing. . . . "The cost of a thing," he writes, "is the amount of what I will call life which is exchanged for it, immediately or in the long run." Exchange brings about the ultimate alienation of man from himself; to engage in buying and selling is not merely to debase the self but to extinguish it, to hurry into death.[30]

Gilmore even notes that Thoreau's critique of commodification and abstract exchange has "certain affinities" with the Marxist critique of capitalism, especially Lukács's idea of reification where "a social relation between men assumes the character of a relation between things."[31] Gilmore uses this evidence of Thoreau's critique of abstract exchange to describe alienation as a problem isolated to the market alone. But for Thoreau, alienation is also represented in broader the broader institutions, habits, and customs of society. His darkest thoughts are often motivated by his recognition of the loss of critical capacities that characterize the ways people think, sense, and experience. Like Adorno, Thoreau moves far beyond the realm of exchange in discussing the effects of this alienation. Thoreau's critiques of the deadening experience of modern society often come in the form of a discussion of the railroad timetables, manners, etiquette, or pastimes such as reading the newspaper or the mail. Alienation, disaffection, extends beyond the market: experience in general has become formulaic, routinized, tamed, and domesticated.

Alienation can also be an experience of psychic suffering that extends beyond the reifying mechanics of abstract exchange. There is a loss that is experienced as suffering, as a sense of psychological pain. The moments of dark frustration and depression in Thoreau's work are often subtly linked to the alienating workings of modern society. If there is a difference between the ideas of reification and alienation, it would seem to be captured by the psychic suffering and pain that is more associated with the concept of alienation, and as we saw in chapter 1, this is the distinction Adorno draws between alienation and reification.

But even more significantly, whereas I describe the problem of alienation as a motivational factor for Thoreau's alternative political practice, Gilmore argues that Thoreau's frustrations with "the curse of trade" ultimately led him to abandon his political project, to retreat away from politics, away from history, into nature, into myth. Gilmore argues that because of Thoreau's frustrations at his inability to sell *Walden,* by his failures at the market, he intentionally sabotaged his own book, in a manner of speaking.[32] By refusing to turn the text into a commodity, Thoreau made it intentionally inaccessible and difficult for the general reader. The market wouldn't have *Walden,* so Thoreau decided to revise the book in ways that made it even more inaccessible to a mass readership: "Though Thoreau begins with the conviction that literature can change the world, the aesthetic strategies he adopts to accomplish political objectives involve him in a series of withdrawals from history; in each case the ahistorical maneuver disables the political and is compromised by the very historical moment it seeks to repudiate."[33]

Thoreau forsakes "civic aspirations for an exclusive concern with 'the art of living well'" reiterating Emerson's phrase about his former disciple. Gilmore sees Thoreau as having sacrificed politics for "living well" and engaging in (for Gilmore) apolitical activities in nature. Thoreau "withdraws" from history and politics by mythologizing his experiences in *Walden.* "By presenting its limited, time-bound conventions as external, the existing order in effect places itself outside time and beyond the possibility of change. Although Thoreau rigorously condemns his society's 'naturalizing' of itself in this fashion, he can be charged with performing a version of the same process on his own life by erasing history from *Walden* and mythologizing his experiment at the pond."[34]

I disagree that history is absent from *Walden.* If we understand Thoreau's motives for withdrawal and look closely at what he *does* when he goes into nature, we better understand how history fits into his writings. Whereas Gilmore thinks that Thoreau identifies alienating tendencies in modern life but then retreats from these forces, I argue that Thoreau's acts of withdrawal are ways to recuperate the critical capacities that allow us to truly be democratic citizens instead of unthinking machines. Huckleberrying, walking, and even hoeing beans, for example, are practices aimed toward working against the problems of alienation that Thoreau identifies in modernity (see chapter 4 in this book). Thoreau's excursions into nature are not apolitical withdrawals but alternative forms of democratically valuable political practice that aim to restore our capacity for critical negation.

Fashion, Manners, and Etiquette

Throughout his work, Thoreau also critiques another form of routine and pattern that seems to emerge from the modernization taking place all around him: etiquette and fashion. He seems to associate the population boom that occurred during his lifetime with a new concern over etiquette, manners, styles, and fashions. Edward Jarvis showed us how people in Concord were becoming increasingly concerned with acting more genteel. Indeed, Jarvis and others associated this refinement with becoming more "modern." But for Thoreau, becoming more refined means becoming more domesticated, tamed, cultivated, and all this adds up to becoming less able to think for ourselves. This tendency is highlighted by the following passage from *Walden*: "When I ask for a garment of a particular form, my tailoress tells me gravely, 'They do not make them so now,' not emphasizing the 'They' at all, as if she quoted an authority as impersonal as the Fates, and I find it difficult to get what I want. . . . When I hear this oracular sentence, I am for a moment absorbed in thought, emphasizing to myself each word separately that I may come at the meaning of it, that I may find out by what degree of consanguinity *They* are related to me, and what authority they may have in an affair which affects me so nearly" (*Walden*, 25).

Thoreau rejects the notion that "They" should have any kind of authority over "I." "They" and "I" are of no relation and share no common blood, but the way he sets up the statement implies that he himself is in the minority in denying that "they" have authority over "I."[35] Fashion is a good stand-in for social authority, for Thoreau. Fashion and style come into being because people follow them: nothing is a fashion unless people conform to it by granting social authority to a trend. Clothing and fashions become a metaphor for the imposition of common forms upon the self. For Thoreau, this kind of formulaic convention is alienating in that social authority is unthinkingly internalized in ways that crowd out a negating self. Being concerned with fashions and clothing are counterproductive to the work Thoreau thinks we need to do to regain our critical capacities. He famously stated: "I say, beware of all enterprises that require new clothes, and not rather a new wearer of clothes" (*Walden*, 23). Elsewhere in

Walden, he says, "We think that we can change our clothes only" (332). But his point does not simply seem to be that clothing distracts us from a more introspective focus on the self, but that concerning ourselves with fashion and styles entails a loss: "They" overtake the "I," the self that can go against the grain of conformity. In one striking sentence, Thoreau says "Sell your clothes and keep your thoughts" (328). This implies that buying clothes detracts from and threatens the thinking and critical self: conversely, we can keep this self by selling our clothes, by rejecting the social authority of style, fashion, and materialism.

Thoreau's thoughts on clothing make a more general statement about the impact of industrialization when we consider that clothing was increasingly produced in the new textile factories in Lowell and other cities: these manufacturing centers represent the most intense example of industrialization during Thoreau's lifetime. Beginning in 1813 in Waltham, Massachusetts, and more than a decade later reaching its pinnacle in Lowell, "Boston capitalists established fully integrated, machine-operated woolen mills" that transformed raw wool into finished cloth all under one roof. Textile mills became towns as women and children "lived in factory dormitories in mill villages where the entire community was organized to fulfill the requirements of the production process."[36] Lowell was a town that originated because of the textile mill: in 1826, a four-square-mile tract of land was cut off from Chelmsford and renamed Lowell, after the founder of the Boston Manufacturing Company, Francis Cabot Lowell. The textile factory was created and it was "truly an instant city." This was the "first company town" and was "an important model of urbanization for Massachusetts and the United States in the nineteenth century."[37] Lowell created the model and hundreds of textile factories followed suit in other northeastern cities. Thoreau's critiques of clothing take on a new light when we consider that the textile industry was booming all around him. His concerns with the ways that clothing and fashion can eclipse the thinking-self map onto a larger critique of industrialization itself.

Manners and etiquette were directly related to the new industrialization, but they also threaten the thinking self. In a striking example that hits close to home for Thoreau, he describes how a concern with the tastes and habits of refined society have taken over "his friend" (most likely Emerson).[38] In a journal entry for October 10, 1851, Thoreau writes "Ah, I yearn toward thee, my friend, but I have not confidence in thee. . . . Even when I meet thee unexpectedly, I part from thee with disappointment. . . . We are almost a sore with one another. Ah I am afraid because thy relations are not my relations. Because I have experienced that in some respects we are strange to one another, strange as wild creatures. . . . We do not know what hinders us from coming together. But when

I consider what my friend's relations and acquaintances are, what his tastes and habits are, then the difference between us gets named. *I see that all these friends and acquaintances and tastes and habits are indeed my friend's self.*"[39]

Thoreau describes a dynamic here where true understanding and relationships are thwarted by the ways that a concern with gentility and refinement can take over the self. Manners and etiquette make us into formulaic, unthinking, and habitual creatures: "we meet at meals three times a day. . . . We have had to agree to a certain set of rules, called etiquette and politeness" (*Walden,* 136). Simply following patterns and not acting as individuals, we experience a real loss and become shells of what we might be when we follow the dictates of these empty conventions.[40]

Losing the Thinking Self in a Modernizing Society

In addition to his broader social critiques, there are many moments in Thoreau's writings where he seems to experience a more personal and direct melancholy or depression. Indeed, these dark moments, in part, have prompted some scholars to wonder for his psychological health and sanity. Here, we explore the nature of Thoreau's experiences of pain and suffering, what forms they take, and most importantly, what seems to prompt them. These experiences are not merely subjective and rooted in his own damaged personality and psyche, but instead are subtly associated with critiques of objective specific social and political conditions, all of which can be easily overlooked but can be illuminating when highlighted and taken together.

In the first example, from his essay "Walking," Thoreau listens to a cock crow; he compares his own mood with that of the crow and finds himself coming up short. It is significant that the bird is a rooster, a morning bird that rouses us out of sleep. As we have seen, "awakening" and "morning" are two tropes that Thoreau continually opposes again states where we are "dull," machinelike, conformist, or too rooted in everyday, common modes of perception. When we are asleep we are not thinking for ourselves, but when we are awake and it is again morning, we are thinking and experiencing in unique, original, and critical ways. The cock's crow "commonly reminds us that we are growing rusty and antique in our employments and habits of thought . . . he has not fallen astern; he has got up early and kept up early and to be where he is is to be in season, in the foremost rank of time. . . . *Where he lives no fugitive slave laws are passed.* . . . When in doleful dumps, breaking the awful stillness of our wooden sidewalk on a Sunday, or perchance, a watcher in the house of mourning, I hear a cockerel crow far or near, I think to myself, 'There is one of us is well, at any rate, —and with a sudden gush return to my senses'" ("Walking," 254; italics mine).

Compared to the rooster, who seems well, Thoreau is unwell. Depressed, he likens himself to a "watcher in the house of mourning," rather than experiencing the awakening that makes it morning no matter what the clock says. He cannot bear the "awful stillness" and is jealous of the bird's comparatively better state. But is this passage just a comment on Thoreau's depression? Not really, because he gives us many clues as to why he is experiencing this dark mood. First, clearly Thoreau is in town, in the village, when he hears the cock crow, for he is on a wooden sidewalk. He is downtown, most likely on a main street in Concord. He is in the epicenter of the very place where the changes wrought by modernization are the most evident. Furthermore, we know what he is thinking about. As he walks downtown past the many shops (which he describes in detail elsewhere), he is ruminating on the economy and on politics.

He walks past the shops and thinks about how modernization has imposed too much uniformity on the ways men make a living, that we have grown "rusty and antique in our modes of employment and habits of thought." Thoreau again draws a connection between the market and conventional employments and our ways of thinking. We unthinkingly conform to habit; we do not live or experiment. Thoreau here conjures an image of being bound in our movements by the market, like the quotation discussed earlier about the shopkeepers who sit with "crossed legs" all day in their shops, but have not yet committed suicide (much to Thoreau's amazement). Thoreau implies that when we cannot experiment in our modes of employment, we will also think in common ways.

But, as the quotation tells us, he is also thinking of politics and specifically the fugitive slave act. Congress passed the Fugitive Slave Law on September 18, 1850, making Northern officials liable to fines for failing to arrest slaves who had escaped to the North. In effect, those officials and institutions were made responsible for enforcing slavery. The law was abhorrent to many Northerners; it was especially contested in Concord, where there was an active underground railroad and where many abolitionists lived. Thoreau's friends and his own family lodged escaped slaves to protect them from being returned to the South. Walter Harding recounts one such instance in his biography of Thoreau:

> On September 30, 1851, Henry Williams, who had escaped to Boston from slavery in Stafford County, Virginia, the previous October, learned that there were warrants out for his arrest and that the police had called for him when he was fortunate enough to be out. Accordingly, he fled to Concord on foot, carrying with him letters of introduction to the Thoreaus from Mr. Lovejoy of Cambridge and William Lloyd Garrison. The Thoreaus lodged him for the night and collected funds to help him along his way. On the morning of October 1, Thoreau went down to the railroad station to buy him a ticket to Burlington,

Vermont. He saw someone there acting so much like a Boston policeman that he retired and waited until the 5 p.m. train when, with the coast clear, he got Williams safely on his way to Canada.[41]

This is only one of several times that Thoreau, his parents, and his sisters, aided fugitive slaves.[42] The fugitive slave act outraged Thoreau: indeed, his essay "Slavery in Massachusetts" ("my thought are murder to the State") was written in response to the famous Anthony Burns case, which was thought to have turned many people in Massachusetts into more ardent abolitionists.[43] Thoreau and his family had long been abolitionists; this incident only confirmed that they already thought. Burns was an escaped slave living in Boston; he was captured and taken back to Virginia, but then purchased and freed by Northern philanthropists.[44]

Thus Thoreau's sentence regarding the fugitive slave law is not just an unimportant line that responds to a topical event. His life and thought testify to a deep and abiding concern with slavery and the fugitive slave law; these are central elements of his critique of mainstream politics. As he argues in "Resistance to Civil Government" and "Slavery in Massachusetts," he cannot engagement with a government that will pass such laws. He says "I cannot for an instant recognize that political organization as *my* government which is the *slave's* government also" ("Resistance," 67). Slavery and a fugitive slave law are created and sustained by unthinking, uncritical men who cannot say no. This is the mechanical way of thinking that characterizes Main Street and conventional political spaces. Thoreau feels a melancholy loss given his location in downtown Concord, yet when he hears the cock, "with a sudden gush," he returns to his senses and is able to shake off the dolefulness that Main Street, and all it stands for, inspires in him.

In another example from "Walking," Thoreau speaks of a forest of pine trees in the woods as though they are a family:

> I was as impressed [by the pine trees] as if some ancient and altogether admirable and shining family had settled there in that part of the land called Concord . . . who had not gone into society in the village,—who had not been called upon. . . . I do not know whether I heard the sounds of suppressed hilarity or not. They seemed to recline on the sunbeams. They have sons and daughters. They are quite well. The farmer's cart-path, which leads directly through their hall, does not in the least put them out, as the muddy bottom of a pool is sometimes seen through the reflected skies. . . . Nothing can equal the serenity of their lives. . . . They are of no politics. There was no noise of labor. I did not perceive that they were weaving or spinning. . . . But I find it difficult to remember

them. They fade irrevocably out of my mind even now while I speak, and endeavor to recall them and *recollect myself.* It is only after a long and serious effort
to recollect my best thoughts that I become again aware of their cohabitancy. If
it were not for such families as this, I think I should move out of Concord.
("Walking," 252; italics mine)

Again, Thoreau seems to compare his own state with that of the pine trees.
Unlike him, they are "quite well" and "serene." Indeed, they are laughing and
barely suppressing their hilarity! But we cannot simply read this as another in-
dication of Thoreau's flawed psyche. For again, he tells us why he is in a darker
state than are the pines. The pines do not have to worry about how they are
going to make a living: they need not "weave and spin." Here, Thoreau is alluding to the "lilies of the field" passage in Matthew 6:28 and Luke 12:27,
where the flowers are also described as being free of worry, work, or spinning.
The pines are far enough away from the market that it does not even bother
them when "the farmer's cart" passes among them. They do not have to worry
about politics: "they are of no politics." Their spatial position is in a forest: they
do not have to go into "society" and have good manners and be polite and call
upon people and "be called upon." No wonder they are laughing.

Thoreau on the other hand, seems lost and is endeavoring to "recollect"
himself and return to "his best thoughts," which he can only do with great effort. What are his "best thoughts"? He does not elaborate here, but at other
times, we know he values the self that can say "no" to convention and experiment with life as the "better part of the man." Thoreau himself seems threatened with losing this vital critical capacity until he removes the village from his
mind and recalls the pine trees.

Thoreau is at his dark best, however, in the "Solitude" chapter of *Walden.*
Here, he grapples with melancholy and loneliness. He speaks of how we might
become more sane, how we might cure ourselves and be healthy; he jokingly
asks what "pill" we might take as a panacea when melancholy strikes. All this
makes the chapter of particular interest to those who want to highlight Thoreau's wounded psyche. Many have written about the "slight insanity" that Thoreau mentions in this chapter. Scholars have also studied this chapter because
of its complex style and frequent paradoxes and contradictions, devices which
have also been seen as evidence of Thoreau's problematic mental state. By
taking the chapter as a whole, however, and asking the questions that Thoreau's
paradoxes prompt, we get a different impression of it: Thoreau seems to consider how the things that modern society both produces and inhibits make public, social spaces the most lonely spaces of all.[45]

He begins the chapter by considering how feelings of melancholy and lone-liness are not always, and even not usually, a function of being alone: "There can be no very black melancholy to him who lives in the midst of nature and has his senses still" (*Walden*, 131). He has experienced such feelings just once and clearly sees the experience of melancholy when one is alone as the exception: "I have never felt lonesome or in the least oppressed by a sense of solitude, but once, and that was a few weeks after I came to the woods, when, for an hour, I doubted if the near neighborhood of man was not essential to a serene and healthy life. To be alone was something unpleasant. But I was at the same time conscious of a slight insanity in my mood, and seemed to foresee my recovery" (131).

Typically, Thoreau notes, we experience the greatest sense of depression, loneliness, and melancholy when we are among others. Feeling alone is not simply a matter of our distance from other people or from society: "What sort of space is that which separates a man from his fellows and makes him solitary? I have found that no exertion of the legs can bring two minds much nearer to one another. What do we want most to dwell near to? Not to many men surely, the depot, the post-office, the bar-room, the meeting-house, the school-house, the grocery, Beacon Hill or the Five Points, where men most congregate, but to the perennial source of our life, whence in all our experience we have found that to issue, as the willow stands near the water and sends out its roots in that direction. . . . this is the place where a wise man will dig his cellar" (*Walden*, 133). For Thoreau, the kinds of spaces that make us solitary are modern social spaces where "many men" (but not men *as such* or men as they might be) congregate. The New England town meeting is typically held up as an exemplar of democ-racy, but, given the kind of men who fill it, even the meetinghouse is not some-thing we want to be "near to." Thoreau implies that we are separated from each other by the institutions of modern society.

Property and the market are especially implicated. Thoreau speaks of one of his "fellow townsman" who was driving his cattle to market and had ac-quired "a handsome property" (*Walden*, 133). He asks Thoreau how he could give up so many comforts of life, and after answering him Thoreau "left him to pick his way thought the darkness and the mud to 'Brighton,—or Bright-town'" and in the next breath speaks of how such "dead men" can be awak-ened (134). The man Thoreau clearly associates with the market, with property accumulation, is the "dead man" who is traveling to a town that promises "bright" things but makes him crawl through the mud to get there.

Given the state of most men in modern society and given the ways that they are dead to themselves and others, Thoreau asks: "Could we not do without the society of our gossips a little while under these circumstances,—have our own thoughts to cheer us? Confucius says truly, 'Virtue does not remain as an abandoned orphan; it must of necessity have neighbors'" (*Walden*, 134). Here is Thoreau at his paradoxical best: on the one hand he is saying we can do without the society of gossips, but on the other hand that virtue necessitates neighbors. Thoreau wants us to be true neighbors to each other but laments the fact that modern society makes it difficult for us to *be* neighbors. We do not want the society of gossips or men who are on their way to the market and hail us only because they want to sell us some property. Such things create spaces between people and separate men from themselves.

At the beginning of the next paragraph in *Walden*, Thoreau sounds positively Emersonian. He speaks of a way of thinking that allows us to stand separate from our context, to exist apart from the people, events, and happenings that rush by us: "With thinking we may be beside ourselves in a sane sense. By a conscious effort of the mind we can stand aloof from actions and their consequences; and all things, good and bad, go by us like a torrent" (*Walden*, 134). But unlike Emerson, Thoreau immediately turns toward a consideration of the negative aspects of this way of holding ourselves apart from our context, of retreating into the mind. When we are aloof, "We are not wholly involved in Nature" and this is rarely, if ever, a good thing for Thoreau (135). He writes, "I only know myself as a human entity . . . and am sensible of a certain doubleness by which I can stand as remote from myself as from another. However intense my experience, I am conscious of the presence and criticism of a part of me, which, as it were, is not a part of me, but a spectator, sharing no experience, but taking note of it, and that is no more I than it is you. . . . This doubleness may easily make us poor neighbors and friends sometimes" (135). In this experience of "doubleness," Thoreau is conscious of a separation within himself. He is alienated from himself, lost to himself. Part of himself does not share in his experience. Given the centrality of really living and really experiencing life for Thoreau, this part of the self that cannot experience "is not a part of me" and "is no more I than it is you." But even more revealingly, it is this doubleness that prevents us from being true neighbors and friends. We already know that Thoreau, agreeing with Confucius, thinks that virtue cannot be alone but requires neighbors. And now we also know that the experience of duality makes us poor neighbors. Thoreau has told us that being a good neighbor is important to him, so this twofold affect seems problematically limiting.

Immediately after saying "This doubleness may easily make us poor neighbors and friends sometimes," Thoreau says "I find it wholesome to be alone the greater part of the time" (*Walden*, 135). At this point, the meaning of Thoreau's paradox seems clearer: he wants to be able to enjoy the society of real neighbors, but he finds them to be rare and so would rather be alone. "I think that I love society as much as most, and am ready to fasten myself like a bloodsucker for the time to any full-blooded man that comes in my way. *I am naturally no hermit,* but might possibly sit out the sturdiest frequenter of the bar-room, if my business called me thither" (*Walden,* 140; italics mine). He recognizes in himself a need to withdraw from other people and from society, but says that this characteristic is not "natural." Is it social, then?

> Society is commonly too cheap. We meet at very short intervals, not having had time to acquire any new value for each other. We meet at meals three times a day, and give each other a new taste of that old musty cheese that we are. We have had to agree on a certain set of rules, called etiquette and politeness, to make this frequent meeting tolerable and that we need not come to open war. We meet at the post-office, and at the sociable, and about the fireside every night; we live thick and are in each other's way, and stumble over one another, and I think that we thus lose some respect for one another. Certainly less frequency would suffice for all important and hearty communications. *Consider the girls in a factory — never alone, hardly in their dreams.* It would be better if there were but one inhabitant to a square mile, as where I live. The value of a man is not in his skin, that we should touch him." (136; italics mine)

Here, Thoreau seems to be responding to the effects of the population boom that took place during his lifetime. An increased population necessitates that people abide by "a certain set of rules, called etiquette and politeness." In this passage, Thoreau explicitly links these social changes with population increases and modernizing tendencies toward refinement and increased gentility. People's actions become formulaic, thoughtless, and superficial. They are not motivated by true feeling, but by a sense of what the rules of politeness and etiquette demand.

But there is also something more disturbing going on here than simply an increased superficiality and concern with gentility. Thoreau implies that various modern forces (busy schedules, rules, etiquette, and the public spaces where we meet) are overtaking the self to the extent that some are, like the factory girls, "never alone, hardly in their dreams." As these women moved from the farm to the factory, their lives changed dramatically.[46] An economic history describes life in the Lowell mills: "On the farm, the rising and setting of the sun, the seasons, and the cycles of crops regulated the patterns of life and work. Now, instead of being guided by nature, work was calibrated to a time clock, a whistle, a bell. Industrialization standardized irregular labor rhythms and made time the measure of work." Nearly every hour of the day was controlled and accounted for. The "operatives," as the factory workers were called, were regulated in nearly every aspect of their daily life: "Work in the Lowell factories was under the watchful eye of a superintendent, his office strategically placed between the dormitories and the mills. Each work room had a foreman, who was responsible for the work and the proper conduct of the operatives. Supervision was thus constant. It was a life without privacy."[47]

Thoreau seems fully aware of how the factory workers were experiencing, in the most intense form, the changes happening all over New England. If he were concerned only about overcrowding, he might have simply left the sentence to read that the factory girls were never alone. But in a haunting addition that remakes the meaning of the sentence, even their dreams are being influenced by their factory life, by modernization. For Thoreau, writing before Freud, dreams seem to be figured as an intensely private, protected, and personal sphere of the self. Thus it is shocking for Thoreau to say that even our dreams are influenced by modernization. Thoreau's reference to the factory girls intensifies the link that he earlier only implies; he connects a more general deadening of social relations in modern society with industrialization by referring to the factory girls at the point where the sentence has built up a great deal of momentum, right before he moves from diagnosing the problem to prescribing a solution. In a way that prefigures Adorno, Thoreau seems to connect formulaic patterns of manners and etiquette with more obviously economic features of modernity, such as industrialization. It is all part and parcel of a cheapening of modern society.

In the final paragraph of the *Walden* chapter, Thoreau turns from diagnosing the problem to proposing a prescription. He asks "What is the pill which will keep us well, serene, contented? Not my or thy grandfather's but our great grandmother Nature's universal, vegetable, botanic medicines, by which she has kept herself young always, outlived so many old Parrs in her day, and fed her health on their decaying fatness. For my panacea . . . let me have a draught of undiluted morning air. Morning air! If men will not drink of this at the fountain-head of the day, why, then, we must even bottle up some and sell it in the shops, for the benefit of those who have lost their subscription ticket to morning time in this world" (*Walden*, 138). He reminds us that he has been concerned all along with how we can be kept "well, serene, contented" and avoid melancholy. Now, humorously, he tells us that the solution is of course not something that can be taken in pill form: it's the "morning air." And for Thoreau, *morning* is one of those recurring terms, like *neighbor* that is shot through with meaning and significance. The morning is when we are awake, when we are not dull and conforming to common sense.

Thoreau, therefore, gives us clues throughout the "Solitude" chapter as to the social origins of this problem. Joel Porte, however, reads the chapter more as a typically Transcendentalist depiction of the Faustian "*zwei Seelen*," two souls, of an existential conflict between the spiritual and sensual sides of the self. Porte argues that all the New England Transcendentalists suffered from this problem: "they were all New England Fausts." And in stating so, he quotes the same passage as above, where Thoreau experiences "doubleness." Porte argues that "Thoreau's admission here of a sense of Faustian doubleness, of a split between experiencing body and judging spirit, carries with it, especially in the searching tentativeness of its rhetoric, a deep note of personal concern, as if what he is saying were causes not only for congratulation but for alarm."[48] But Porte's reading differs from mine in that he does not see this passage regarding "the duplex soul" (to borrow Porte's term) in light of the rest of the chapter, where Thoreau to attributes this internal divide to an alienating modern society, to the new modern developments such as industrialization, the population boom, and the increasing concern with etiquette and manners. The entire "Solitude" chapter seems a meditation on the nature and origins of this sense of alienation, but Porte reads the passage on "doubleness" on its own, without linking it to other illuminating moments in the chapter. And too, Porte depicts Thoreau's notion of "doubleness" as a typical problem of Transcendentalism and Emersonianism without discussing the ways we know Thoreau often uses language that sounds Emersonian, toward very different ends. Even if this problem of the loss of self is a common problem for both Emerson and Thoreau, they approach the nature and origins of it very differently: Thoreau links it to external conditions of modernity, while for Emerson, as we have seen, it is more of an internal problem of clouded vision, of not maintaining the correct focal distance.

The final example of the experience of alienation comes from "The Village" chapter of *Walden*. Thoreau describes a trip into the village of Concord: "It is a surprising and memorable, as well as valuable experience, to be lost in the woods any time . . . not till we are completely lost, or turned round,—for a man needs only to be turned round once with his eyes shut in the woods to be lost,—do we appreciate the vastness and strangeness of nature. Every man has to learn the points of the compass again as often as he awakes, whether from sleep or any abstraction. Not till we are lost, in other words not till we have lost the world, do we begin to find ourselves, and realize where we are and the infinite extent of our relations" (*Walden*, 170).

This passage sounds fairly Emersonian at first glance. Thoreau speaks of "losing the world," which conjures up images of retreating into the mind and losing the real material world in favor of building a world in our own minds. But in the context of the entire chapter, the quotation has a different meaning. Thoreau describes this sense of losing and finding himself as he is telling us about his walks home from the village. He describes a "village of busy men, as curious to me as if they had been prairie-dogs, each sitting at the mouth of its burrow, or running over to a neighbor's to gossip. I went there frequently to observe their habits. The village appeared to me a great news room; and on one side, to support it, as once at Redding & Company's on State Street, they kept nuts and raisins, or salt and meal and other groceries" (*Walden*, 167). But the most striking parts come as Thoreau describes what it felt like to walk down the main street of Concord. He feels suffocated by "the vitals of the village: such as "the grocery, the bar-room, the post-office, the bank" where "signs were hung out on all side to allure him [the traveler]; some to catch him by the appetite, as the tavern and victualling cellar; some by fancy, as the dry goods store" (168). Material items and conveniences all call out to him and tempt him. Because Thoreau lives in the woods and is more removed from the village, he finds it easier to resist these siren songs, but even he feels the need to dash away to escape their lure. Sometimes he "bolted suddenly, and nobody could tell my whereabouts" for he "never hesitated at a gap in the fence" (169). Thoreau then writes of walking home from the village at night and getting lost in the woods, and then generalizes in a more abstract style about being lost in a seemingly more existential sense.

Coming after this description of the material charm of the village, "the world" that Thoreau finds it valuable to escape from is actually a specific, historical context: the world of the village, Main Street. Only when we have lost this particular kind of modern world do we begin "to find ourselves, and realize where we are and the infinite extent of our relations." But in what ways does such a world limit and corrupt our relations? What relations is Thoreau referring to?

In "The Village," Thoreau describes the market men, the shop owners greedy for customers; the central thoroughfare where shops and houses are close together "so that every traveler had to run the gauntlet, and every man, woman, and child might get a lick at him" (*Walden*, 168). These closely placed houses and the shops are things that try to trap us, that must be dodged and skillfully eluded. They exert a power and a pull on us that we must try to "bolt" from, escaping them by leaping over fences.

In this passage, the influence of the shops and the market men is especially strong. But buying and selling are ways of relating that extend even to the government. Immediately after encouraging us to find the infinite extent of our relations, Thoreau tells us how after one trip to the village, he was jailed for not paying his poll tax because he would not recognize the authority of "the State, which buys and sells men, women, and children, like cattle at the door of its senate-house" (*Walden*, 171). After a night in jail, Thoreau tells us he went huckleberrying on Fair Haven Hill.[49] Thus for Thoreau, both the market and the state represent superficial and corrupt ways of relating to one another that limit and restrict our relations. The world of the market and of politics represents worlds that Thoreau wants to lose: we "find" ourselves once we distance ourselves from such spaces and realize other ways of relating to one another that transcend those of buyer and seller.

Thoreau, Adorno, and Modern Alienation

As we saw in chapter 1, in the section on alienation and damaged life, for Adorno, people wear masks of "exuberant health." Those who are the sickest appear normal: they unhesitatingly do and say the expected and appropriate thing, with a bland formalism, a "slick stupidity." The most alienated are those who move without awkward gestures or anything unexpected or unconventional. They have "push-button behavior patterns." They are not neurotic, because that would imply an internal struggle against the authority of society. They are not anxious; they are unthinkingly "normal"—the regular guy, the popular girl. But for Adorno this is not life, but death. These are not humans, but machines. The nonidentical has been erased and behavior has been smoothed out, made to fit into abstract patterns of etiquette, tact, manners. These tendencies are rooted in the logics of abstract exchange and identity, which work violently upon difference to tame and absorb it. Adorno practices negative dialectics to rupture the illusion of harmony, to upset this mask of equilibrium, to make people aware that their capacity to think and negate is being replaced with knee-jerk reactions that affirm the collective authority of society.

And here, we can see the resemblances between Adorno and Thoreau's characterization of modern alienation. Like Adorno, Thoreau links the mechanical conformity to abstract patterns of behavior with death, with sleeping, with not living. Although he does not describe a nearly all-encompassing system in the way Adorno does, Thoreau does see a relationship between this alienated sensibility and the ways that abstract exchange and the logic of the market erase difference and particularity. For Thoreau, there seems to be a kind of nascent network connecting things like manners, fashion, politics, and the workings of the economy.

Thoreau and Adorno describe similar objective conditions of alienation, despite their many differences. They also work against these forces in sympathetic ways as Thoreau's practices of withdrawal are undertaken with the ends of upsetting conventional patterns, formulas, and illusory harmonies. While Adorno's negative dialectics highlights the nonidentical, Thoreau walks in a quest for the wild. He walks to dislodge from his mind the whistle of the railroad that, unconsciously, becomes a timetable for daily activities, a timetable organized around the business back and forth from Boston. He walks in different patterns to remind himself that life need not be modeled from existing molds.

4

Huckleberrying toward Democracy

Thoreau's Practices of Withdrawal

> That government is best which governs not at all; and when men are prepared for it, that will be the kind of government which they will have.
> Henry David Thoreau

> Is a democracy, such as we know it, the last improvement possible in government? Is it not possible to take a step further toward recognizing and organizing the rights of man?
> Henry David Thoreau

In his book *The Senses of Walden*, Stanley Cavell reads *Walden* word by word, sentence by sentence. His goal is to unravel the layers of meaning and decipher some of the mysteries of Thoreau's excursionary, metaphorical, and allegorical style: "My opening hypothesis is that this book is perfectly complete, that it means in every word it says, and that it is fully sensible of its mysteries and fully open about them." In parsing the words and sentences of *Walden*, Cavell brings his reader to the doorstep of many interesting lines of inquiry but leaves a fuller exploration of some questions to others. He says, "I have come to the end of the questions I have wanted to pose about *Walden*. That I leave them incompletely explored will not matter if I have left them faithful and prompting enough for the book to take them out of my hands, to itself, for strangers."[1]

One of Cavell's questions prompts a deeper exploration of the relationship between Thoreau and democratic politics. How does Thoreau, by withdrawing, separating, and distancing himself from society and politics, actually end up enacting a unique form of democratic politics? How does he, by these separations, enact practices that prove valuable in a democracy? As Cavell puts it: "*Walden* is, among other things, a tract of political education, education for membership in the polis. It locates authority in the citizens and it identifies citizens—those with whom one is in membership—as 'neighbors.' What it shows is that education for citizenship is education for isolation. . . . The writer of *Walden* . . . resists society by visibly withdrawing from it. . . . The writer's strategy, which enforces his position as neighbor, is to refuse society his voice."[2] But what does this mean? How can education for citizenship be about isolation? How can we become neighbors by refusing and withdrawing from society?

Thoreau's work is fraught with paradoxes, but perhaps the most central one concerns the seemingly contradictory attitude he takes toward other people, to society, to questions of the common good, and to politics. That his education for citizenship takes the form of education for isolation strikes to the heart of this paradox. How can a thinker who is often seemingly misanthropic, egoistic, and excessively individualistic be said to offer a political education? The target of his advice is most often the individual, and Thoreau usually denigrates "the mass of men," but at the same time he often shows concern for the common good, for society as a whole. He worries about the path that these men proceed down but has little hope for effecting broad social change by reform movements. He criticizes organized institutions, parties, reformers, and philanthropists who seek to "do good." At the same time, he expresses concern for mainstream ways of living and wants to offer us advice, presumably so we can change. He is concerned about those who fail to contribute to the common good and makes it clear that he *does* seek to "do good," albeit in an unusual way.

In "Life Without Principle," Thoreau criticizes those who are so concerned to make money that they neglect their duty to contribute to society. As he says, "The day went by, and at evening I passed the yard of another neighbor, who keeps many servants, and spends money quite foolishly, while he adds nothing to the common stock" ("Life," 157). This was the era of the Gold Rush and Thoreau criticizes people who flocked to prospect in California: "That so many are ready to live by luck, and so get the means of commanding the labor of others less lucky, without contributing any value to society!" (162). And regarding the gold-digger again, "What difference does it make, whether you shake dirt or shake dice? If you win, society is the loser" (163). Thoreau, as we will see, idealizes the "West" in his essay on "Walking," but it functions more as a metaphor for freedom from taming and domestication. Surprisingly, given the tenor of his thought on modernization, Thoreau does not consider actually moving westward to the frontier: he figures that as an escape from contributing to the common good.

In another passage, Thoreau says that he is concerned with showing "the mass of men" how to "improve" their lives and their times: "I do not speak to those who are well employed, in whatever circumstances, and they know whether they are well employed or not—but mainly to the mass of men who are discontented, and idly complaining of the hardness of their lot or of the times, when they might improve them" (*Walden*, 16). Again, in the advice giving mode, Thoreau says, "I would fain say something, not so much concerning the Chinese and Sandwich Islanders as you who read these pages, who are said to live in New England; something about your condition, especially your outward condition or circumstances in this world, in this town, what it is, whether it is necessary that it be as bad as it is, whether it can be improved as well as not" (4). Thoreau seems to want to give us an example of his ways of overcoming these bad outward circumstances. He says he is going to give a "simple and sincere account of his own life," while we are supposed to listen to see if his practices can heal our own desperation, to see if the coat he wore fits us: "I trust that none will stretch the seams in putting on the coat, for it may do good service to him whom it fits" (4).

Thoreau's efforts at helping others, however, look unusual: regaining the critical parts of the self, ceasing to act as a machine, becomes its own democratically valuable contribution to the common stock. But because mainstream society and conventional politics are the sources of alienation, working to counteract these ill effects involves an initial separation, a distancing. Thus we end up with Cavell's paradoxical statement that education for citizenship is indeed education for isolation. Thoreau's ideal, however, is not a state of isolation and solitary withdrawal in these borderlands. He longs for true "neighbor"-hood, but cannot find it in mainstream modern society. Like Adorno, Thoreau has harsh words for the society of his own day, but not society *per se*, not as it might be differently imagined. Thoreau envisions a true neighborhood of travelers, of people who also move back and forth between the woods and fields and Main Street. He wants to surround himself with people who are also not "at home" and comfortable in the village, but continually seek out rupturing and uprooting experiences in the borderlands and other withdrawn spaces. Thoreau does not become a permanent resident of these spaces of withdrawal: he always returns, after his excursions, to the town, having recovered the critical capacities that allow him to avoid thinking like a machine—even when he is in the village, surrounded by shops, and being hailed by market men. But it is not that Thoreau's democratic politics begin *properly* when he has returned to the public spaces: instead, his practices of withdrawal are themselves enactments of his unique democratic politics. Like Adorno's negative dialectics, Thoreau's practices of walking, huckleberrying, and confronting the "wild" pay attention to particularity and find a rupturing, contradictory quality in objects that is drawn out toward a more general critique of society. And like Adorno, Thoreau identifies the critical capacities that come from these practices of withdrawal as democratically valuable. The frustration and pain that Thoreau experiences in his own historical context, under a market that increasingly shapes the timetable of daily life and under a slaveholding government, motivate practices that seek to disrupt the status quo toward a more democratic possibility.

Walking

"Walking" is usually read as the story of Thoreau's method of escaping from society and from politics. In this essay, he criticizes what is "civilized" and "domesticated" over what is "wild" and "natural." In the first paragraph, he says: "I wish to speak a word for Nature, for absolute freedom and wildness, as contrasted with a freedom and culture merely civil,—to regard man as an inhabitant, or a part and parcel of Nature, rather than a member of society" ("Walking," 225). Thoreau walked every day and saw these excursions as necessary to his health and mental well-being. He says "I think I cannot preserve my health and spirits unless I spend four hours a day at least—and it is commonly more than that—sauntering through the woods and over the hills and fields, absolutely free from all worldly engagements" (227). In this passage and in other places, Thoreau seems to describe nature as a retreat from the society and politics that drain his most important critical qualities: "In my afternoon walk, I would fain forget all my morning occupations and my obligations to society. But it sometimes happens that I cannot easily shake off the village. The thought of some work will run in my head and I am not where my body is,—I am out of my senses. In my walks I would fain return to my senses" (229).

When he is able to "shake off the village," he shakes off the habits of the machine and "returns to his senses." In another passage, Thoreau traces the etymology of the word "village," finding its roots in the Latin *villa:* "Hence, too, the Latin word *vilis* and our vile; also *villain*. This suggests what kind of degeneracy villagers are liable to" ("Walking," 231). In this essay, and as is seen in these passages, Thoreau often speaks of Nature and walking as two forms of retreat from the vile village. To give one more example, he says: "Let me live where I will, on this side is the city, on that the wilderness, and ever I am leaving the city more and more, and withdrawing into the wilderness" (234).

These are the kinds of passages that seem to confirm a reading of Thoreau as a misanthropic hermit. But there are other passages in "Walking" that complicate the story considerably. While Thoreau goes into nature out of a need to regain parts of the self, his withdrawals are not retreats from politics. Rather, Thoreau is trying to carve out a new space for his own variety of politics *within* nature. He may go into nature to reject the alienating village and mainstream politics ("what is called politics"), but he goes there with a mission, a crusade to carve out a new space for a new type of democratic politics, to create a new type citizen.

In this way, "Walking" as an essay has a great deal in common with Thoreau's essay on "Resistance to Civil Government," though it is typically interpreted as a "nature essay" unconnected with Thoreau's more overtly political essays. In "Resistance to Civil Government," Thoreau overtly describes himself as at war with the State "after his own fashion"; but "Walking" shows *how* Thoreau will wage his war against the State. It describes the practices that can constitute a new breed of real citizens whose critical stance against unjust State practices will constitute a bloodless, but sustained, war. "Walking" articulates how men can be "prepared" for a government that "governs not at all."

A few pages into the essay, it becomes clear that walking is not just about putting one foot in front of the other and sauntering in the woods (though it is also that). On a deeper level, walking is a revolutionary activity that seems capable of changing our lives forever. Thoreau says "We should go forth on the shortest walk, perchance, in the spirit of undying adventure, never to return,— prepared to send back our embalmed hearts only as relics to our desolate kingdoms. If you are ready to leave father and mother, and brother and sister, and wife and child and friends, and never see them again,—if you have paid your debts, and made your will, and settled all your affairs, and are a free man, then you are ready for a walk" ("Walking," 226).[3] Walking may begin with a sense of "undying adventure" but rapidly descends into the darker prospect of death and dying. Even though the passage as a whole seems to be exaggerated, the hyperbole moves from light to dark, from adventure to death in a way that seems significant. Thoreau seems to imply that walking is an adventure—but a serious one that should not be taken lightly. It can force us to leave behind not only those we love but also our comfortable life. The strangeness of this passage is alarming: Why do we need to be ready to die before we are ready to walk? It makes no sense with any of our traditional understandings of the significance of walking. But when we begin to think of walking as a form of political activity, the dangers associated with it become clearer. Thoreau is still using his characteristic "extra-vagant" language that wanders outside of traditional bounds to better convey a truth.[4] Instead, he may be trying to convey the radical nature of walking, the fact that it is transformative and will change our life as we know it, that walking kills the citizen-as-machine within us. We had better be ready to leave that old life behind before we begin walking in earnest.

In the next passage, Thoreau further develops the significance of walking. He says, "To come down to my own experience, my companion and I, for I sometimes have a companion, take pleasure in fancying ourselves knights of a new, or rather an old, order,—not the Equestrians or Chevaliers, not Ritters or Riders, but Walkers, a still more ancient and honorable class, I trust. The chivalric and heroic spirit which once belonged to the rider seems now to reside in, or perchance to have subsided into, the Walker,—not the Knight, but Walker, Errant. He is a sort of fourth estate, outside of Church and State and People" ("Walking," 226). In the *ancien régime,* the First Estate was the clergy (the Church,) the Second Estate was the nobility (the State), and the Third Estate was the Commoners (the People). The Fourth Estate is the free press, the "watchdog" of government. According to the *Oxford English Dictionary,* the earliest use of the term Fourth Estate to mean the press is found in Thomas Carlyle's book *On Heroes, Hero Worship and the Heroic in History* (1841) in which he wrote: "[Edmund] Burke said there were three Estates in Parliament; but in the Reporters' Gallery . . . there sat a Fourth Estate more important far than they all." Though the *OED* also notes it has not been able to confirm that these words were actually spoken by Burke, we do know that Thoreau read Carlyle's book on heroes. In fact, Thoreau wrote a review essay of Carlyle, "Thomas Carlyle and His Works" (1847), and cited that text in particular as an excellent specimen of Carlyle at his best.[5]

Playing on Carlyle's idea that the press performs an invaluable and important service in keeping a critical eye trained on the government and on the other estate, Thoreau says the Walker is also "sort of a fourth estate." Like the press, the walker must be separated from conventional politics, the better to criticize the State. Thoreau also associates, but distinguishes, the walker with knights. But what does the walker have in common with such a person? He says the walker is like the knight-errant or a traveling knight, but the word *errant* also means to stray outside conventional boundaries. In this way, Thoreau defines the walker as someone who occupies a new space for an unconventional critical politics. The knight's role was to protect the king and defend the state. But Thoreau's walker takes up a more oppositional attitude: he is deeply critical of the state. In "Resistance to Civil Government," Thoreau tells is that he is at war with the state: "In fact, I quietly declare war with the State, after my fashion." ("Resistance," 84). And so, if the walker is like a knight in Thoreauvian terms, he is attacking the state, not defending it.

To add to these perplexing descriptions, in "Walking" Thoreau also calls the walker a "crusader." In tracing the etymology of the word "saunterer," Thoreau mentions that some say the word came from pilgrims who were going to the Holy Land or *à la Sainte Terre*. Thus, when Thoreau alludes to walkers as crusaders: "For every walk is a sort of crusade, preached by some Peter the Hermit in us, to go forth and reconquer this Holy Land from the hands of the Infidels" ("Walking," 225), he may be referring to the Holy Land in this context as the realm of politics, not of nature. Thoreau abhors any domestication or instrumentalization of nature and certainly would not describe this as a realm to be "reconquered." Politics and the state are more consistently the source of his scorn and appear to be in need of being reclaimed (from "citizens"). Thoreau also describes walking as a crusade carried out by some "Peter the Hermit" within us. In other words, to crusade against the state, we must go out walking alone. Thoreau may look like a hermit, but he is actually on a mission against the state.

In addition to the image of the walker as a "sort of fourth estate," a knight or a crusader, Thoreau also calls walkers such as himself "moss-troopers."[6] He says "For my part, I feel that with regard to Nature I live a sort of border life, on the confines of a world into which I make occasional and transient forays only, and my patriotism and allegiance to the State into whose territories I seem to retreat are those of a moss-trooper" ("Walking," 251). Moss-troopers were bandits, marauders, and plunderers who operated out of the bogs on the border between England and Scotland in the seventeenth century, attacking those who would pass by. Thoreau says that he has no patriotism or allegiance to the state but rather adopts a position of attack against it. He never fully retreats against this state, either, but only "seems to" when he has to return from walking.

Like the moss-trooper, Thoreau will attack the state even from the swampy bogs. For "Walking" does not just describe meandering in pastoral and scenic nature. One of the most vivid images in the essay comes in Thoreau's discussion of the swamps, which offer the greatest hope for towns and society.

> Hope and the future for me are not in lawns and cultivated fields, not in towns
> and cities, but in the impervious and quaking swamps. . . . I derive more of my
> subsistence from the swamps which surround my native town than from the cul-
> tivated gardens in the village. . . . Bring your sills up to the very edge of the
> swamp, then (though it may not be the best place for a dry cellar), so that there
> be no access on that side to citizens. . . . Yes, though you may think me perverse,
> if it were proposed to me to dwell in the neighborhood of the most beautiful
> garden that ever human art contrived, or else of a Dismal Swamp, I should cer-
> tainly decide for the swamp. How vain, then, have been all your labors, citizens,
> for me! . . . My spirits rise infallibly in proportion to the outward dreariness. . . .
> When I would recreate myself, I seek the darkest wood, the thickest and most
> interminable and to the citizen, the most dismal swamp. I enter the swamp as a
> sacred place—a *sanctum sanctorum*. There is the strength, the marrow of Nature.
> ("Walking," 241–42)

Thoreau directly addresses this passage to "citizens," who are, as we now
know, those unthinking conformists who blindly serve the state as machines.
The "you" he is speaking to is the conventional citizen: "you may think me per-
verse . . . How vain, then, have been all your labors, citizens, for me!" Thoreau
values the swamp because it is hostile to citizens, and consequently to "what is
called politics" and the state.[7] It is dismal to the citizen and he is blocked out of
it: there is "no access on that side to citizens." And yet, the swamp is a sacred
place of "re-creation." To re-create what? Thoreau implies that in the swamp,
we can mold ourselves in opposition to the citizen. Throughout his work, Thoreau uses building metaphors to describe the building of the self. Here, he tells
us to build a house in the swamp, to refashion ourselves there. In this space,
we can distance ourselves from "lawns and cultivated fields," from "towns and
cities," and from the ways these places tame and domesticate us, make us like
the mechanical citizen.

Indeed, Thoreau describes these swamps as the saving grace of towns and
the place where a true "Reformer" can be re-created: "A town is saved, not
more by the righteous men in it than by the woods and swamps that surround
it. A township where one primitive forest waves above while another primitive
forest rots below,—such a town is fitted to raise not only corn and potatoes, but
poets and philosophers for the coming ages . . . and out of such a wilderness
comes the Reformer eating locusts and wild honey" ("Walking," 242).[8] Out of
the swamp, out of the wilderness, comes the Reformer, sustaining himself with
what is wild instead of what is tame and cultivated. By turning to the swamp,
Thoreau is not turning away from politics as such, but is actually using this
withdrawn space to become the kind of critical thinker whose thoughts are not

manufactured for him to fit the needs of his society and his state: such a Reformer, a walker, can "save" the town.

Walking also seems to work against Thoreau's main criticisms regarding the alienating effects of modernization. Walking is an experiment each time we set out: there is no preset pattern to our walking. Thoreau could walk almost anywhere. He undertook his walks with a spirit of adventure where anything could happen. He moves leisurely through the woods and fields, not staying on roads or highways. Thoreau says that "Roads are made for horses and men of business. I do not travel in them much, comparatively, because I am not in a hurry to get to any tavern or grocery or livery stable to which they lead" ("Walking," 231).[9] He associates the road with the alienating world of politics and the market, recognizing that politics is increasingly shaped by the market: "If you would go to the political world, follow the great road, —follow that market-man, keep his dust in your eyes, and it will lead you straight to it" (230). By avoiding the roads that lead toward both the market and the state, Thoreau seeks also to escape the conventional ways of thinking that characterize these well-traveled paths. The experimental, adventurous nature of his daily walks opposes the modern conventions for what we should think and how we should behave. By walking as an experiment, Thoreau works against becoming like a machine.

Thoreau also "saunters." Whereas Thoreau's modernizing Concord was becoming increasingly fast-paced and tied to a busy schedule, walking is slow. He walks for the sake of walking itself, not quickly as a means of exercise: "But the walking of which I speak has nothing in it akin to taking exercise . . . but is itself the enterprise and adventure of the day" ("Walking," 228). And he thinks while he walks: "Moreover, you must walk like a camel, which is said to be the only beast which ruminates when walking" (228). Walking is a practice that is in stark contrast to the busy-ness Thoreau associates with modernization.

Walking is also hostile to the market in important ways.[10] Walking produces nothing that can be sold: it is a leisure activity that has no relation to market society. Time spent walking is time away from working. But walking is not just unrelated to the market, but oppositional to it: walking also teaches us to see in a way that works against the abstracting gaze of the exchange economy. While walking slowly and thinking, Thoreau perceives in a careful, particularizing way. He walks and looks at flora and fauna in minute detail: each wild apple, each plant, each huckleberry is studied for itself. Thoreau's mode of perception while walking opposes the gaze of the market, which abstracts way from particular qualities and sees objects in terms of their value as means of exchange.

"Walking," then, is less a tranquil essay about nature than a declaration of war against the state and a plan for refashioning a new, less alienated citizenry that is closely linked to the more overtly political ideas we see in "Resistance to Civil Government." In "Walking," we learn about the practices necessary for carrying out the ideals Thoreau articulates in "Resistance": "That government is best which governs not at all;" and *when men are prepared for it*, that will be the kind of government which they will have" ("Resistance," 63; italics mine). "Walking" is a way of preparing men for this time when the government will not "govern" so much, when the state will not form citizens into obliging wooden men without critical judgment. When men have developed the critical, thinking selves that walking fostered, they will be capable of true democratic "self-government."

Thoreau's Excursions and Rousseau's Reveries

Is there something about walking itself that tends to stimulate this kind of thought?[11] Thoreau is not the only writer to connect the act of walking with a critique of society. In the political theory canon, the most famous parallel to Thoreau's excursions are Rousseau's solitary reveries.[12] In *Reveries of the Solitary Walker,* Rousseau labels each chapter of the book as a "walk": "First Walk," "Second Walk," and so on up to "Tenth Walk." In each, Rousseau wanders, alone, most often through the countryside. He keeps "a faithful record of my solitary walks and the reveries that occupy them, when I give free rein to my thoughts and let my ideas follow their natural course, unrestricted and unconfined."[13] But, when unconstrained, his thoughts continually return to the inauthenticity of modern society. Ironically, in his detachment and withdrawal from the world, his reveries are completely caught up with society. Rousseau's reveries are similar to Thoreau's walks in that he thinks about society in a space of withdrawal, but importantly different.

Rousseau feels that his lack of guile and cunning made it impossible for him to be truly himself in a society based on artifice, lies, deception, and intrigue. He describes how society corrupts our natural virtues and spontaneous good intentions; we are not ourselves when we "unthinkingly and imprudently" follow conventions that go against our nature and the urgings of our heart. He concludes that he has "never been truly fitted for social life." "If I had remained free, unknown and isolated, as nature meant me to be, I should have done nothing but good, for my heart does not contain the seeds of any harmful passion."[14] In the famous Fifth Walk, during an idyll on the island of St. Pierre, in Switzerland, Rousseau implies that true happiness and peace are best found apart from modern society, and indeed, he implies, nearly outside of history itself:

But is there is a state where the soul can find a resting-place secure enough to establish itself and concentrate its entire being there, with no need to remember
the past or reach into the future, where time is nothing to it, where the present
runs on indefinitely but this duration goes unnoticed, with no sign of the passing
of time, and no other feeling of deprivation or enjoyment, pleasure or pain, desire or fear than the simple feeling of existence, a feeling that fills our soul entirely, as long as this state lasts, we can call ourselves happy, not with a poor, incomplete, and relative happiness such as we find in the pleasures of life, but with
a sufficient, complete and perfect happiness which leaves no emptiness to be
filled in the soul. What is the source of our happiness in such a state? Nothing external to us, nothing apart from ourselves and our own existence; as long as this
state lasts we are self-sufficient like God. The feeling of existence unmixed with
any other emotion is in itself a precious feeling of peace and contentment.[15]

But Rousseau could only experience this kind of happiness, literally, on an island: "it must be admitted that this happened much more easily and agreeably
in a fertile and lonely island, naturally circumscribed and cut off from the rest
of the world."[16]

There is a slight tinge of sour grapes that runs throughout the *Reveries*. One
has the feeling that Rousseau wants so deeply to be embraced by his fellow man,
but since he has been rejected, he tries to convince himself that he is better off
apart from the world. He renounces the world that he feels has rejected him.
But the *Reveries* also embody the paradox that runs throughout Rousseau's
works: he identifies a nobility in solitude and a corrupting of virtue in modernity, yet at the same time sees fellowship and society as deeply important to
man, not least of all for Jean-Jacques.

But Rousseau's withdrawal from the world is very different from Thoreau's
in that Rousseau does not seem to engage in critical practices aimed at allowing
him to return to modern society, to better cope with the alienating effects of
modern society. Rousseau is critical of modern society, but his reveries are not
political practices aimed to recuperate the critical capacities necessary if we are
to reenter society as more truly democratic citizens. His renunciation of society
seems more final, more complete. Written only two years before his death in
1778, Rousseau seems to be searching for a more personal explanation for why
he has been rejected, or at least not more fully embraced, by his fellow man. *Les
rêveries* are like daydreams; for Rousseau, they are personal musings that aim to
make sense of why society has forsaken, rejected, and abandoned him.
Rousseau's walks in nature are recuperative in that his distance from society allows him to see its corrupting influence, but his critique seems aimed toward

justifying his ultimate abandonment of society rather than preparing him for a return. Since he has not found it among men, Rousseau, at this point in his life at least, most desires a peace apart from society.

Despite these central differences, for both thinkers walking stimulates a critique of modern society. Something about the *promeneur solitaire* seems to motivate Rousseau's reveries. The phenomenological, physical experience of putting one foot in front of the other in the countryside seems to lend itself to such thoughts. The practice of walking itself contains particularly paradoxical and subversive tendencies in the way it contains two senses, which conflict with each other. Walking is a form of physical locomotion that itself encapsulates possibilities that subvert our conventional definitions of it. In modern society, it most typically connotes a means to an end, a way of getting from point A to point B. In this conventional mode of walking, heads down, scurrying to get somewhere, perhaps to get to work, it seems consistent with the busy, unthinking, mechanical, instrumental tendencies of modern society. But walking also contains the possibility of meandering, sauntering, strolling, or wandering. When we stop hurrying about to get somewhere, when we walk slowly, looking about us and thinking, we move in a way that appears at odds with the pace of modern society. We may not be going anywhere at all, we are walking for the sake of walking.

But walking as sauntering may make us realize how it has become harder and harder to wander in modern life. There are fewer free places in which to wander; everything is fenced off, private property, no trespassing. There is also less time in which to wander. When we are alone, walking slowly, it is easy to become critical of the bustle of modern society. When we engage in such a simple and elemental human activity as putting one foot in front of the other, our thoughts may more easily turn to the artificiality of social conventions and customs. We might trace these thoughts back to the paradox contained in the practice of walking itself, between wandering and going somewhere quickly to do something. Rousseau's reveries and Thoreau's excursions seem to similarly draw inspiration from the physical act of walking in spaces removed from society, even if their critiques seem aimed toward different ends.

Huckleberrying

The practice of huckleberrying helps us understand Thoreau's extension of the sphere where democratically valuable activities can take place.[17] He did indeed write an essay titled "Huckleberries," but huckleberries also figure into his best-known essay, "Resistance to Civil Government." In the final pages of this essay, Thoreau says that as soon as he was released from jail, he led a huckleberry party into the fields to pick the small fruit. He says "I was put into jail as I was going to the shoemaker's to get a shoe which was mended. When I was let out the next morning, I proceeded to finish my errand and, having put on my mended shoe, joined a huckleberry party, who were impatient to put themselves under my conduct; and in half an hour,—for the horse was soon tacked,—was in the midst of a huckleberry field, on one of our highest hills, two miles off, and then the State was nowhere to be seen" ("Resistance," 83). Thoreau creates a relationship between huckleberrying and his jail sentence in this passage. He opposes the huckleberry field with the jail, a judicial arm of the government. From the huckleberry field, "the State was nowhere to be seen." There are several possible ways of reading this passage. Thoreau might be describing huckleberrying as an apolitical act that is the opposite of the acts of civil disobedience that landed him in jail in the first place. He might be describing berry picking as a retreat away from politics into nature, an escape from the more traditional political realm represented by the jail and the judicial system. If we go along with the traditional interpretation of Thoreau as a misanthropic egoist unconcerned with politics, this reading would seem to corroborate that view. But we get a more satisfying interpretation by trying to read Thoreau on his own terms.

Here, Thoreau uses the practice of huckleberrying to model his own particular version of democratic politics. Thoreau contrasts huckleberrying with the jail, the judicial system, and politics as it is commonly understood to highlight the unique nature of his own version of politics and of democratic political practices. He leaves the jail to practice another kind of politics, in the huckleberry fields, to enact a new kind of politics that he seems to think will be more conducive to creating the kind of citizens who can relate to the state as individuals and neighbors, not as machines.

In describing how he left the jail and immediately went huckleberrying, Thoreau also signals his reluctant and ambivalent position as a protester. He rejects a state that supports slavery and other abhorrent practices and institutions. But, just as he criticizes "reformers" and "do-gooders" and "philanthropists," he also seems repelled by traditional political practices of protest. This is ironic, since Thoreau's essay on civil disobedience has been a touchstone for mass political movements and protests. But it is important to remember that Thoreau refused to pay his poll tax for six years before he was jailed for it. And he did nothing to call attention to his refusal to pay the tax. He simply did not pay it without saying anything about it. He was not trying to lead a mass protest against the government by spending a night in jail. He was not trying to convert others to his cause. His war with the state was intense ("my thoughts are murder to the State") but quiet and personal. For Thoreau, mass-based protests would share too many of the symptoms of mainstream politics, for in them we stop thinking for ourselves and become subjects, if not of the government then of the movement itself. So in distinguishing his choice to go huckleberrying with his unintended night in jail, Thoreau is signaling the kinds of practices that are most valuable to his own notion of democratic politics, that are vital to his own war against the state, to politics after his own fashion. And he chooses to engage in this alternative politics through huckleberrying. Thoreau is reluctant to lead a protest, but he is willing to lead a huckleberry party. It seems important that Thoreau is always given the role of the "leader," "commander," or "captain" of the huckleberry party to signal how importantly he took this activity.

Unfortunately, the theoretical and political significance of huckleberrying has been missed and, when perceived, misunderstood. Most famously, in a eulogy Emerson delivered after Thoreau's death, he criticized Thoreau for not living up to his full potential by being "only" the "leader of a huckleberry party"; Emerson thought Thoreau was born for greater leadership positions and more important commands.[18] Emerson's eulogy helped solidify the dominant interpretation of Thoreau as not concerned enough with society and politics; in keeping with this way of thinking, Emerson criticizes Thoreau for "only" huckleberrying when he might have been a social engineer.[19] "Had his genius been only contemplative, he had been fitted to his life, but with his energy and practical ability he seemed born for great enterprise and for command; and I so much regret the loss of his rare powers of action, that I cannot help counting it a fault in him that he had no ambition. Wanting this, instead of engineering for all America, he was the captain of a huckleberry party. Pounding beans is good to the end of pounding empires one of these days; but if, at the end of years, it is still only beans!"[20] But in criticizing Thoreau for leading a huckleberry party instead of heading up an empire, Emerson misunderstands his project.

The parallel Emerson sets up is similar to the one Thoreau created between huckleberrying and the jail, except Emerson creates a dichotomy between being a social engineer and being the leader of a huckleberry party. But whereas I have argued that Thoreau is trying to redefine huckleberrying as a politically important activity, Emerson uses huckleberrying to argue that Thoreau did not do enough to effect social change. But Emerson's notions of political and social leadership are limited to conventional understandings of politics, in terms of public action, participatory engagement, and wide-scale social change. Emerson rightly understands that Thoreau had strong opinions about social problems, but he does not appreciate that being a social engineer and "pounding empires" is antithetical to Thoreau's critiques of modern society. Such actions would be prey to all the alienating effects he associated with mainstream society and conventional politics. Ultimately, Emerson misrepresents Thoreau's choice: he sees Thoreau as having chosen contemplation over action, mindlessly leading huckleberry parties instead of engaging in democratic political action oriented toward change. But for Thoreau, huckleberrying is itself a political practice oriented toward social change.

The essay "Huckleberries" begins with two themes: "little things" and "education." Thoreau tells us that he is going against conventional wisdom to speak about little things often deemed insignificant: "Many public speakers are accustomed, as I think foolishly, to talk about what they call *little things* in a patronising way sometimes"[21] He says that "what is thought to be covered by the word *education*—whether reading, writing or 'rithmetic—is a great thing, but almost all that constitutes education is a little thing in the estimation of such speakers as I refer to" ("Huckleberries," 468). Here Thoreau contrasts "what is thought to be covered by the word education" with his own definition of education: he is going to show us how education is really about these little things and how they educate us.

But then, in a move that is typical of his excursionary style of walking around a topic and looking at it from various angles, Thoreau shift gears and moves immediately into a micro-level analysis of the berries. He tells us about the different varieties of berries: the Late Whortleberry, the Hairy Huckleberry, the Deerberry or Squaw Huckleberry, to name just a few. He tells us when these berries are at their prime, telling us when and where different varieties ripen. His microscopic gaze is so acute that he is able to tell us that "if you look closely at a huckleberry you will see that it is dotted, as if sprinkled over with a yellow dust or meal, which looks as if it could be rubbed off" ("Huckleberries," 471). He observes the changes the huckleberry has gone through, from the nineteenth of June to early August (470). He tells us where they grow and what they taste like. He gives us the etymology of the names of the various varieties.

He appraises and assesses the value of the fruit and finds it primarily in the act of huckleberrying itself, in the gathering of them. Thoreau says he was lucky to be appointed the family huckleberry collector: "They at home got nothing but the pudding, a comparatively heavy affair—but I got the afternoon out of doors. . . . They got only the plums that were in the pudding, but I got the far sweeter plums that never go into it" ("Huckleberries," 491). Thoreau learned more in the huckleberry field than he ever learned in school: "I well remember with what a sense of freedom and spirit of adventure I used to take my way across the fields with my pail . . . and I would not now exchange such an expansion of all my being for all the learning in the world. Liberation and enlargement—such is the fruit which all culture aims to secure. I suddenly knew more about my books than if I had never ceased studying them. I found myself in a schoolroom where I could not fail to see and hear things worth seeing and hearing—where I could not help getting my lesson—for my lesson came to me" (492). In fact, huckleberrying was such an important activity for Thoreau that he speaks of it as a career: "I served my apprenticeship and have since done considerable journeywork in the huckleberry field" (491).

Thoreau still has not spelled out in explicit terms exactly *what* he has learned from huckleberrying, though: he has not told us precisely how little things educate us. Nevertheless he goes on to argue for the creation of parks for the preservation of natural, primitive, wild spaces. He says the heads of states and towns should see the preservation of nature as politically important and as an investment in the polity ("Huckleberries," 496). But why are these spaces in nature politically important? How is huckleberrying a politically important education, as Thoreau understands the terms "political" and "education"? This seems to be the topic of his essay, yet these are the questions seemingly left unanswered.

Thoreau's answer, in part, comes in the following passage: "As in old times they who dwelt on the heath, remote from towns, being backward to adopt the doctrines which prevailed in towns, were called heathen in a bad sense, so I trust that we dwellers in the huckleberry pastures, which are our heathlands, shall be slow to adopt the notions of large towns and cities, though perchance we may be nicknamed huckleberry people" ("Huckleberries," 491). Huckleberrying teaches us how to be heathens with respect to the mainstream ways of life that Thoreau sees as alienated. For him, alienation is about a loss of critical faculties, a loss of the ability to negate, to think for ourselves. In calling for the preservation of natural spaces, Thoreau signals that alienation is indeed a political problem: he thinks that citizens act like machines, and he wants to teach them how to act like critical, independent individuals. Huckleberrying is action oriented toward change, but the individual is the target; the practice of huckleberrying teaches us how to begin to recover some of these lost parts of the self. The huckleberry fields are a space where this political education can take place, where we can work against the tendency to act like conformist and unthinking citizens and work on being heathens who hesitate to accept prevailing doctrines and ways of life. But again, we see that the space of democratic politics, the space of where we are educated in politically important ways, is separated and distant from the town. Because of the alienating forces of Main Street and the conventional ways of thinking it represents, the only way to be "slow to adopt the notions of large towns and cities" is to distance oneself from them.

Ultimately, though the entire essay might seem like a digression from Thoreau's initial stated topic, we see that it has been an extended enactment of how we might see the world if we could learn to be "huckleberry people," if we could let ourselves be educated by these little things. Throughout the piece, Thoreau employs a microscopic gaze: he pays such close attention to these small berries that he is able to describe them in the most minute detail. There are many pages with precise descriptions of Thoreau's observations of these small berries. Thoreau is critical of the idea that huckleberries are a self-evident universal category. Rather, each variety of huckleberry is treated as unique, each gets individual consideration and is differentiated from other types in several ways. Each type of huckleberry is different at different times of year and in different localities, and Thoreau thinks it is important and vital to perceive these particularities. This, he believes, is the only way we can truly understand huckleberries. The fundamental difference between Thoreau's mode of perception and Emerson's is that Emerson's eye abstracts and universalizes whereas Thoreau's specifies and particularizes. Thoreau, like Adorno, counteracts the alienating force of conventional ways of thinking by looking for particularity and uniqueness.

In his essay, Thoreau gives us an example of how the heathen huckleberryer negates the "common sense." The prevailing opinion of his day said that white settlers "discovered" huckleberries, but Thoreau emphasizes that Native Americans taught white settlers about huckleberries, not the other way around, and argues for the restoration of the berries' aboriginal names. He outlines a counterhistory of Native American use of huckleberries, which begins in 1615 and continues to the mid 1800s: "Hence you see that the Indians from time immemorial, down to the present day, all over the northern part of America—have made far more extensive use of the whortleberry [huckleberry]—at all seasons and in various ways—than we—and that they were far more important to them than us" ("Huckleberries," 484). Thoreau describes the Native Americans' extensive use of the huckleberry and lauds them for living simply on natural resources instead of supporting themselves by growing tobacco, with all its concomitant evils. Thoreau associates huckleberrying with paying attention to particularity in a way that also works against the logic of abstract exchange that increasingly characterizes the society around him. Huckleberrying gives "preponderance to the object," to borrow Adorno's phrase: we get to know the berries in all their uniqueness instead of just seeing them as objects to be exchanged for another object of equal value. Under the logic of abstract exchange, we abstract away from the particular features of the object and think only of its fungibility and exchange value (see chapter 3 in this book for a fuller discourse on the huckleberry and the logic of abstract exchange). When abstract exchange makes disparate things fungible, we do not experience things for themselves, but think of objects as means to other ends. Here, huckleberries become solely a means to profit and are reduced to "mere provender," mere food to eat or to sell as nourishment.[22] In choosing to discuss huckleberries, a notoriously market-resistant fruit, Thoreau also signals the increasing pervasiveness of the market and the drive toward commodification. Despite the difficulties, attempts were being made to ship these fragile berries to Boston markets during Thoreau's time, which he expounds upon in order to give an extreme example of the reach of the logic of exchange and the market.

Another writer, more famously, also linked huckleberries with resistance to the domesticating logics of civilization. Think of Mark Twain's classic rascal, Huckleberry Finn. In his article "Huckleberries and Humans: On the Naming of Huckleberry Finn," James L. Colwell explores the question of how Finn got his name, concluding that Twain, like Thoreau, was capitalizing upon the huckleberry's resistance to being tamed or cultivated. Colwell notes the sympathy between the boy who resists polite society and can't be "sivilized" and the berry that resists domestication: "Twain chose well—probably better than he knew—when he named Huck, for there is a characteristic of that small berry that makes it a superb symbol for the boy and his life. Through all of the history of American civilization, the huckleberry has resisted attempts at its domestication." In addition, both the berry and the boy prefer spaces that are withdrawn from mainstream society and conventional ways of life. "Twain's Huckleberry, too, never reaches the city. He, in his way, was a determined social innocent, preferring to flee the American society rather than submit to its domestication. Wealth and most other human possessions were as burdensome to him as to any Thoreauvian: he wanted no part of 'sivilization.' . . . At the end of his *Adventures,* he is preparing to 'light out for the territory ahead of the rest' rather than suffer any further efforts at taming him."[23]

Huckleberries, then, have a deeper connection to modern American history than we might have initially guessed. And it is a history of opposition to those taming, domesticating, civilizing forces that we associate most closely with modernization. Drawing out the wild qualities of these little things, Thoreau is inspired to make broader critiques of modern society and work against the common sense and the logic of abstract exchange. Huckleberrying fosters the changes in perception that Thoreau thinks will help us become critical citizens who are capable of true self-government.[24] For Thoreau, paying attention to particularity helps us learn to see for ourselves, which helps us learn to think for ourselves: we will be more critical of the dominating logic of conventional categories and become more conscious of ways that an abstracting gaze violates particularity. As Thoreau makes clear, the universal category of huckleberries actually tells us nothing about these wild fruits. Such categories are worse than useless, because to the extent that we rely on abstractions and try to make huckleberries a common unit of exchange, we lose their defining wildness and uniqueness. Ultimately, despite the smallness and almost comic insignificance of the fruit, huckleberrying is a practice that changes the way we perceive in politically important ways.

It is especially important for Thoreau that practices of withdrawal, such as walking or huckleberrying, be bodily and physical. As Thoreau says in *Walden*, "My head is hands and feet" (*Walden*, 98). We change what the head does by changing what the hands and feet do; the recuperation of our critical capacities, for Thoreau, is strongly connected to his body's movement in space. This is an important difference from Adorno's less corporeal and more cognitive practice of negative dialectics. Although both work toward sharpening our capacities for critical negation, for Thoreau, the changes in how we think and perceive seem to come from how we move our bodies, how we shift the spatial arrangements of our bodies. When we move our bodies out of the everyday, familiar, landscapes of mainstream society, something happens that affects how we think and perceive. Through practices of withdrawal, we can become heathens with respect to conventional ways of acting and thinking.

Wild Apples

Thoreau begins his "Wild Apples" essay by explicitly calling attention to the historical significance of this fruit, a connection only implied in "Huckleberries."[25] As he notes in the opening sentence, "It is remarkable how closely the history of the Apple-tree is connected with that of man" ("Wild Apples," 444). For Thoreau, the attempt to cultivate, domesticate, and commodify wild apples reflects a broader trend in modern society: the apples that are most common, most popular, are also the tamest. He describes several varieties of indigenous wild apples in North America, but notes that the cultivated apple, the rosy, milder-tasting orchard apple, was brought to America by the British, who got it from the Romans: "We have also two or three varieties of indigenous apples in North America. The cultivated apple tree was first introduced into this country by the earliest settlers, and it is thought to do as well or better here than anywhere else. Probably some of the varieties which are now cultivated were first introduced into Britain by the Romans" (445).

In one sentence he names two empires, the Roman and the British. Having already told us that the history of humans and the apple reflect one another, Thoreau now draws a parallel between imperialism and the cultivated apple.

The Romans passed on varieties of cultivated apples to the British, after conquering them to extend the Roman empire. Interestingly, Thoreau says these apples have thrived in America as in few other places. He draws a connection between the cultivation of apples and acts of conquering and empire. This makes sense, as both seek to homogenize, control, and domesticate.[26] Just as he critiques the ways modernity tames humans, Thoreau also denigrates cultivated apples. He says they may be sweet-smelling and uniformly pretty, but he thinks they have been drained of their "spirited flavor," are "mild," and "commonly turn out to be very tame" ("Wild Apples," 458).

Not surprisingly, these are also the apples that are most commonly exchanged on the market. Thoreau makes the same argument regarding the violence of abstract exchange with apples that he made with huckleberries. He describes how the essential quality of an apple is lost when it is sold on the market and becomes mere "pomace." He speaks of a "certain volatile and ethereal quality," which represents the apple's "highest value, and which cannot be vulgarized, or bought and sold" ("Wild Apples," 448). To sell an apple, then, is to engage in a violence upon their highest quality: their wildness, their nonidentity, to use Adorno's term.

For Thoreau, the most noble apple is also the wildest, wholly inaccessible to any efforts at cultivation, taming, or domestication. He extols the virtues of one particular apple tree, growing in a forbidding, rocky terrain on the side of a cliff. This tree was never planted intentionally, and it is in a place too inhospitable and distant for the farmer to bother with it at all. The farmer is not even aware that he "owns" the tree, thus it is wholly outside the reach of the market. The fruits of the tree cannot be sold, and it cannot even be eaten, since it grows in such an inaccessible place on a cliff. The apples from this tree will never be circulated, never exchange on the common market.

> It was a rank wild growth, with many green leaves on it still, and made an impression of thorniness. . . . The owner knows nothing of it. . . . When I go by this shrub thus late and hardy, and see its dangling fruit, I respect the tree, and I am grateful for Nature's bounty, even though I cannot eat it. Here on this rugged and woody hill-side has grown an apple-tree, not planted by man, no relic of the former orchard, but a natural growth, like the pines and oak. Most fruits which we prize and use depend entirely on our care. Corn and grain, potatoes, peaches, melons, etc., depend on our plantings; but the apple emulates man's independence and enterprise. . . . Even the sourest and crabbedest apple, growing in the most unfavorable position, suggests such thoughts as these, it is so noble a fruit. ("Wild Apples," 451)

This tree's utter and complete resistance to cultivation is what ennobles it. Its freedom from being tamed or domesticated connotes the qualities of independence that Thoreau wants to encourage in humans. Everything about this tree is unharmonious and uneasy. It grows on a precipice. Never having been touched by human hands, it would likely yield the most mottled, speckled, wormy, apples. Its taste would not be mild or sweet but would have the real sourness, "zest," "*tang*" or "*smack*" that Thoreau relishes ("Wild Apples," 458; italics in original). These apples, even in their flavor, wake us up, startle and unsettle us. Such fruits work against the domestication of all that is different and nonidentical, a tendency that, like the cultivated apple, has especially thrived in America.

Thoreau says that there used to be more wild apples, indeed whole wild apple orchards, "standing without order" that would "spring up wild" and thrive ("Wild Apples," 451). But the imperialist tendency to drive out its volatile and ethereal qualities, to do violence against what is nonidentical, is only getting stronger and is driving out the wild apples: "The era of the Wild Apple will soon be past. It is a fruit which will probably become extinct in New England. You may still wander through old orchards of native fruit of great extent, which for the most part went to the cider mill, now all gone to decay. . . . Ah, poor man, there are many pleasures which he will not know! . . . I see nobody planting trees today in such out-of-the-way places, along the lonely roads and lanes, and at the bottom of the dells in the woods. Now that they have grafted trees, and pay a price for them, they collect them into a plat by their houses, and fence them in,—and the end of it all will be that we shall be compelled to look for our apples in a barrel" (467). Thoreau foresees a future where there are no wild apples left, where all trees are grafted and fenced in as property. Every owner will account for his trees, and the only apples we will get will be the ones we can buy. Given the connections he has established between human history and the apple, this is a dire pronouncement. The taming and domestication of apples also marks the alienation and conventionalization of human lives and human thoughts. This is why walking and huckleberrying become democratically valuable countervailing practices that work against modern alienation: they protect our ability to think wildly against the force of convention.

Courting "the Wild"

Thoreau discusses this concept most extensively in his essay "Walking." The wild is typically understood as a confrontation with untamed, uncivilized, undomesticated nature, with wilderness. Thoreau contrasts the wild with the East Coast, with civilization, with the village, with society. The wild is adventure, experimentation, the unexpected, the unconventional. He says "Life consists with wildness. The most alive is the wildest" ("Walking," 240). And further, "Give me a wildness whose glance no civilization can endure" (240). Jane Bennett's *Thoreau's Nature: Ethics, Politics, and the Wild* contains the most sustained and thoughtful scholarly treatment of this aspect of Thoreau's work. She describes the wild as "that which disturbs and confounds settled projects, techniques, and myths." Thoreau's "notion of the Wild speaks to the idea that there always remains a surplus that escapes our categories and organizational practices, even as it is generated by them." Bennett continues, "[Thoreau] takes comfort in the thought that the Wild is indestructible, that complete domestication is impossible because every act of organization engenders elements that escape it."[27] But for Bennett, the project for Thoreau is re-creation, not recovery. She argues that Thoreau displays a "postmodern sensibility," and calls his activities of "fronting the Wild" "techniques of the self." Bennett ascribes a postmodern notion of subjectivity to Thoreau that does not allow for the recuperation of lost parts of the self. However, as I suggest, Thoreau's understanding of the wild entails courting unsettling experiences that upset conventional patterns of thought and action, but also work toward fostering a recovery of the critical capacities.

Like Adorno's notion of the nonidentical, the wild exceeds categorization, unsettles conventions, and resists domestication. At times, Thoreau associates the wild with experiences of radically Other, wild, savage, untamed nature, such as the experience he describes when he climbed Mount Ktaadn, in his book *The Maine Woods*. As he mounts the summit, nature presents itself to him as gray, cloudy, and hostile, craggy with sharp rocks. He says "this was primeval, untamed, and forever untamable *Nature*."[28] He encounters what he calls "pure Nature" and finds it "vast and drear and inhuman," "savage and awful, though beautiful . . . Here was no man's garden, but the unhandselled globe" (*Maine Woods*, 70). Thoreau feels he is encountering pure matter: "Talk of mysteries!—Think of our life in nature,—daily to be shown matter, to come in contact with it,—rocks, trees, wind on our cheeks! the *solid* earth! the actual world! the *common sense*! *Contact! Contact! Contact! Who* are we? *where* are we?" (71). Just as Adorno's notion of the nonidentical disrupts "smooth logic" and unsettles in highlighting disjunctures in conventional ways of thinking, so the wild unsettles Thoreau's conventional self, disrupts the tendency to fall back on comfortable, alienated, common sense. But the wild also fosters a recuperation of the self; the wild is "Not yet subdued to man . . . its presence refreshes him" ("Walking," 240). It restores something, fills something up, replaces something vital and essential to life itself that is, unfortunately, drained out of us by "Main Street," by the machinelike, formulaic, predictable patterns of our behavior in mainstream modern society.

Damaged Natural Spaces in Thoreau's Concord

But we do not need to climb to the top of Mount Ktaadn to experience the wild. Thoreau usually courts the wild in border spaces. The woods, fields, swamps, and huckleberry fields that he writes about are at a remove from the town—but neither are they deep in the wilderness. These spaces are not wholly primitive or uncultivated. Thoreau may have romanticized raw, untouched, wild nature and the untamed Western frontier, but he stayed in Concord and walked in places where the effects of modernization would have been all too evident. He does not abandon the tainted natural landscape of Concord, which was overfarmed and overtimbered even in his day, for a more pure and primitive nature. Instead, Thoreau seems to value spaces that bear scars, that have been used as instruments to serve society's need for timber or arable farmland.[29]

Two of the spaces Thoreau emphasizes most as spaces of self-recovery—the dismal swamp and the huckleberry field—are also spaces that were themselves recovering from the effects of modernization. During Thoreau's day, the majority of Concord's surrounding forests were cut down to meet the town's growing needs for fuel. Huckleberry bushes sprang up in the copsewoods that developed in areas that had been recently burned or deforested. Swampland became increasingly valuable in Concord as farmland. The swamps were drained, cleared of trees, and cultivated, prized for their rich soil and resistance to drought. Thoreau would have abhorred this short-sighted abuse of the land for immediate gains, but it is important that he targets these areas as spaces of recovery. He is not simply trading a tainted society for virgin nature. Instead, he withdraws to borderlands that bear clear marks of modernizing society. But in these spaces, Thoreau is also able to regain the critical qualities that are necessary for the kind of democracy he imagines. Thoreau withdraws to spaces that are at a distance from mainstream Concord but still bear its marks in ways that may have stimulated Thoreau's critique and motivated his political practice.

In his essay "The Forests and Fields of Concord: An Ecological History, 1750–1850," Brian Donahue describes a Concord that is rapidly being depleted of timber and of good farmland. Because of the great need for firewood, the forests of Concord were reduced to about half the town's surface by the end of the colonial era. "Nearly all 'virgin' forest was probably cut at least once. Some was allowed to regrow undisturbed into mature second growth, while a large part of the remaining oak woods was transformed into copsewood by repeated cutting." Copsewood are regrowth thickets of small shrubs and bushes. Donahue notes that by the nineteenth century, "the bulk of Concord's remaining forest was found in swamps and on steeper hillsides" because every flat surface had already been cleared of timber. By 1850 only 11 percent of Concord remained wooded. "The most important thing about the forest in this period is that it was being wiped out. In Concord, 'woodland' dropped from roughly a quarter to about a tenth of the land surface of the town. The drop was particularly sharp after 1820." And by 1860, "virtually all of the forest in Concord was either managed woodlot or 'new woods' that had occupied abandoned farmland. There was no 'virgin' forest left; and most of the mature second growth timber had been cut as well."[30]

Donahue continues, "In the first half of the nineteenth century, Concord practiced a 'system of husbandry' that must have been progressively deteriorating its own lands." By the mid 1800s, the soils of Concord were also exhausted and depleted of nutrients due to overfarming. In an effort to find arable farmland that would be more drought resistant and also to find additional sources of timber, the swamps began to be "reclaimed": "Besides the greater richness of its soil, a second advantage of reclaimed swamp is its resistance to drought. . . . In 1825, the *New England Farmer* points out that: 'As a country becomes cleared of timber, it becomes more liable to droughts; and these will be more or less severe according to climate. . . . Another way to avoid the effects of droughts is, to cultivate swamp lands more extensively. . . .' Thirty years later, Dr. Joseph Reynolds remarked to the Concord Farmers' Club, that 'the frequent droughts to which we are subjected, are teaching us to set a higher value upon [reclaimed swamp] than we have hitherto done.'"[31] Clearing swamps worsened the ecological situation, leading to flooding in other areas, as what had previously been a water reservoir was turned into farmland.

Thoreau would certainly have been aware of these husbandry methods, and they shed light on his very real anxieties about the increasing domestication of wilderness and instrumentalization of nature. Thoreau articulates these concerns most explicitly in his 1843 essay "Paradise (to be) Regained," where he reviews a book by J. A. Etzler, *The Paradise within the Reach of all Men, without Labor, by Powers of Nature and Machinery*. Etzler's book presents a Fourier-inspired plan to harness all of nature's power by machinery and make nature work for the benefit of man. He promises to create luxury and leisure for every man if his plans are adopted at the national level. He promises that "the whole face of nature shall be changed into the most beautiful forms."[32] To create this paradise within ten years, Etzler proposes to "level mountains, sink valleys, create lakes, drain lakes and swamps, and intersect the land everywhere with beautiful canals, and roads for transporting heavy loads of many thousand tons, and for traveling one thousand miles in twenty-four hours" ("Paradise," 115). Thoreau is (often comically) skeptical of the viability of Etzler's plans. He dislikes the search for quick comforts and conveniences: "the chief fault of this book is, that it aims secure the greatest degree of gross comfort and pleasure merely" (136). He is skeptical of the scale and amount of money needed for Etzler's reforms and thinks he would do better to start with the individual: "He who wants help wants everything. True, this is the condition of our weakness, but it can never be the means of our recovery. We must first succeed alone, that we may enjoy our success together" (133). But his critiques return to Etzler's willingness to instrumentalize nature to increase man's comfort and luxury: as he says "How meanly and grossly do we deal with nature!" (117).

One passage in Etzler's book in particular helps us understand the passage in "Walking" where Thoreau praises the regenerative potential of the swamplands. Etzler writes of converting swamps into useful land: "Any wilderness, even the most hideous and sterile may be converted into the most fertile and delightful gardens. The most dismal swamps may be cleared of all their spontaneous growth, filled up and levelled and intersected by canals" ("Paradise," 126). Thoreau's essay "Walking" was presented in its earliest form as lectures beginning in 1851, refined throughout the 1850s, and finally published in the *Atlantic Monthly* in 1862. The use of the phrase *dismal swamp* echoes Etzler's use of the term, but it also brings to mind the Great Dismal Swamp, the enormous ecosystem that divides southwestern Virginia and northeastern North Carolina. Thoreau would likely have been familiar with this name and area. As early as 1763, George Washington organized the Dismal Swamp Land Company in an attempt to utilize the area by logging it, draining parts of it, and building a canal through it.

Thoreau would also have been aware of efforts to utilize swampland closer to home, in Concord, since many other places were also being logged and cultivated. Why does Thoreau choose swamps to symbolize a space of recovery and rebuilding that is hostile to the alienated citizen? Thoreau may find swamps a particularly evocative symbol of how "life" is being cultivated away in modern society. Swamps are known hotbeds of biodiversity: they are a symbol for life. Once again, in opposing the swamp with the citizen, Thoreau juxtaposes "life" with the alienated state of mainstream politics and society. On three occasions, he makes it clear that although he loves the swamp, the citizen would find it inhospitable. First, he urges us to "Bring your sills up to the very edge of the swamp, then . . . so that there be no access on that side to the citizen" ("Walking," 241). Then he says that he would choose to live in a swamp over a beautiful garden and taunts "How vain, then, have been all your labors, citizens, for me!" (242). Lastly, Thoreau says that he would "re-create" himself in "the thickest and most interminable, and, to the citizen, most dismal swamp" (242). The swamp is an evocative representative symbol for how life is being cultivated away. But there is also a sense that Thoreau wants to defend the swamp from the citizen. He wants to keep away the citizen by building his house in the wildest, most dismal swamp. He recognizes that citizens labor to make him prefer cultivated gardens instead of alive, wild swamps. The swamp is a valuable symbol to highlight the extent of the modern instrumentalization of nature. Swamps would seem to be a last resort: as Donahue notes, in Concord, people began to think about cultivating the swamps only after every other more hospitable and accessible place has been deforested and turned into farmland. Swamps would also seem resistant to the pull of the market. A lot of work must be done before swampland can become arable land. So when Thoreau seeks to "re-create" himself, he chooses the "darkest wood, the thickest and most interminable" swamp: these superlatives are necessary because perhaps only this most inhospitable, least useful kind of bog would escape being "reclaimed."

Like the swamps, the huckleberry fields in Thoreau's time were not tracts of virgin, undeveloped land. The bushes grew most abundantly in those copsewood areas where trees had been cut down or burned. In "Huckleberries," Thoreau describes how huckleberry bushes "reclothe the hills when man has laid them bare" and how nature "heals the scar" with huckleberries when the woods are cut down:

> If you look closely you will find blueberry and huckleberry bushes under your feet, though they may be feeble and barren, throughout all our woods, the most persevering Native Americans, ready to shoot up into place and power at the next election among the plans, ready to reclothe the hills when man has laid them bare and feed all kinds of pensioners. What though the woods be cut down; it appears that this emergency was long ago anticipated and provided for by Nature, and the interregnum is not allowed to be a barren one. She not only begins instantly to heal that scar, but she compensates us for the loss and refreshes us with fruits such as the forest did not produce. As the sandal wood is said to diffuse a perfume around the woodman who cuts it—so in this case Nature rewards with unexpected fruits the hand that lays her waste. I have only to remember each year where the woods have been cut just long enough to know where to look for them. It is to refresh us thus once in a century that they bide their time on the forest floor. If the farmer mows and burns over his overgrown pasture for the benefit of grass, or to keep the children out, the huckleberries spring up there more vigorous than ever." ("Huckleberries," 478)

Thoreau's association between huckleberries and politics continue in this passage; he describes these bushes as "ready to shoot up into place and power at the next election." Huckleberry bushes, with their unique capacity for recovery, emerge to achieve a rare kind of regenerative power that Thoreau links with politics. "Elections" are not a typical metaphor for the growth of plants, but given that Thoreau associates huckleberries with a political education, we are not completely unprepared for this image. If huckleberrying is a practice aimed toward recuperating the critical, negating qualities necessary for people to become real citizens, then it makes sense that huckleberry bushes symbolize an optimistic hopefulness that nature can indeed be a space that "compensates us" for loss, and "refreshes us." Border spaces and border practices such as huckleberrying can regenerate the alienated politics of the citizen as well, if we follow Thoreau's excursionary line of thought. But, again, we cannot engage in this recovery in spaces that are completely removed from the influence of modern society and politics. Thoreau does not withdraw to forget about modern society but to find a way to cope with it. Total escape is not an option; we must exist within society; with frequent pilgrimages to the borders that offer the kind of critical distance that allow one to remember what was lost, so as to be able to recover those qualities.

Ultimately, Thoreau thinks we can confront the wild even in damaged spaces, even in the scarred woods around Concord. This is significant, because if the wild could be encountered only in savage, untouched places, it would be far less useful as an everyday way of working against alienation. But this seems not to be the case: in "Walking," Thoreau implies that the wild can also be confronted in nature that bears the scars of modernization. "One who pressed forward incessantly and never rested from his labors, who grew fast and made infinite demands on life, would always find himself in a new country or wilderness, and surrounded by the raw material of life. He would be climbing over the prostrate stems of primitive forest trees" ("Walking," 240). Thoreau says here that we can find ourselves in a wilderness even if we are actually in a place where the trees have been cut down.

For Thoreau, nature in not an edenic, pristine, space fully preserved from the taint of modern society, but neither is modernity an all encompassing system. In the border spaces Thoreau is most interested in, the instrumentalization of nature is evident but not complete. As we have seen, he is most interested in border spaces that bear the scars of modernization. He walks, huckleberries, and confronts the wild in spaces where the line between "nature" and "society" has been blurred. Yet even in damaged landscapes, he shows how particular things, when we look closely, inspire criticisms of "what is" and contain alternative possibilities that rupture the status quo.

Thoreau, Adorno, and Practices of Withdrawal

Thoreau was born and died in Concord, Massachusetts, a place whose name is synonymous with accord and agreement. And yet, his thought is deeply antithetical to the harmonizing tendencies that the name of this place evokes; his political practices of withdrawal seek to fracture, break apart, and negate. Through confronting the wild, Thoreau pays attention to particular objects, lingers with them, and draws out their rupturing potential to critique modern conventions and institutions. He awakens us to what is violated and lost through the abstract ways of thinking that increasingly dominate his rapidly modernizing society. Thoreau's thought is discordant and dissonant, much like the atonal music by Alban Berg and Arnold Schönberg that Adorno listened to and modeled his own compositions on. Adorno's equally atonal philosophy of negative dialectics helps us see the theoretical and political importance of these strains in Thoreau's writings, which may be missed if we read him through the lens of Emersonian Transcendentalism.

Adorno values the negative, that which ruptures the affirmative synthesis of the idealist dialectic. He values nonreconciliation; he fractures and breaks apart unified systems; he emphasizes disjuncture, and his thought is opposed to harmony. Thoreau also values these dissonant qualities. In this chapter, we have seen him use such onomatopoeic words as "quaking," "thorny," "acidic," "crabbed," "sour," "sharp" in praise of these qualities. Thoreau indeed seeks out jarring experiences. Both Thoreau's practice of confronting the wild and Adorno's negative dialectics emphasize the value of discord, of seizing upon contradictions and drawing out their implications for modern society, of negating comfortable, familiar patterns.

Employing something like Adorno's microscopic gaze, Thoreau walks slowly and looks at the little things, wild apples or huckleberries. The wild and volatile qualities of these particular objects, their resistance to taming, reveal the false equilibrium of the market and highlight instead its violence. Paying attention to the particular works against modern tendencies toward abstract, formulaic ways of thinking and stimulates our critical capacities of negation, toward realizing the contingency of "what is." And just as life is contained in the nonidentical for Adorno, for Thoreau confronting the wild is the opposite of common sense, of sleeping. and represents really being alive, living life to its fullest. Both engage in practices that work against the monotonous and dead ways of experiencing that characterize modernity. Confronting the wild, like the practice of negative dialectics, allows a momentary recuperation of the critical capacities that are threatened by an alienated modern landscape, but vital to true democracy. And yet these practices occur at a distance from the shared, public, intersubjective spaces of conventional politics. In this way, reading Thoreau with Adorno expands the parameters of democratic politics into spaces of withdrawal that have previously, by definition, been seen as apolitical or undemocratic.

5

Traveling Away from Home

Thoreau's Spaces of Withdrawal

> So there is one *thought* for the field, another for the house. I would have my
> thoughts, like wild apples, to be food for walkers, and will not warrant them
> to be palatable, if tasted in the house.
>
> Henry David Thoreau

Robert Frost's poem "The Death of a Hired Man" poignantly captures an enduring image of the way we typically imagine home.[1] Here, Silas, a former employee with a less than stellar track record as a worker returns to the farm of Warren and Mary, where he is found "Huddled against the barn-door fast asleep / A miserable sight, and frightening, too."[2] Mary says that Silas has "come home to die," which raises the question of what they should do with him, given that "he's nothing to us anymore." Warren says, mockingly, "Home is the place where, when you have to go there, / They have to take you in." Mary frames it a different way: "I should have called it / Something you somehow haven't to deserve." In both Mary and Warren's definitions, home is figured as a space where your belonging is not up for debate, neither on the part of those giving refuge (frustratingly for Warren) or on the part of those seeking refuge (luckily for Silas). "The Death of a Hired Man" gives us an image of home as a place to lay your head and let down your burdens, a kind of refuge from the questions, criticisms, and debates that characterize our lives in other spheres, most particularly in the realm of the political.

Given these characteristics, democratic theorists tend to see "home" as something dangerous, while ascribing democratic value to states of psychic "homelessness."[3] In an essay on the politics of the ideological space of home, Bonnie Honig characterizes it as a place removed from political involvement, a space of "safety and withdrawal from the tumult of politics."[4] For Honig, democratic politics requires that we "give up on the dream of a place called home, a place free of power, conflict, and struggle, a place — an identity, a form of life, a group vision — unmarked or unriven by difference or untouched by the power brought to bear upon it by the identities that strive to ground themselves in its place." She sees this dream of home as dangerous because it "exacerbates the inability of constituted subjects — or nations, to accept their own internal differences and divisions, and it engenders zealotry, the will to bring the dream of unitariness or home into being." The dream of home motivates people to do one of two things: either they try to withdraw from conflicts "to a supposedly safe home that is elsewhere, away from all this tumult" or they engage in acts of conquering "that tumultuous disorder in order to build a supposedly safe home here."[5]

Thomas L. Dumm depicts the dangers of home in a similar way. In a chapter subtitled "Democracy and Homelessness," Dumm asks "How might democracy be connected to homelessness?" He writes "For many people, fear of democracy is associated with a desire for home, which remains, as it has for the history of our experience of united states, the solution to all of our problems, the comfort we might find when the demands and challenges of political life become too great." For Dumm, "home" is figured today as an easy solution rather than a difficult challenge, a comfortable place where we might seek refuge from politics: it is "a private place, a place of withdrawal from the demands of common life, a place of fixed meaning, where one is protected from disorientation, but also from the possibility of democratic involvement." Being at home relieves us of the hard work of having "to think for ourselves, think impertinently." If fears of being thrown upon our own critical resources push us to seek refuge at home, then democracy is about overcoming this desire for submission to authority, for clear directions, answers, and firm foundations: "Democracy is connected to a form of homelessness, in that it requires that one overcome the desire to be at home. . . . Hence one might say that democratic life requires one to overcome the fear of homelessness, to develop the courage to leave home (embracing another fear) without knowing when or whether one will return."[6]

Thoreau, like Adorno, is animated by a similar desire to escape the thoughtless, stultifying, conventional life that is associated with the ideological space of home. But there is an important difference between Thoreau's travels away from home and the characterizations we have seen in Honig and Dumm's works. Both of these authors associate home with a space of withdrawal: for Honig, it is withdrawn from the "tumult of politics," and for Dumm, it is withdrawn from "the demands of common life" and "democratic involvement." Here, again, we see how the notion of withdrawal is presented in opposition to democratic politics, as it is more typically understood: as a public, participatory, space of collective engagement. But once again, Thoreau cuts through this traditional opposition. He travels away from the ideological space of home to engage in the kind of critical thinking that he identifies as necessary to the true possibility of democratic self-government. But the paradoxical, unhomelike places that he travels to are located in areas withdrawn from Main Street and distanced from our conventional notion of politics as something that takes places in a shared, public, common space. His travels are undertaken with a spirit of democratic homelessness that works to disrupt a desire for easy answers, comfort, safety, unity, identity, and fixed meaning. Again, Thoreau expands the parameters of democratic politics to include these spaces of withdrawal.

Thoreau's Homelessness

Despite his ideological tendencies toward homelessness, Thoreau is deeply associated with his hometown in Massachusetts. He was born in Concord and lived there his whole life, with only brief excursions to other states and to Canada. His thought is informed by, and responds to, the topography of his hometown. There is, in many ways, a profound domesticity in Thoreau's writings, seen most strikingly when he writes about his cabin on the shore of Walden Pond. But at the same time these temporary, borrowed quarters are in no way a conventional "home" in the way he understands the term. The cabin at Walden Pond might be a home in the literal sense that he lived there, but it is not (for Thoreau) a home in the metaphorical sense — that is exactly its value. He goes there to live deliberately, to think critically, not to be at home and comfortably numb, so to speak. Thoreau's deep love of certain places does not contradict his fears about the settled, conventional kind of thinking that occurs when we feel at home.

Indeed, the places that Thoreau loves most are places that deliberately unsettle us and work against the loss of our critical capacities that he identifies as the experience of modern alienation. Despite his local attachments, Thoreau consistently makes efforts to decenter and displace himself. Thoreau identifies himself as a "traveler," as an itinerant border dweller. Thoreau's home may have been Concord, but he travels back and forth from the woods and fields outside of town to the main street. Thoreau was not forced into exile (as was Adorno), but both find value in a kind of homelessness. Thoreau took on a voluntary status of displacement; he tried to make himself a traveler within the territory of his own hometown.[7]

Paradoxically, in the places that Thoreau most idealizes, we are displaced, not "at home" in the conventional sense. He values being scraped about, windblown, and even frightened on the craggy top of Mount Ktaadn in Maine because it reminds him that earth is "no man's garden" and cannot always be domesticated. He loves nature, in part, because it can be wildly unsettling. Elsewhere, such as in "Walking," Thoreau imagines building his home in a swamp, a place that lacks "a firm foundation," one specifically chosen because it would be inaccessible (or undesirable) to the "citizen," a trope to describe the alienated sensibility with which we are by now familiar. In the "Housewarming" chapter of *Walden*, Thoreau describes an ideal house but speaks of its inhabitants as "travelers," who seem to be only temporary guests. Similarly, in "The Landlord," Thoreau muses on where we might find the perfect, ideal house and concludes that it is the tavern, an inn for "travelers" that exists on a highway outside of town, a stopping place on the route to somewhere else. All of these houses share an element of displacement: Thoreau chooses places designed to unsettle the conventional self, such as the swamp, or else his visions of home are spaces to accommodate and shelter the wandering traveler, who stays only temporarily before continuing on his journey. The larger implication is that there is value in *not* feeling completely at home, as Thoreau's "homes" are not at all "homey." To be completely at home is too close to the comfortable, complacent, uncritical attitude that Thoreau associates with the citizen-as-machine. The traveler and the neighbor have the capacities to negate that the citizen-as-machine lacks; he is too easily "at home" in the towns and cities, too comfortable, too unthinkingly set in his conventional ways.

Thoreau's homelessness is not an existential problem, but a particularly modern problem. The alienated "citizen" experiences a deadening of critical capacities because of certain aspects of modernization. Thoreau does not describe this loss as an abstract, ahistorical feature of the human condition, but he roots it in the transformations of his own nascent modern society. Furthermore, Thoreau's notions of the "traveler" and the "neighbor" seem formed in distinction to his concept of the citizen-as-machine in ways that also seem to be reactions to specifically modern experiences, another form of withdrawal that works against the alienating effects of a rapidly modernizing society. Voluntary displacement and a degree of homelessness counter the tendency to become too masterful in our domains, too dominating of other people and things, too materialistic, too much in the thrall of commodities and an increasingly powerful market society. The detachment, material simplicity, and lack of luxury are part of what he seems to value in these "homes" for travelers. Thoreau fears that when one owns a home, the home actually owns you. Houses entrench their owners in the market economy and in an acquisitive lifestyle.[8]

In *The Senses of Walden*, Stanley Cavell undertakes a reading of the famous passage where Thoreau describes how he lost a hound, bay horse, and turtledove. In this passage from *Walden*, Thoreau says: "I long ago lost a hound, a bay horse and a turtle-dove and am still on their trail. Many are the travelers I have spoken with concerning them, describing their tracks and what calls they answered to. I have met one or two who had heard the hound, and the tramp of the horse, and even seen the dove disappear behind a cloud, and they seemed as anxious to recover them as if they had lost them themselves" (*Walden*, 17). His loss of these creatures is metaphorical.[9] But in Cavell's reading, this passage conveys the sense of existential loss that pervades *Walden*. For Cavell, whose writings on Thoreau are also influenced by Heidegger, estrangement is a fundamental aspect of the human condition. We are all always on the outside and lost to ourselves; some of us just are more sensitive to this state than others. For Cavell, Thoreau is not writing about the modern condition, but the human condition as such, and he sees Thoreau's experiences of loss as a reaction to the experience of "having a self" and "being human."[10]

> The writer comes to us from a sense of loss; the myth does not contain more than symbols because it is no set of desired things he has lost but a connection between things. Everything he can list he is putting in his book: it is a record of losses. . . . He is not fully recovered. He has come back, "a sojourner in civilized life again." He was a sojourner there before, and now again he sojourns there instead of at Walden. . . . The little myth of the horse, hound and turtledove refers to "one or two"—viz., travelers, hence strangers—who had heard and seen what he has lost, and seemed as anxious to recover them as if the losses were theirs. Here the writer fully identifies his audience as those who realize that they have lost the world, i.e., are lost to it. The fate of having a self—of being human—is one in which the self is always to be found; fated to be sought, or not; recognized, or not. . . . It is those who accept this condition of human existence that the writer accords the title of traveler or stranger. It is the first title he accords himself (after writer).[11]

Instead of seeing Thoreau's treatment of travelers as a way of confronting a modern problem, Cavell thinks it describes an existential problem of homelessness and estrangement. But we can only come to Cavell's conclusion if we ignore how the traveler and the neighbor relate to Thoreau's depiction of the citizen-as-machine as a specifically modern problem. Cavell misses the historical situatedness of Thoreau's project in saying that the displaced context of the traveler is a feature of human existence itself. In part, Cavell might miss the links Thoreau makes between the citizen, the traveler, and the neighbor because he reads *Walden* as a text complete in itself, apart from the rest of Thoreau's corpus. But Cavell also does not appreciate how the value of traveling is intimately related to Thoreau's discussions of homes and homeownership and how they trap us within a modern society that threatens the critical capacities of the self. Ultimately, Thoreau's discussions of traveling do not occur in a vacuum but are linked to the alternative democratic politics he proposes as a countervailing practice to modern alienation.

The House That "Got" the Man

In *Walden*, Thoreau writes "And when the farmer has got his house, he may not be the richer but the poorer for it, and it be the house that has got him" (*Walden*, 33). But what are we trapped by? What has "got" us? Thoreau seems critical of the idea of home and homeownership for several reasons. First, he writes of how a concern with luxury, commodities, and material wealth distracts us from ourselves: we focus on the external instead of the internal. Thoreau describes the richness and luxury with which we decorate our houses and our lives: "now, a taste for the beautiful is most cultivated out of doors, where there is no house and no housekeeper" (38). Possessions end up dominating us. In his journal, Thoreau contrasts the homelessness of the Native American and the walker with the homeowner:

> The charm of the Indian to me is that he stands free and unconstrained in Nature, is her inhabitant and not her guest, and wears her easily and gracefully. But the civilized man has the habits of the house. His house is a prison, in which he finds himself oppressed and confined, not sheltered and protected. He walks as if he sustained the roof; he carries his arms as if the walls would fall in and crush him, and his feet remember the cellar beneath. His muscles are never relaxed. It is rare that he overcomes the house, and learns to sit at home in it, and roof and floor and walls support themselves, as the sky and trees and earth. It is a great art to saunter.[12]

We come to see our house as a burden we must hold and drag around with us. It oppresses us; we tax ourselves to sustain it. It imprisons us instead of sheltering us. It makes it difficult for us to be walkers, to saunter. We take on "the habits of the house" and think tame, domesticated kinds of thoughts.

Thoreau is concerned that houses and possessions root us too much in this modern world. He writes that "the very simplicity and nakedness of man's life in the primitive ages imply this advantage, at least, that they left him still but a sojourner in nature. . . . He dwelt, as it were, in a tent in this world." (*Walden*, 37). He wants to limit his attachments to the alienating modern world, to plant only shallow roots. This seems partly to insulate himself from the threat to the self that Thoreau associates with the town and mainstream society, but also because he does not want to participate in such a flawed form of conventional life. Owning a home roots us too firmly in a modern world that eviscerates the critical capacities of the self. And this is why Thoreau values homes where we are treated as travelers and guests.

In another passage from *Walden*, Thoreau draws even more stark parallels between owning houses and the ways we may be "owned" by the forces of mainstream society: "Shall we forever resign the pleasure of construction to the carpenter? What does architecture amount to in the experience of the mass of men? I never in all my walks came across a man engaged in so simple and natural an occupation as building his house. We belong to the community. It is not the tailor alone who is the ninth part of a man; it is as much the preacher, and the merchant, and the farmer. Where is this division of labor to end? And what object does it finally serve? No doubt another may also think for me; but it is not therefore desirable that he should do so to the exclusion of my thinking for myself" (*Walden*, 46). His thought bounces several ideas off one another: he speaks of walking, house-building, the division of labor, the ways we can belong to the community where others think for us. How do all these pieces fit together? Here, as elsewhere in *Walden*, Thoreau draws a parallel between building a house and building the self. But there is an ominous overtone to this discussion: when Thoreau speaks about belonging to the community, he seems to mean we are overtaken by the community. The tailor, merchant, farmer, and preacher make up part of the man. They divide their labor in constructing the self, each taking responsibility for a part. But what is the object of this division of labor? Thoreau implies that it aims toward allowing the community (which in Thoreau's description is comprised primarily of tradesmen) to think for us. In a comic understatement, Thoreau says that yes, others *may* think for us, but this is not "desirable." So, building a house in a "natural" and "simple" sense seems parallel to building the self in deliberate, critical ways, and this works in contrast to having the community build the self for us, to think for us. But Thoreau also implies that most men are not engaged in this occupation: most have both their selves and their houses built for them by others, have their thinking done for them by others—again, a parallel between "home" and an unthinking complacency.

Thoreau's own home for about two years, at Walden Pond, was an exercise in the value of this kind of displacement. Here, Thoreau practiced a radical simplicity geared toward reducing his reliance on the market and enhancing his ability to focus on the internal without distraction. Thoreau's daily life was geared toward reducing his attachments to mainstream society. This kind of simplicity and detachment figures prominently in his other idealizations of home. But, like the cabin at Walden Pond, all of Thoreau's paradoxical homes are also in physical locations of withdrawal: this is true of his portrait of the tavern located on the highway outside of town or his vision of the swamp-house. Importantly, these unhomelike homes become spaces for an alternative democratic politics to work against the alienating mentality of the citizen-as-machine.

The Swamp-House

Thoreau says that he was always attracted to the "impermeable and unfathomable bog," the "impervious and quaking swamps" when assessing the best locations for building a house ("Walking," 241). Imagining the building of his swamp-house, he says "Bring your sills up to the very edge of the swamp, then (though it may not be the best place for a dry cellar,) so that there be no access on that side to citizens" (241). He says he would always choose to dwell in a "dismal swamp" instead of "in the neighborhood of the most beautiful garden that ever human art contrived" and then exclaims, joyfully, "How vain, then, have been all your labors, citizens, for me!" (241–42). The swamp literally is a place that unsettles: it is "quaking," unstable. It is particularly not a good place to build a firm foundation. And this seems to be what Thoreau likes about the site—it is both undesirable and inaccessible to citizens. These are exactly the kind of people who desire the kind of firm foundations that Thoreau eschews.

In his excellent essay "*Walden*'s False Bottoms," Walter Benn Michaels argues that Thoreau continually defies his readers' attempts to find a "hard bottom," a reality that is not contingent, but fully "real," not human or man-made. Michaels sees *Walden* as posing a paradox oriented between two poles. On the one hand, Thoreau seems to want to get to the bottom, to get to reality, to experience the most raw and real; on the other hand, he continually undermines the possibility of such a foundation. Thoreau's discussion of whether or not Walden Pond has a bottom or is bottomless encapsulates this theme. At one point, Thoreau imagines the pond as bottomless, infinite. But then at another point he says that he in fact measured the pond, and it had a depth of 102 feet. It also appears in Thoreau's discussions of Nature: sometimes he presents Nature itself as a "hard bottom," as something that is "real," but then at other times he shows how it has been domesticated and cultivated by man. We look for what is "real" in Nature and at times, Thoreau presents Nature as fully Other, as non-human, such as when he comes face to face with the wild on top of Mount Ktaadn. But conversely, in other moments, he shows Nature as more mediate, as something that is cultivated and shaped by human hands. Michaels highlights this search for firm foundations: we keep looking for something that is real, Other, and not shaped by human hands, but we keep seeing our own face reflected back to us.

Ultimately, Michaels implies that the foundation of *Walden* is a commitment to upsetting foundations: "To read *Walden*, then, is precisely to play at Kittlybenders, to run the simultaneous risks of touching and not touching the bottom. If our reading claims to find a solid bottom, it can only do so according to principles which the text has both authorized and repudiated; thus we run the risk of drowning in our certainties. If it doesn't, if we embrace the idea of bottomlessness and the interest of the ice itself, we've failed *Walden*'s first test, the acceptance of our moral responsibility as deliberate readers. It's heads I win, tails you lose. No wonder the game makes us nervous."[13] Kittlybenders is a child's game of running over thin, rubbery ice that bends under one's weight. Part of the word's etymology is rooted in the Scottish word "kittle," which indicates something ticklish or tricky. In the "Conclusion" to *Walden*, Thoreau writes "It affords me no satisfaction to commence to spring an arch before I have got a solid foundation. Let us not play at kittly-benders. There is a solid bottom everywhere." But in the next few sentences, Thoreau tells the story of a traveler who "asked the boy if the swamp before him had a hard bottom. The boy replied that it had. But presently the traveler's horse sank up to the girths, and he observed to the boy, 'I thought you said that this bog had a hard bottom.' 'So it has,' answered the latter, 'but you have not got half way to it yet.' So it is with the bogs and quicksands of society; but he is an old boy that knows it" (*Walden*, 330).

So what are we to think? Is there no ultimate reality that is "natural," presocial, and not just historical and contingent? Or have we just not yet discovered this foundation? Thoreau leaves these questions unanswered, but Michaels shows how his writing style enacts "the principle of uncertainty" that is built into *Walden*. This uncertainty is productive: Thoreau's paradoxes and contradictions ask the reader continually to make "interpretative decisions which call into question both his notion of the coherence of the text and of himself."[14] *Walden*'s style continually uproots hierarchies, overturns conventions, and makes us rethink authority in valuable ways.

Thoreau anticipates our desire to build a solid foundation underneath ourselves, a "solid bottom," a grounding for authority, a truth, and then, as if to
chasten us, continually pulls that ground out from underneath us with his style
of writing.

> Thoreau's concern in *Walden* is, of course, to show us that we do have choices
> left and, by breaking down hierarchies into contradictory alternatives, to insist
> on our making them. But this breakdown, which creates the opportunity, or
> rather the necessity for choosing, serves at the same time to undermine the ra-
> tionale we might give for any particular choice. If there is no hierarchy of val-
> ues, what authority can we appeal to in accounting for our decisions? What
> makes one choice better than another? This is what the search for a solid bot-
> tom is all about, a location for authority, a ground upon which we can make a
> decision. *Walden* insists upon the necessity for such a search at the same time
> that it dramatizes the theoretical impossibility of succeeding in it.[15]

Calling into question the possibility of foundations is also about repudiating the
search for authority. Thoreau wants to help us recognize contingency and the
possibility of alternatives to "what is" instead of searching for an authority that
will remove the necessity for independent critical thought. But, as critics since
Emerson have noted, for this reason, Thoreau's style of writing can be nerve-
wracking; reading Thoreau's paradoxes and contradictions made Emerson
"nervous and wretched."[16] Michaels himself notes that Thoreau's own game of
kittly-benders makes us anxious. We are only fully at home when we think we
can resolve all paradoxes and contradictions. But when we *are* fully there in this
sense, we are also unthinking and complacent. This is why Thoreau exhorts his
readers to avoid such foundations, to learn to be travelers or neighbors. This is
why he tells us to build our houses in swamps, spaces that would be undesirable
to alienated citizens. Whereas Emerson's writings often seek to reassure and to
affirm, Thoreau favors making us feel nervous.

"The Landlord"

This short essay, published in 1843, before either "Walking" or "Huckleberries," begins with a meditation on where one might find the ideal house. Thoreau decides that "the gods who are most interested in the human race preside
over the Tavern, where especially men congregate."[17] The tavern, or inn, is
granted special distinction as an ideal house because it is a shrine to hospitality
and the place where all "pilgrims without distinction resort" ("Landlord," 108).
The inn is ideal because it offers shelter to travelers, those who do not have
homes or are away from home. It is a place "where the traveler shall really feel
in, and at home" (108). But the inn is an ideal home only when it is located in

remote places, in border spaces: "In these retired places the tavern is first of all a house—elsewhere, last of all, or never—and warms and shelters its inhabitants" (109). Unless it is in a place quite removed from town, the inn cannot be a home at all: it cannot warm and shelter travelers. The implication being that if the inn is located in the middle of a town, it is too much a part of the modern problem. The ideal home, then, is about not being a resident but being in the position of a traveler stopping along the way.

The ideal man, the innkeeper, in this essay, occupies a border position and is surrounded by travelers. Thoreau describes this landlord in terms that are weighted heavily with positive value in Thoreau's lexicon. He "loves men, not as a philosopher, with philanthropy, nor as an overseer of the poor, with charity, but by a necessity of his nature" ("Landlord," 108). In other words, the innkeeper is not a "do-gooder" or a reformer but is simply a good person. He also lives the kind of rustic and simple life that Thoreau thinks is so important to our physical and mental health: "The Landlord stands clear back in nature, to my imagination, with his axe and spade felling trees and raising potatoes with the vigor of a pioneer . . . and he is not so exhausted, nor of so short a stride, but that he comes forward even to the highway to this wide hospitality and publicity" (110). "Surely he has solved some of the problems of life. He comes in at his back door, holding a fresh log cut for the hearth upon his shoulder with one hand, while he greets the newly arrived traveller with the other" (110). At the innkeeper's hearth, "here the real and sincere life which we meet in the streets was actually fed and sheltered" (110). The landlord is healthy in a hearty, simple way, "Hence it will not do for the Landlord to possess too fine a nature. He must have health above the common accidents of life, subject to no modern fashionable diseases" (110). Thoreau sees him as "the true house-band, and centre of the company—of greater fellowship and practical social talent than any" (113).

These are all positive qualities in Thoreau's work. But seeming contradiction and paradox enters his description of the innkeeper, in illuminating ways, when he begins to list qualities this man possesses which typically have a negative connotation in Thoreau's work. For example, the innkeeper "never wants to be alone, but sleeps, wakes, eats, drinks sociably" ("Landlord," 111). Being alone is typically a valuable state for Thoreau, so it seems odd that this innkeeper, whom he praises, does not need or want to be alone. Thoreau says the innkeeper "entertains no private thought, he cherishes no solitary hour, no Sabbath day, but thinks—enough to assert the dignity of reason—and talks, and reads the newspaper" (111). Even worse, the innkeeper reads the mail: "the mail might drive through his brain in the midst of his most lonely soliloquy, without disturbing his equanimity, provided it brought plenty of news and passengers" (111).[18] Compare Thoreau's mild description of how the innkeeper reads newspapers and the mail with his attack on these trivial engagements in his essay "Life Without Principle." Here, Thoreau describes these activities that distract us from the "inward and private" work of truly living. He says of newspapers: "Not without a slight shudder at the danger, I often perceive how near I had come to admitting into my mind the details of some trivial affair,— the news of the street; and I am astonished to observe how willing men are to lumber their minds with such rubbish—to permit idle rumors and incidents of the most insignificant kind to intrude on ground which should be sacred to thought. Shall the mind be a public arena, where the affairs of the street and the tea-table chiefly are discussed? Or shall it be a quarter of heaven itself?" ("Life," 171).

And of the mail: "Just so hollow and ineffectual for the most part is our ordinary conversation. Surface meets surface. When our life ceases to be inward and private, conversation degenerates into mere gossip . . . in proportion as our inward life fails, we go more constantly and desperately to the post-office. You may depend on it, that the poor fellow who walks away with the greatest number of letters proud of his extensive correspondence has not heard from himself this long while" ("Life," 169). And yet, the innkeeper reads the newspaper and mail in a way that would seem to taint this "quarter of heaven," as Thoreau calls the mind in "Life Without Principle." All this happens without "disturbing his equanimity" ("Landlord," 111). How can the innkeeper engage in these seemingly corrupting activities *without* being corrupted? Thoreau's praise of the innkeeper is sincere, not tongue-in-cheek praise. So what separates the innkeeper from other men, whose minds are so easily tainted by news and mail?

Two aspects of the innkeeper's job make him unique. First, Thoreau explicitly positions this ideal inn-keeper on a highway, outside of the town. Neither fully in the wilderness nor in town, the innkeeper is also a liminal figure who lives a kind of "border life." The tavern is not located in town but in the countryside and is "plain and sincere." The inn is "located in no Tarrytown, where you will receive only the civilities of commerce, but far in the fields it exercises a primitive hospitality, amid the fresh scent of new hay and raspberries, if it be summer time, and the tinkling of cow-bells from invisible pastures; for it is a land flowing with milk and honey, and the newest milk courses in a broad deep stream across the premises" ("Landlord," 109). Interestingly, Tarrytown, New York, was the home of Washington Irving, author of the well-known short stories "The Legend of Sleepy Hollow" and "Rip Van Winkle." Thoreau must have been familiar with Irving's works, and in light of how Thoreau uses the tropes of "sleep" to convey an alienated sensibility and juxtaposes it with "morning" and being "awake," it seems significant that he distinguishes the inn from a Tarrytown, where we might languish, like Rip Van Winkle, for a hundred years, dozing in a sleepy hollow.

Thoreau distinguishes the inn from the sleepy "common sense" and "commerce": its location insulates it in valuable ways. Only in such places can the inn truly be a home to weary travelers without running the risk of turning them into "citizens." The landlord occupies a border position that insulates and allows him to engage in activities like reading the newspaper and the mail without being threatened with a loss of self. Thoreau thinks that when we inhabit mainstream, public spaces, we must adopt more of a defensive position with respect to these activities, indulging in them sparingly lest they overtake us. But the landlord need not defend himself against the alienating forces of society, since he already inhabits a space of withdrawal.

The position of the innkeeper is also unique because of another aspect of his job: his clientele. They are truly travelers, seekers, on the way somewhere else. In Thoreau's lexicon, "travelers" are those discontented souls who are searching for something that was lost and who sympathize with the experience of loss. The landlord deals with such "travelers" each day and this, in part, accounts for his disposition and character. The landlord is not a "man of genius" who "sits afar and retired, off the road, hangs out no sign of refreshment for man and beast, but says, by all possible hints and signs, I wish to be alone—goodbye—farewell. But the landlord can afford to live without privacy. . . . The dust of travel blows ever in his eyes, and they preserve their clear, complacent look" ("Landlord," 111). He does not need to be alone and can afford to be with others, to read the newspaper and the mail because he never forgets that we are all travelers. The landlord is able, then, to be magnanimous, honest, sincere, friendly, and hospitable. He doesn't fall into the trap of thinking that life is stable, too comfortable, or familiar. He is not prey to becoming unthinkingly conformist or overly comfortable in a superficial existence: "To his imagination all things travel save his sign-post and himself" (109).

His admiration of the innkeeper shows that Thoreau is not unconditionally interested in withdrawal or separation from men and society. Indeed, Thoreau desires and relishes the "true community" of men that is possible at the tavern. Thoreau's praise also seems especially relevant because he applauds the public and politically valuable work that innkeepers perform. As he often does, and as we have seen before, Thoreau invokes terminology associated with conventional politics in these spaces of withdrawal. He says that the innkeeper is a model of public service, a "more public character than a statesman—a publican, and not consequently a sinner; and surely he, if any, should be exempted from taxation and military duty" ("Landlord," 113). Similarly, Thoreau notes "How many fragrant charities and sincere social virtues are implied daily in this daily offering of himself to the public" (114). These traits may not apply to all innkeepers, but Thoreau says he is speaking about the "true and honest Landlord" (108). And how is the innkeeper like a statesman or a "publican"? The *Oxford English Dictionary* defines a "publican" as one who collects "taxes, tributes and customs." Biblically, a publican is also "a person regarded as a heathen; a person cut off from the Church or excommunicated." Finally, a "publican" is a keeper of a public house, such as a tavern.[19]

We know Thoreau chooses his words carefully and in this instance, he seems to draw on all the valences of this word. In "Huckleberries," Thoreau values the "heathens" who keep free of the habits of the town because they dwell in a removed space on the "heath." Like the "huckleberry people," the landlord is also a heathen. But the publican also collects taxes and customs, meaning tolls or duties. Could Thoreau mean the landlord collects people's customs (meaning habits) and conventions, as they pass through his inn? Does he lighten the burden of these travelers by collecting their socially ingrained practices?

The landlord has been excommunicated, set apart from society, but he is not a sinner; instead, he is more like a statesman. To be a statesman is to serve the public in some socially important work and to try to ameliorate political problems. In every sense of the word, this publican helps the traveler "shake off the village." The innkeeper engages in public work by ministering to lost travelers, helping them to become heathens with respect to modern society, collecting their conventional ways of thinking as a tax. The inn is a public house for those who enact Thoreau's practices of withdrawal, those travelers who walk and huckleberry and are launching their own attacks against an alienating society. Thoreau's innkeeper is providing a public service to help cultivate a new type of citizen.

"Housewarming" and Thoreau's Ideal of "Neighborhood"

At several points in his writings, Thoreau contrasts the present necessity of aloofness (given the forces of modern alienation) with a future possibility of greater fellowship and cooperation. In the "Economy" chapter of *Walden*, Thoreau describes building his cabin on Walden Pond, interlacing practical talk about building with metaphorical references to building the self. He prefers a solitary dwelling, though he realizes that it may be as easy to house two or more people in one house and share a common roof and cellar—all you require is a common wall to divide.

> But for my part, I prefer the solitary dwelling. Moreover, it will commonly be cheaper to build the whole yourself than to convince another of the advantage of the common wall; and when you have done this, the common partition, to be much cheaper, must be a thin one and that other may prove a bad neighbor and not keep his side in repair. The only coöperation which is commonly possible is exceedingly partial and superficial; and what little true coöperation there is, is as if it were not, being a harmony inaudible to men. . . . To coöperate in the highest as well as the lowest sense, means to get our living together. I heard it proposed lately that two young men should travel over the world, the one without money, earning his means as he went, before the mast and behind the plough, the other carrying a bill of exchange in his pocket. It was easy to see that they could not long be companions or coöperate, since one would not *operate* at all. They would part at the first interesting crisis in their adventures. Above all, as I have implied, the man who goes alone can start today; but he who travels with another must wait till that other is ready, and it may be a long time before they get off. (*Walden*, 71)

At first, Thoreau seems to be straightforwardly talking about building a house. But it soon becomes clear that building a dwelling place serves as a metaphor for the more important discussion about cooperation. Thoreau is yearning for a truer form of cooperation than is commonly possible. Most men, it seems, do not truly "coöperate" (by getting their living together) but instead simply adapt to the mode of life of "whatever company he is joined to." Now Thoreau juxtaposes two modes of life: first, there is a mode of life where one has few possessions and earns payment for his simple lifestyle by working as necessary. This is the lifestyle that resembles Thoreau's own: he picked up work as a surveyor or made pencils in his father's factory when he needed a few dollars. In the other mode, that of the rest of the world, we live according to the market and "carry a bill of exchange" in our pocket. Thoreau implies that these two modes are incompatible. But, it seems, we cannot wait for the rest of the world to realize the impoverishment of life organized by the market and abstract exchange. Thoreau finishes the paragraph by implying that the traveler should not wait for the world to learn how to truly cooperate, but should set out on his own and distance himself as much as possible from the dominant mode of living.

To really live, in Thoreau's lexicon, means to live a life where we have recovered the part of the self often lost to society, the ability to oppose, to negate, to critically think for ourselves. Thoreau experiments with this mode of truly, fully living, alone on Walden Pond, but his dream seems to be a cooperative effort where we "get our living together" as a society. Ideally, Thoreau seems to say, we would not need to separate, to withdraw, to go to a Walden Pond. In the "Housewarming" chapter of *Walden,* Thoreau gives us a hint about what our living arrangement might look like if we could truly get our living together. Thoreau describes another ideal house, and again, it is communal and a space that ministers to travelers:

> I sometimes dream of a larger and more populous house, standing in a golden age, of enduring materials, and without gingerbread work, which shall still consist of only one room, a vast, rude, substantial, primitive hall, without ceiling or plastering, with bare rafters and purlins supporting a sort of lower heaven over one's head . . . a cavernous house, wherein you must reach up a torch upon a pole to see the roof; where some may live in the fireplace, some in the recess of a window, and some on settles, some at one end of the hall, some at another, and some aloft on rafters with the spiders, if they choose; a house which you have got into when you have opened the outside door, and the ceremony is over; where the weary traveler may wash, and eat, and converse, and sleep, without further journey; such a shelter as you would be glad to reach in a tempestuous night. . . .
> A house where the inside is as open and manifest as a bird's nest, and you cannot go in at the front door and out at the back without seeing some of its inhabitants; where to be a guest is to be presented with the freedom of the house, and not to be carefully excluded from seven eights of it, shut up in a particular cell, and told to make yourself at home there,—in solitary confinement. Nowadays the host does not admit you to his hearth, but has got the mason to build one for yourself somewhere in his alley, and hospitality is the art of *keeping* you at the greatest distance. . . . I am aware that I have been on many a man's premises . . . but I am not aware that I have been in many men's houses. (*Walden,* 243)

Thoreau describes a "more populous" house with no walls separating its inhabitants. The whole house is one common room where people congregate, where they cannot help but see one another and be sociable as they go in and out of the house. There is community: no "weary traveler" or "guest" is shut up in his individual cell "in solitary confinement." Everything in this house is simple and rustic; there is no formality, no refined ceremonies, no etiquette. This is a house whose inside is "as open and manifest as a bird's nest."

This is truly the kind of place where it is possible to be a neighbor to another person, where people are not separated from themselves or each other by the trappings of modernity, by artifice, by superficial manners, or concerns with style and etiquette. In such a place, we would not need walls to separate us because we would not be threatened with an alienating loss of self. This ideal of community reflects the picture of neighborhood that we saw in "The Landlord."

And clearly, for Thoreau, this is still the ideal. For now, at least, he must live in a solitary dwelling where he is divided from neighbors (who are often but "poor neighbors" anyhow). Is this because we cannot trust society to produce good neighbors? To cooperate in the highest sense is to get our living together, to "live" in a more ideal communal space, in unalienated ways. But we should not put off our pilgrimage until we find the best companions. For Thoreau, we cannot wait for society to change for the better, because society will change only when individuals change. If we cannot have true neighbors, we have to go it alone. But going it alone and living in unalienated ways will have the side effect of contributing to the common good of society. Society will have neighbors when we, as individuals, learn how to act like neighbors.

With the concept of the neighbor, Thoreau invokes a space where we are valuably distanced from other people while also experiencing some degree of fellowship. For Thoreau, the neighbor is contrasted most explicitly with the citizen and the subject. As he says in "Resistance to Civil Government," "I am as desirous of being a good neighbor as I am of being a bad subject" ("Resistance," 84). Citizens are all those who "serve the state thus not as men but as machines," with "no free exercise whatever of the judgment or of the moral sense" (66). The neighbor seems to be the opposite of the citizen and the subject: his most prominent characteristic is that he thinks for himself and possesses the ability for critical thinking, for oppositional thinking, that society erases from the citizen.

The concept of the neighbor allows Thoreau to connect with others, while also maintaining a degree of withdrawal. This metaphor allows Thoreau to describe community while also preserving a self that can exist apart enough to still be a critical, negating, unalienated self. Being a good neighbor, then, seems to be about making connections while still respecting individuality. Used as a verb, *to neighbor* something is to exist next to it. Neighbors are also those who reside next to each other and live in the same community and are connected to each other in various ways. But the divisions have not been erased. Neighbors are not intrusive, but are also not entirely disengaged or separate. The notion of a good neighbor is typically someone whom we like and can connect with but also respects our personal space. This trope works to protect the thinking, critical self in necessary ways in an alienating society, but it points toward a future where the community side of the equation is more amplified. Thoreau wants us to try to be neighbors now, even in an alienated society, but he acknowledges that we may find it impossible to "truly get our living together" because bad neighbors abound. The concept also pushes toward even greater community and true neighborhood, where there are fewer citizens and more neighbors, where we can truly "get our living together" in the populous house with no dividing walls.

There is an interesting parallel between Thoreau's discussion of neighbors and Robert Frost's poem "Mending Wall."[20] Frost's poem depicts two neighbors engaging in an annual springtime ritual of replacing loose stones on the .wall running between their two properties. Each man stands on his own side of the wall and they walk the fields, replacing stones that have fallen during the winter; they walk to "set the wall between us once again" and "keep the wall between us as we go." This is a tradition, the thing that their fathers have done before them. But the narrator of the poem begins to question why the wall is necessary: they have no livestock and "my apple trees will never get across / and eat the cones under his pines." The narrator questions whether they need to mend wall: "something there is that doesn't love a wall / That wants it down." He says "before I built a wall I'd ask to know / What I was walling in or walling out." But his neighbor says this is the way things have always been done: "good fences make good neighbors." The neighbor "will not go behind his father's saying / and he likes having thought of it so well / He says again, 'Good fences make good neighbors.'"

Frost's poem makes us question this adage. Don't we wall each other out too if this is how we view our relationships with each other? Shouldn't being neighbors entail a richer relationship? Frost seems critical of arranging our relationships in ways that unthinkingly conform to tradition; the poem pushes us to consider how we might order our relationships without the weight of conventional wisdom, tradition, and reified social institutions. Like Thoreau, Frost too gets us thinking about the double meaning of "neighbor," as a separation (perhaps necessary) but also as a connection (holding greater possibilities). Thoreau uses the notion of the neighbor in ways that retain a certain distance, yet also evoke community and connection.

But when we think of this concept more as a verb, *neighboring* also shares some of the displacement of traveling. To neighbor is to adjoin, to be next to, to be close to something else. When we neighbor something else, we are in a border space; we are next to something but not in it. Neighboring entails a certain amount of distance that Thoreau sees as valuable. But distance from what? Both neighboring and traveling involve a distance from home. The traveler travels away from home and the neighbor exists "next to" home. Even in the "The Landlord," Thoreau does not idealize a situation where the traveler is "at home." Instead, he praises the innkeeper for ministering to travelers, for accepting their homeless state and accommodating them in their travels. But why is this displacement from home so important for Thoreau?

To travel, to experiment, to venture outside the comfortable patterns, to walk outside of well-worn paths: for Thoreau, these are the activities that protect us from the thoughtless, comfortable complacency of the citizen-as-machine. Thoreau uses the "traveler" trope frequently in his writings but seems to intend it like other quasi-metaphors he uses. On the one hand, he means it literally: "traveling" as physical displacement to border spaces outside of town. But the traveler also seems to work more generally as a metaphor for the person who seeks unsettling, wild experiences that disrupt conventional patterns. In this way, walking and huckleberrying work similarly to traveling. Thoreau confronts the wild and seeks experiences that shake us out of familiar ways of thinking or living that have become second nature. Just as Adorno's practice of negative dialectics disrupts and unsettles in order to highlight disjunctures in conventional ways of thinking, so the wild unsettles the conventional self for Thoreau in ways that protect us from becoming too unthinkingly at home in the world.

Thoreau, Adorno, and Thoughts of Home

In the essay "Wild Apples," Thoreau makes a distinction between the grafted, cultivated apple that is palatable to those who are "indoors," inside the "house" and "frequent the markets" and those apples savored by the walker. The grafted apple, the market, and the house seem to connote taming and domestication, doing violence to the concept of the wild. At home, the palate rejects all that is wild and demands milder flavors: "All apples are good in November. Those which the farmer leaves out as unsalable, and unpalatable to those who frequent the markets, are the choicest fruit to the walker. But it is remarkable that the wild apple, which I praise as so spirited and racy when eaten in the field or woods, being brought into the house, frequently has a harsh or crabbed taste. The Saunterer's Apple not even the saunterer can eat in the house. The palate rejects it there . . . and demands a tamed one; for there you miss the November air, which is the sauce it is to be eaten with" ("Wild Apples," 459). Eaten inside the house, even the wild apple loses its attractive tang and simply tastes harsh, so Thoreau says that wild apples must be eaten outside: "The apples have hung in the wind and frost and rain till they have absorbed the qualities of the weather or season, and thus are highly *seasoned*, and they *pierce* and *sting* and *permeate* us with their spirit. They must be eaten in *season*, accordingly, — that is, out-of-doors. To appreciate the wild and sharp flavors of these October fruits, it is necessary that you be breathing the sharp October or November air. The out-door air and exercise which the walker gets gives a different tone to his palate, and he craves a fruit which the sedentary would call harsh and crabbed. They must be eaten in the fields" (459).

But now, Thoreau takes this discussion to an entirely different level and makes more explicit the connection between the kind of tamed, domesticated thinking that he associates with being at home and the rupturing, critical thought of the walker and the traveler. Thoreau makes it clear that the image of the wild apple reflects a certain kind of thinking: "So there is one *thought* for the field, another for the house. I would have my thoughts, like wild apples, to be food for walkers, and will not warrant them to be palatable, if tasted in the house" ("Wild Apples," 461). He makes no guarantee that his thoughts will be palatable or easy to swallow for those who are inside, at home, but they seem designed to jar, rupture, and unsettle those who are comfortably ensconced in familiar surroundings. The terms Thoreau associates with the wild apple and with the walker are words that fly in stark opposition to what is smooth and harmonious. The thoughts of the walker correspondingly rupture, break apart, and fracture abstract conventions and comfortable identities as he seeks the wild and travels away from home.

Whereas Thoreau's walker creates a self-imposed exile, Adorno's exile was forced upon him, yet both identify a valuable critical distance in the experience of homelessness we can achieve in spaces of withdrawal. Both identify a political danger in the feeling of comfortable self-assurance. In his aphorism "Refuge for the Homeless" (*"Asyl für Obdachlose"*), Adorno cautions the emigrant against surrendering to an easy and consoling private life and states that "the best mode of conduct" (given historical circumstances) is to lead an "uncommitted, suspended" life that is not deeply entrenched in the social order (*Minima Moralia,* 39). For both Adorno and Thoreau, homeownership and settling down seem to give tacit consent to a problematic status quo.

Adorno identifies particular dangers in our mentality when we feel comfortably at home. In "Memento" (see chapter 1 in this book), Adorno cautions against the writer who "sets up house" in his writing and thinking: "Just as he trundles papers, books, pencils, documents untidily from room to room, he creates the same disorder in his thoughts. They become pieces of furniture that he sinks into, content or irritable. He strokes them affectionately, wears them out, mixes them up, rearranges, ruins them." Adorno links such a home with a "slackening of mental tension," a tendency to "drift along idly," and to "generate a warm atmosphere" (*Minima Moralia,* 87). We must be wary of making such a nest for ourselves. Home for Adorno is a place that generates a dangerous tendency to sink down comfortably in entrenched conventions; thoughts too can become solid, weighty, like pieces of furniture. When we feel this way, we may do nothing, may be lulled into a false sense of complacency; when we feel this way, we might indeed create the conditions for fascism. If this is the state of affairs in our physical and psychic homes, it is better to seek a critical border position, the withdrawn, marginal space of the walker or the exile.

Thoreau, like Adorno but unlike Emerson, is highly attuned to the dangers of a sense of self-assurance. Consequently, Thoreau's houses are designed with an eye that is wary of any sort of harmony or comfort. He seeks out the withdrawn space of the dismal swamp. Like Adorno, Thoreau is relentless in trying to upset and unsettle identity. Unlike Emerson though, there is no building a home in spirit or the universal mind—there is only continual walking, sauntering, and traveling. Through Adorno and Thoreau's practices of withdrawal, both try to wake us up to the dangers that home can present to the possibility of true democracy.

Conclusion

Alienation and
the Anti-Foundationalist Foundation of the Self

Writing independently, separated by time and space, Thoreau and Adorno enter into a kind of fellowship in exploring the experience of alienation in modernity and the politics of withdrawal we might enact to work against that alienation. In this way, Thoreau becomes the kind of friend Adorno would have especially valued. As Susan Buck-Morss notes, Adorno loved to discover sympathetic criticisms with writers in other spaces and times and thought such confluence confirmed the validity of his responses to objective modern conditions: "The uniquely individual experiences of critical subjectivity ran parallel because they focused on particulars which reflected the same objective reality, and it followed that collaboration was possible among intellectuals even when they worked alone. Nothing pleased Adorno more than when a friend came to similar insights independently, for he considered it a validation of their correctness."[1] Adorno would likely have taken great pleasure in the similarities that exist, over and against many differences, between him and Thoreau.

Reading Thoreau with Adorno, I have articulated their paradoxical politics of withdrawal, analyzed the experience of alienation that motivates them, and explored how these practices might be a valuable part of democratic politics. This is not to trump other conceptions of politics, nor to say that these more typical and traditional definitions of politics are wrong, but reading Thoreau with Adorno renders another kind of democratic politics visible and expands the parameters of democracy beyond their more usual participatory boundaries. Despite many recent contestations and expansions of the borders of democratic politics, "withdrawal" and "democracy" are still typically thought of as two mutually exclusive terms, the oil and water of contemporary political thought. But if only participatory actions in shared, public spaces count as democratic actions, we both misunderstand Thoreau's politics and miss his unique contributions. Adorno helps cast an illuminating spotlight on exactly those elements of Thoreau's thought that have met with the greatest confusion.

In addition to broadening our understanding of democracy beyond conventional public, intersubjective, participatory parameters, Thoreau and Adorno also help us develop an understanding of alienation that overcomes some limitations in previous approaches. Although the last two chapters focused on the democratic value of practices of withdrawal, it is important to remember what motivates those acts of self-distancing for Thoreau and Adorno. Both are pushed toward marginal spaces and borderlands because of the alienating effects of modern life, because of a loss of the critical capacities they see as both central to a notion of selfhood and vital to democratic self-government. Thoreau's and Adorno's novel approaches to alienation, identifying it as a political problem, might also help revitalize this method of analysis.

Concerns over the loss of self were a popular topic for theorists in the 1960s and 1970s, but today much less is written on the subject.[2] This is likely due to many different factors. But one part of the explanation may concern the shift away from social explanations toward more biological and neuroscientific understandings of things like anxiety, melancholy, and a sense of loss.[3] In *Escape from Freedom* Erich Fromm describes anxiety, a loss of self, psychological neuroses, and a longing for submission to authority as problems of modern democratic society. Similarly, Adorno notes that "there are profound links between history and the consciousness of the mentally ill."[4] But today, in the so-called age of the brain, the explanations for these subjective states are far more likely to involve discussions of serotonin levels and neurotransmitters. Forms of psychic unrest such as anxiety and melancholy are increasingly explained as chemical imbalances, as physical illnesses rooted in the brain. Today, explanatory power regarding psychic unrest is increasingly placed not on society but on the biology of the brain.[5] Surgeon general David Satcher reflected the logic behind what is variously called the new "biological materialism," "scientific materialism," or "the medical model": "Science . . . says that the bases of mental illness are chemical changes in the brain, and therefore physical changes,

changes in the basic cells of the brain. . . . Mental illnesses are physical illnesses. They're related to physical changes in the brain."[6]

For complex reasons, the focus has shifted from society to biology. But, as many critics have noted, biology has become an explanatory variable that threatens to eliminate all other perspectives on the roots of psychic dis-ease.[7] Or as Adorno wrote, "Terror before the abyss of the self is removed by the consciousness of being concerned with nothing so very different from arthritis or sinus trouble" (*Minima Moralia*, 65). This is not a topic my project explores, but it seems important to mention it as at least one part of the reason for why more socially embedded discussions of feelings of alienation have fallen out of favor as of late. The crowding out of social theory in this area seems especially damaging given the valuable ways that Adorno and Thoreau link feelings of psychic unease to complex social forces.

A very different kind of reason for the decreased popularity of the topic of alienation may concern the influence of what we may call postmodern understandings of subjectivity. Such theories tend to conflict with the notion of a socially rooted loss of the critical capacities of the self in two ways. First, the problem of alienation does not seem to exist if we imagine the self as always already produced and created by society: the self cannot experience a loss at the hands of an alienating society if it can be created only from the ground up by that society in the first place. This is why a thinker such as Foucault, who is deeply concerned with problems of madness, disease, and civilization, does not focus on the problem of alienation in the same way that Adorno does, for example. For Adorno, the capacities of the individual can be lost and painfully lamented, but for Foucault they can only be produced and cultivated. The sense of pathos and nostalgia that characterizes Adorno's work has no place in Foucault's writings, given his different understanding of subjectivity. Second, due to the influence of postmodern theories today, there is greater skepticism regarding any claims for a utopian wholeness. The problem of the loss of self begs to be overcome with a return to self, a fulfillment of what was lost, but many theorists today (correctly) tend to see this kind of complete recovery as impossible and argue instead that the self can only ever be fragmented, partial, contingent, relational, shifting, and unstable.

The gap between more postmodern ways of thinking and the problem of alienation seems even more expansive given that, when we think of the problem of social and political (as opposed to existential) alienation at all, it probably appears in our minds in its Marxist form. And even later Marxists (such as Adorno) grew critical of Marx's plans for solving the problem of alienation through wide-scale economic reforms. We still perhaps tend to associate the experience of alienation with the limited and often problematic diagnosis of the problem given by Marx. We view his prescription more warily too, skeptical of the possibility and desirability of the kind of massive social change that Marx saw as a corrective to the experience of alienation.

But both Thoreau and Adorno discuss alienation in ways that differ from our more conventional understanding of the problem. Neither Thoreau nor Adorno imagines a primordial self or an essential self that is wholly prior to society: the ways that we think are shaped by society, which is why the self can become alienated. But for both, as we have seen, there *is* one feature that is central to the possibility of our collective experience as humans, and that is the ability to negate, to critique, to think against convention. For Adorno, objects contain contradictory qualities that can stimulate this praxis of thinking, if we grant preponderance to them. Similarly, little things like wild apples and huckleberries contain dissonant qualities from which Thoreau draws a social critique. For both Thoreau and Adorno, we experience a loss when this capacity for critical negation is threatened. The thinking self is "liquidated," to use Adorno's trope, and humans become more like "machines," to draw on the metaphor that both use.

Ultimately, Thoreau seems critical of any notion of identity that is stable or grounded in some foundational truth. The value Thoreau places on traveling as a metaphor for experiences of displacement highlights the strong antifoundationalist strain that runs through his work. But Thoreau's antifoundationalism is unique in that he does see humans as having a defining quality that, if lost, is to be lamented; for Thoreau, however, to be human and to live life is the ability to think against conventions, to negate, to experiment with our lives. In other words, there is a kind of antifoundationalist foundation to Thoreau's notion of subjectivity. This balancing act is another point of sympathy with Adorno: Thoreau and Adorno are both critical of naturalized institutions in ways that point toward more postmodern, antifoundationalist ways of thinking. The unsettling, disruption, and disjuncture of settled conventions play important roles in both these men's thoughts. Both articulate a notion of what we share as humans that is based on the capacity for thinking and critical negation. Yet there is a foundation and a core to their notions of what unites humans, however modest, that stops short of a full antifoundationalism. This thin notion of subjectivity exists as the antifoundationalist foundation for their thought, making it possible for them to speak of an alienating loss of self. Their practices of withdrawal aim toward the recovery of these critical capacities, but neither imagines that these recuperative practices will culminate in a complete, whole, or fully restored subject.

When we read Thoreau and Adorno together, we appreciate that working against alienation is a continual, daily practice; neither thinker is optimistic that the problem of alienation can be solved or escaped but rather, for both, it can only be held at bay every day in small ways. We cannot fully regain the capacity for critique in a final way but can only struggle (with greater or less success) to recover, however temporarily, the capacity to negate, to think against convention. For Thoreau, we can reclaim these characteristic features of the self by withdrawing to border-spaces to engage in practices that teach us to see for ourselves, to pay attention to particularity, to be wary of abstraction, and to question conventions. For Thoreau, to act in these ways is to truly live, but these experiences are fleeting: the fruits of walking or huckleberrying are not permanent but must be continually reclaimed. For Adorno, working against alienation is about reclaiming the possibility of thinking as a (potentially shared) praxis. Negative dialectics aims toward thinking against what is given, against instrumentalism, to preserve the possibility of alternative ways of living. But neither thinks that walking, huckleberrying, or negative dialectics will culminate in a complete and whole self, a restored self. These countervailing practices to alienation are absolutely necessary if we are to live even a pale shade of life, yet at the same time they are ultimately incapable of complete success.

Walking, huckleberrying, and negative dialectics are practices that help us pay attention to particularity, appreciate what is unique despite the force of sameness, and think for ourselves against the power of convention. They are modestly enacted in ways that are small-scale, daily, and might at first glance seem insignificant. Practices of withdrawal are not spectacular events; they are not the kind of politics that will get coverage on the evening news. Nor are they the kinds of grand events that historians will write about. They are inglorious and inconspicuous acts, but Thoreau and Adorno try to help us to recognize their value, to see that they have a potential that exceeds their humble appearance. Together, Thoreau and Adorno help us appreciate how practices of withdrawal, separation, and self-distancing can be politically valuable in a democracy, though at first glance they seem like minor acts of hermitage and hibernation.

Notes

Preface

1. In the section from *Negative Dialectics* titled "After Auschwitz," Adorno reflects on the survivor's guilt of one who "was spared": "But it is not wrong to raise the less cultural question whether after Auschwitz you can go on living—especially whether one who escaped by accident, one who by rights should have been killed, may go on living. . . . By way of atonement he will be plagued by dreams such as that he is no longer living at all, that he was sent to the ovens in 1944 and his whole existence since has been imaginary, an emanation of the insane wish of a man killed twenty years earlier." Theodor Adorno, *Negative Dialectics*, trans. E. B. Ashton (New York: Continuum, 1973), 363.

2. Tom Huhn, "Thoughts Beside Themselves," in *Cambridge Companion to Adorno*, ed. Tom Huhn (New York: Cambridge University Press, 2004), 1.

3. Theodor Adorno, "Aldous Huxley and Utopia," in *Prisms* (Cambridge: MIT Press, 1983), 97.

4. Theodor Adorno, "Critique," in *Critical Models: Interventions and Catchwords* (New York: Columbia University Press, 1998), 281.

5. Robert Putnam, *Bowling Alone: The Collapse and Revival of American Community* (New York: Simon & Schuster, 2001).

6. Robert A. Dahl, *On Political Equality* (New Haven, CT: Yale University Press, 2006).

7. Robert Bellah et al., *Habits of the Heart: Individualism and Commitment in American Life* (Berkeley: University of California Press, 1985; reprint, 1996).

8. Michael Sandel, *Liberalism and the Limits of Justice* (New York: Cambridge University Press: 1982; reprint, 1998); Michael Sandel, *Democracy's Discontents: America in Search of a Public Philosophy* (Cambridge, MA: Belknap Press, 1998); Michael Sandel, *Public Philosophy: Essays on Morality in Politics* (Cambridge, MA: Harvard University Press, 2006).

9. Quoted in Seyla Benhabib, "The Democratic Moment and the Problem of Difference," in *Democracy and Difference: Contesting the Boundaries of the Political*, ed. Seyla Benhabib (Princeton, NJ: Princeton University Press, 1996), 6–7.

10. For Habermas, "alienation phenomena" include "loss of meaning," "anomie," and "psychopathologies." These phenomena result from "systematically distorted communication" that develops when the "lifeworld," which is supposed to be characterized by intersubjective forms of communicative rationality, is "colonized" by an instrumental, purposive, means-end rationality. Jürgen Habermas, *The Theory of Communicative Action*, vol. 2: *Lifeworld and System: A Critique of Functionalist Reason*, trans. Thomas McCarthy (Boston: Beacon Press, 1987), 143, 384.

11. Sheldon S. Wolin, "Fugitive Democracy," in Benhabib, *Democracy and Difference*, 43.

12. For Wolin, these moments are "rare" and "episodic," in contrast with what he calls "politics," which we might think of as politics as usual, concerned with who gets what, when, and where: "*Politics* refers to the legitimized and public contestation, primarily by organized and unequal social powers, over access to the resources available to the public authorities of the collectivity." Ibid., 31.

13. Wolin states, "Here I should like to point out that the words 'public,' 'common,' and 'general' have a long tradition of usage which has made them synonyms for what is political." Sheldon Wolin, *Politics and Vision: Continuity and Innovation in Western Political Thought* (Princeton, NJ: Princeton University Press, 2004), 10.

14. *Oxford English Dictionary*, s.v. "agon."

15. "The key claim of those supporting agonistic encounters is that moral conflict and engagement across differences is a valuable and indispensable part of social and political life. Such conflict is good for the body politic, and both groups and individuals within it." David Schlosberg, "The Pluralist Imagination," in *The Oxford Handbook of Political Theory*, ed. Bonnie Honig, John S. Dryzek, and Anne Phillips (New York: Oxford University Press, 2006), 150. Chantal Mouffe expresses a similar sentiment: "In a democratic polity, conflicts and confrontations, far from being a sign of imperfection, indicate that democracy is alive and inhabited by pluralism." Chantal Mouffe, "Democracy, Power, and the 'Political,'" in Benhabib, *Democracy and Difference*, 255.

16. Bonnie Honig, *Political Theory and the Displacement of Politics* (Ithaca, NY: Cornell University Press, 1993), 2.

17. As Honig notes, these "displacements" have "antidemocratic resonances, if by democracy one means a set of arrangements that perpetually generates popular (both local and global) political action as well as generating the practices that legitimate representative institutions." Ibid., 4.

18. Honig, "Difference, Dilemmas, and the Politics of Home," in Benhabib, *Democracy and Difference*, 260. See also chapter 5 in this book.

19. William Connolly sees pluralism as an inevitable part of society generally, but also of our identity as individuals: "*Intrasubjective* and *intersubjective* difference opens up relational possibilities of agonistic respect, studied indifference, critical responsiveness, and selective collaboration between interdependent, contending identities." William E. Connolly, *The Ethos of Pluralization* (Minneapolis: University of Minnesota Press, 1995), xvii. Bonnie Honig states, "Difference is what identity perpetually seeks (and fails) to expunge,

fix, or hold in place. In short, difference is a problem for identity, not one of its adjectives." She outlines this decentered subject in the following terms: "In opposition to this fantasy of safety and impermeability, however, another conception of subjectivity emerges, a coalitional (and psychoanalytic) conception in which the fragments, differences, and identities that constitute subjectivity do not simply coexist within a single if plural self but actually cross-cut and inhabit each other, cooperating with and waging war against each other in a perpetual motion of mutuality, engagement, struggle, and debt." Honig, "Difference, Dilemmas, and the Politics of Home," 258, 271.

20. William E. Connolly, *Identity/Difference: Democratic Negotiations of Political Paradox* (Minneapolis: University of Minnesota Press, 1991), ix, x. Honig also describes how decentered subjects will "energize" social democracies: "Social democracies—in so far as they are committed to the perpetuity of political contest and to the generation of new (domestic as well as international or extrastatist) social movements *in addition* to the more rather than less egalitarian distribution of scarce resources—have the greatest potential to permit and even energize the sorts of mobilities and settlements that these renegotiations require. And when decentered subjects, aware of the role that difference plays in relation to identity, engage in these renegotiations they, in turn have the power to energize their social democracies, while pressing upon them claims of justice, fairness, fidelity, and ethicality on behalf of those difference to which social democratic regimes tend to become deaf in their eagerness to administer to represented identities that are established, stable, and familiar." Honig, "Difference, Dilemmas, and the Politics of Home," 272.

21. Consider, for example, Seyla Benhabib's anthology *Democracy and Difference: Contesting the Boundaries of the Political*. Even though this collection of essays is subtitled, "contesting the boundaries of the political," we see, in fact, that "the political" is still primarily defined in terms of collective interaction in a common, public space. "Democratic politics" is not contested beyond these particular borders.

22. Dana Villa, *Socratic Citizenship* (Princeton, NJ: Princeton University Press, 2001). Villa's understanding of Socratic citizenship is in some ways sympathetic to my understanding of a politics of withdrawal, but there are also significant differences concerning why Thoreau and Adorno withdraw, how they withdraw, and to what end. In addition, my reading of Thoreau's politics differs in important ways from Villa's (all of which I discuss more in the next chapter, in the section on withdrawal).

23. Bob Pepperman Taylor, *America's Bachelor Uncle: Thoreau in the American Polity* (Lawrence: University of Kansas Press, 1996), 7.

24. Alexis de Tocqueville, *Democracy in America and Two Essays on America*, trans. Gerald E. Bevan (New York: Penguin Books, 2003), 297, 298.

25. In a way that is often sympathetic with, but also different from, the democratic practices of withdrawal that I examine, Thomas Dumm writes about the loneliness of the modern individual. He sees loneliness as "fundamental to the very constitution of our selves" and "foundational, in the sense that in the end we all understand ourselves as being alone in the world." For Dumm, loneliness is also a "profoundly political experience because it is instrumental in the shaping and exercise of power, the meaning of

individuality, and the ways in which justice is to be comprehended and realized in the world." Thomas Dumm, *Loneliness as a Way of Life* (Cambridge, MA: Harvard University Press, 2008), 26, 30, 29.

Introduction

1. The sources for the epigraphs, in the order they are referenced, are: Michael Meyers, *"Several More Lives to Live": Thoreau's Political Reputation in America* (Westport, CT: Greenwood Press, 1977), 11; Philip Abbott, "Henry David Thoreau, the State of Nature, and the Redemption of Liberalism," *Journal of Politics* 47, no. 1 (1985): 183; Bob Pepperman Taylor, *America's Bachelor Uncle: Thoreau in the American Polity* (Lawrence: University of Kansas Press, 1996), 7.

2. Henry David Thoreau, "Slavery in Massachusetts," in *The Higher Law: Thoreau on Civil Disobedience and Reform,* ed. Wendell Glick (Princeton, NJ: Princeton University Press, 2004), 108. Hereafter cited in text as "Slavery."

3. Mary Elkin Moller, *Thoreau in the Human Community* (Amherst: University of Massachusetts Press, 1980).

4. Taylor, *America's Bachelor Uncle.*

5. George Kateb, *The Inner Ocean: Individualism and Democratic Culture* (Ithaca, NY: Cornell University Press, 1992); George Kateb, "The Moral Distinctiveness of Representative Democracy," *Ethics* 91, no. 3 (1981); George Kateb, "Walt Whitman and the Culture of Democracy," *Political Theory* 18, no. 4 (1990).

6. Jack Turner, "'Performing Conscience': Thoreau, Political Action and the Plea for John Brown," *Political Theory* 33, no. 4 (2005).

7. Jane Bennett, *Thoreau's Nature: Ethics, Politics and the Wild* (Thousand Oaks, CA: Sage, 1994). See chapter 4 in this book for a discussion of my sympathies with Bennett, but also a further exploration of how my reading of Thoreau differs from hers in significant ways.

8. Brian Walker, "Thoreau on Democratic Cultivation," *Political Theory* 29, no. 2 (2001).

9. Morris B. Kaplan, "Queer Citizenship: Thoreau's Civil Disobedience and the Ethics of Self-Making," in *Sexual Justice: Democratic Citizenship and the Politics of Desire* (New York: Routledge, 1997). For a different kind of queer reading of Thoreau, see also Michael Warner, "Thoreau's Bottom," *Raritan* 11, no. 3 (1992).

10. Vincent Buranelli, "The Case against Thoreau," *Ethics* 67, no. 4 (1957).

11. Abbott, "Henry David Thoreau, the State of Nature, and the Redemption of Liberalism."

12. Richard Bridgman, *Dark Thoreau* (Lincoln: University of Nebraska Press, 1982).

13. Hannah Arendt, "Civil Disobedience," in *Crises of the Republic* (New York: Harcourt, Brace and Jovanovich, 1969), 62–63. Because of some strong sympathies, yet even stronger divergences, Arendt provides an illuminating foil to Thoreau and Adorno. Arendt is also centrally concerned with the potentially tyrannical implications of

thoughtlessness. She also wants us to be critical, to "think what we are doing," as she says in *The Human Condition*. But for Arendt the arena of politics is *necessarily* and by definition the proper public space for us to appear to each other to debate, deliberate, create shared meanings together, and bring the new into the world. She laments as "worldlessness" and "world alienation" the modern tendency to withdraw into the self. For Arendt, the idea of a "politics of withdrawal" would be an oxymoron: politics, in her normative sense, is by definition opposed to practices of withdrawal as she sees withdrawal as synonymous with a dangerous apathy and disengagement. The disagreement between Arendt, on the one hand, and Thoreau and Adorno, on the other, seems to be rooted in Arendt's sharp distinction between the private and public realms and her argument that truly free action and politics can take place only in the intersubjective realm of the public. Arendt's conclusions about politics seem to stem from her method: as her biographer Elisabeth Young-Bruehl puts it, "She called her method 'conceptual analysis'; her task was to find 'where concepts come from.' With the aid of philology or linguistic analysis, she traced political concepts back to the concrete historical and generally political experiences which gave rise to those concepts. She was then able to gauge how far a concept had moved from its origins" (318). Hannah Arendt, *The Human Condition* (Chicago: University of Chicago Press, 1958). See also Elisabeth Young-Bruehl, *Hannah Arendt: For Love of the World*, 2nd ed. (New Haven, CT: Yale University Press, 2004).

14. Nancy Rosenblum, "Thoreau's Militant Conscience," *Political Theory* 9, no. 1 (1981).

15. See also Nancy Rosenblum, *Another Liberalism: Romanticism and the Reconstruction of Liberal Thought* (Cambridge, MA: Harvard University Press, 1987), chapter 5, "Heroic Individualism and the Spectacle of Diversity"; and Nancy Rosenblum, "The Inhibitions of Democracy on Romantic Political Thought: Thoreau's Democratic Individualism," in *Lessons of Romanticism: A Critical Companion*, ed. Thomas Pfau and Robert F. Gleckner (Durham, NC: Duke University Press, 1998).

16. Joel Porte, *Emerson and Thoreau: Transcendentalists in Conflict* (Middletown, CT: Wesleyan University Press, 1966), 150. In *Consciousness and Culture*, a compilation of essays published more recently, Porte sees Thoreau as straddling a paradox that also characterizes "the whole American experience": Thoreau rejects the society that surrounds him, as well as society as such, and flies away to the woods to avoid "the complications, responsibilities and conformities of American life." Joel Porte, *Consciousness and Culture: Emerson and Thoreau Reviewed* (New Haven, CT: Yale University Press, 2004), 146.

17. Michael T. Gilmore, *American Romanticism and the Marketplace* (Chicago: Chicago University Press, 1985). See chapter 3 in the present work for another aspect of Gilmore's chapter, regarding abstract exchange.

18. Leo Marx, *The Machine in the Garden: Technology and the Pastoral Ideal in America* (New York: Oxford University Press, 1964, 2000), 265.

19. Leigh Kathryn Jenco, "Thoreau's Critique of Democracy," *Review of Politics* 65 (Summer 2003), 356, 363, 357. Jenco's reading of Thoreau differs from mine in other

important ways. Whereas I focus on Thoreau's nature writings as well as his political essays, she draws her argument only from Thoreau's overtly political "reform" writings ("Resistance to Civil Government," "Slavery in Massachusetts," "Life without Principle," and the "Higher Law" chapter of *Walden*). Whereas I show the many ways that Thoreau departs from Emerson, Jenco understands Thoreau as an Emersonian Transcendentalist, grounding Thoreau's morality in Emerson's notion of a higher law.

20. Rosenblum, "The Inhibitions of Democracy on Romantic Political Thought," 61.

21. Dana Villa, *Socratic Citizenship* (Princeton, NJ: Princeton University Press, 2001), 17, xii.

22. Ibid., 55.

23. Ibid., 29.

24. Henry David Thoreau, "Resistance to Civil Government," in *The Higher Law: Thoreau on Civil Disobedience and Reform,* ed. Wendell Glick, 84. Hereafter cited in text as "Resistance."

25. Villa, *Socratic Citizenship,* xi–xii.

26. Ibid., 21.

27. Theodor Adorno, *Negative Dialectics,* trans. E. B. Ashton (New York: Continuum, 1973), 203. Hereafter cited in text as *Negative Dialectics.* In the original German version of *Negative Dialektik,* the last part of this quote reads "Weh spricht: 'vergeh.'" *Vergehen* has a slightly different, more negative connotation than "Go," which would be *gehen. Vergehen* means something more like "go away." Theodor Adorno, *Negative Dialektik* (Darmstadt: Wissenschaftliche Buchgesellschaft, 1998). I have used English translations of Adorno's texts but checked the passages I quote against the German. See notes for the original German texts where there seems to be a confusing, weak, or unclear translation. Adorno employs many stylistic devices that are difficult if not impossible to fully render in English, thus the close relationship between the style of his writing and the content of his ideas does not come through as clearly in English. For an interesting essay on translating Adorno, see Samuel Weber's introductory essay to Adorno's *Prisms,* where he discusses the difficulties of rendering Adorno's thoughts in English. Samuel Weber, "Translating the Untranslatable," in *Prisms* (Cambridge, MA: MIT Press, 1981).

28. See the epigraph that prefaces *Minima Moralia.* Theodor Adorno, *Minima Moralia: Reflections from Damaged Life,* trans. E. F. N. Jephcott (London: Verso, 1974).

29. Adorno helpfully distinguishes alienation from reification by calling it "the subjective state of consciousness that corresponds" to reification, again stating that consciousness is not the source of this state of suffering: "The cause of human suffering, meanwhile, will be glossed over rather than denounced in the lament about reification. The trouble is with the conditions that condemn mankind to impotence and apathy and would yet be changeable by human action; it is not primarily with people and with the way conditions appear to people. Considering the possibility of total disaster, reification is an epiphenomenon, and even more so is the alienation coupled with reification, the

subjective state of consciousness that corresponds to it. Alienation is reproduced by anxiety; consciousness—reified in the already constituted society—is not the *constituens* of anxiety" (*Negative Dialectics*, 190).

30. Henry David Thoreau, *Walden*, ed. J. Lyndon Shanley (Princeton, NJ: Princeton University Press, 2004), 136. Hereafter cited in text as *Walden*.

31. Henry David Thoreau, "Walking," in *Collected Essays and Poems*, ed. Elizabeth Hall Witherell (New York: Library of America, 2001), 254. Hereafter cited in text as "Walking."

32. See chapter 2 in this book for a discussion of these influences on Emerson's thought.

33. Thoreau, in fact, seems to have read German better than Emerson and enjoyed reading German texts more. Emerson preferred not to read texts in their original language if a translation was available, while Thoreau liked to read texts in their original language, even when translations were at hand. Thoreau read Greek, Latin, French, and German.

34. Lukács says, "A considerable part of the leading German intelligentsia, including Adorno, have taken up residence in the 'Grand Hotel Abyss' . . . 'a beautiful hotel, equipped with every comfort, on the edge of an abyss, of nothingness, of absurdity. And the daily contemplation of the abyss between excellent meals or artistic entertainments, can only heighten the enjoyment of the subtle comforts offered.'" Georg Lukács, *The Theory of the Novel* (Cambridge, MA: MIT Press, 1994), 22.

35. Martin Jay, *Adorno* (Cambridge, MA: Harvard University Press, 1984), 55. The quotation originally comes from Habermas's "Consciousness-Raising or Redemptive Criticism: The Contemporaneity of Walter Benjamin," *New German Critique* 17 (1979): 43.

36. Theodor Adorno, *The Culture Industry*, ed. J. M. Bernstein (New York: Routledge, 1991), 198. Hereafter cited in text as *Culture Industry*.

37. Ralph Waldo Emerson, introduction to *Walden and Other Writings* (New York: Modern Library, 2000), xxviii.

38. Adorno, *Minima Moralia: Reflections from Damaged Life*, 26. Hereafter cited in text as *Minima Moralia*.

39. See chapter 1 of this book, which focuses on Adorno, where I elaborate further on how negative dialectics manifests itself as a kind of political praxis. In later chapters I explore the corporeality of Thoreau's practices of changing the way we think and perceive with Adorno's less corporeal, more disembodied discussion of thinking.

40. The phrase "a distanced nearness" is *Nähe an Distanz* in the original German ("nearness by distance"). Theodor Adorno, *Minima Moralia: Reflexionen aus dem Beschädigten Leben*, ed. Rolf Tiedemann et al. (Darmstadt: Wissenschaftliche Buchgesellschaft, 1997), 100.

41. Alexander Hamilton, James Madison, and John Jay, *The Federalist Papers with Letters of "Brutus,"* ed. Terence Ball (New York: Cambridge University Press, 2003). See especially *Federalist Papers* #10 and #51, where these mechanistic images are developed.

42. Henry David Thoreau, "Life without Principle," in *The Higher Law: Thoreau on Civil Disobedience and Reform,* ed. Wendell Glick, 177. Hereafter cited in text as "Life."

43. Henry David Thoreau, *The Journals of Henry D. Thoreau,* vol. 8–14 (New York: Dover, 1962), 28.

44. Theory and vision have a long history. The word *theory* derives from the Greek *theoria,* which is defined as the practice of looking at, viewing, or seeing something, but also contemplating or speculating about it. How we look at things, what our eyes focus on, what is seen and unseen, shapes our view of the world and our theory of it. As Sheldon Wolin says, each theorist views problems "from a different perspective, a particular angle of vision. This suggests that political philosophy constitutes a form of 'seeing' political phenomena and that the way in which phenomena will be visualized depends in large measure on where the viewer 'stands'" (17). At the same time, there is an imaginative element in how we see: "The impossibility of direct observation compels the theorist to epitomize a society by abstracting certain phenomena and providing interconnections where none can be seen. Imagination is the theorist's means for understanding a world he can never 'know' in an intimate way" (19). Sheldon Wolin, *Politics and Vision: Continuity and Innovation in Western Political Thought* (Princeton, NJ: Princeton University Press, 2004).

45. Adorno used this term in reference to Walter Benjamin's work. But Adorno, influenced by Benjamin, also adopted this "microscopic gaze." Susan Buck-Morss, *The Origin of Negative Dialectics* (New York: Free Press, 1977), 74.

46. Theodor Adorno, "Critique," in *Critical Models: Interventions and Catchwords* (New York: Columbia University Press, 1998), 281.

47. Henry David Thoreau, *A Week on the Concord and Merrimack Rivers,* ed. Carl A. Hovde, William L. Howarth, and Elizabeth Hall Witherell (Princeton, NJ: Princeton University Press, 2004), 78.

48. For the German, see Adorno, *Minima Moralia: Reflexionen aus dem beschädigten Leben.*

49. Thanks to Sean Franzel and Samuel Frederick, for their feedback and advice on my translations of *Minima Moralia.*

50. Gillian Rose, *The Melancholy Science: An Introduction to the Thought of Theodor W. Adorno* (New York: Columbia University Press, 1978), 13.

51. Ibid., 14.

52. Ibid., 11.

53. In his *Journals,* Thoreau associates exaggeration with a kind of deeper truth that must be spoken to men with a loud voice: "Exaggeration! Was ever any virtue attributed to a man without exaggeration? Was ever any vice, without infinite exaggeration? Do we not exaggerate ourselves to ourselves, or do we often recognize ourselves for the actual men we are? The lightening is an exaggeration of light. We live by exaggeration. Exaggerated history is poetry, and is truth referred to a new standard. To a small man every greater one is an exaggeration. No truth was ever expressed but with this sort of emphasis, so that for the time there was no other truth. The value of what is really valuable can

never be exaggerated. You must speak loud to those who are hard of hearing; so you acquire a habit of speaking loud to those who are not." Thoreau, *Journals of Henry D. Thoreau*, 121.

54. Joseph J. Moldenhauer, "The Extra-Vagant Maneuver: Paradox in *Walden*," in *Critical Essays on Henry David Thoreau's Walden*, ed. Joel Myerson (Boston: G. K. Hall and Company, 1988), 98.

55. Henry David Thoreau, *The Correspondence of Henry David Thoreau*, ed. Carl Bode and Walter Harding (Westport, CT: Greenwood Press, 1974), 478.

56. Interestingly, though, in his *Journal*, Thoreau transcribes a conversation he had with a traveler who was searching for his lost dog. This passage, with additions and changes, morphs into the famous horse, hound, and turtledove passage from *Walden*: "'Have you seen my hound, sir? I want to know—what! A lawyer's office? Law books?— if you've seen anything of a hound around here. Why what do you do here?' 'I live here. No, I haven't' 'Haven't you heard one in the woods anywhere?' 'oh, yes, I heard one this evening.' 'What do you do here?' 'But he was some way off.' 'Which side did he seem to be?' 'Well, I should think he was on the other side of the pond.' 'This is a large dog; makes a large track. He's been out hunting from Lexington for a week. How long have you lived here?' 'Oh, about a year.'" The traveler is shocked the discover a man living with books in the woods. But the main point is that he had lost a hound. Thoreau, having experienced his own unique form of loss, which remains unexplained, draws from this conversation with the traveler in writing his passage in *Walden*. Thoreau, *Journals of Henry D. Thoreau*, 118.

57. Ibid., 21.

58. For example, Nancy Rosenblum sees Thoreau's style as part of his aggressive militancy and understands Thoreau's use of paradox as something intended to "shock and insult" as "an attack on common understanding and as a way of withholding consent from shared meaning, paradox is the literary expression of Thoreau's militancy. It proceeds by inversion and disorientation, undermining argument, persuasion, and common sense. The same aggression is apparent in Thoreau's technique of 'ontological assassination.' . . . Accepted notions are not just wrong, they *are not*" (*Another Liberalism*, 113). These linguistic markers of Thoreau's militancy are figured as potentially dangerous to traditional notions of democratic politics.

59. As Walter Benn Michaels recounts, Emerson thought Thoreau's form was rooted in his "old fault of unlimited contradiction. The trick of his rhetoric is soon learned: it consists in substituting for the obvious right word and thought its diametrical antagonist. . . . It makes me nervous and wretched to read it." Walter Benn Michaels, "*Walden*'s False Bottoms," in Myerson, *Critical Essays on Henry David Thoreau's Walden*, 132. Three years after Thoreau's death, James Russell Lowell wrote disparagingly of Thoreau's style as a reflection of his flawed personality. Perhaps most famously, Vincent Buranelli used Thoreau's style to make a case for his mental instability ("The Case against Thoreau").

Chapter 1. Damaged Life, the Microscopic Gaze, and Adorno's Practice of Negative Dialectics

1. The epigraph source is J. M. Bernstein, "Negative Dialectics as Fate," in *Cambridge Companion to Adorno,* ed. Tom Huhn (New York: Cambridge University Press, 2004), 38.

2. Theodor Adorno, *Negative Dialectics,* trans. E. B. Ashton (New York: Continuum, 1973), 27.

3. The word translated as "fundamentally akin" is *urverwandt* in the original German. Adorno wants to say that the exchange or barter principle (*Tauschprinzip*) is originally and foundationally related to the principle of identification: it is an *ur*-relationship. Theodor Adorno, *Negative Dialektik* (Darmstadt: Wissenschaftliche Buchgesellschaft, 1998), 149.

4. Bernstein, "Negative Dialectics as Fate," 36.

5. Susan Buck-Morss, *The Origin of Negative Dialectics* (New York: Free Press, 1977), 63.

6. Seyla Benhabib, *Critique, Norm, and Utopia* (New York: Columbia University Press, 1986), 181.

7. Theodor Adorno, "On Subject and Object," in *Critical Models: Interventions and Catchwords* (New York: Columbia University Press, 1998), 256. Hereafter cited in text as "On Subject and Object."

8. Indeed, Adorno argues that there is a paradoxical kind of ideological function to this idealist positing of the transcendental subject: "The more individuals are in effect degraded into functions within the societal totality as they are connected up to a system, the more the person pure and simple, as a principle, is consoled and exalted with the attributes of creative power, absolute rule and spirit" ("On Subject and Object," 248). The notion of an idealist transcendental subject is itself a response to changing historical contexts and meets the needs of a new kind of systematized society. The less absolute individuals actually are, the more powerful the notion of a transcendental subject.

9. In fact, Adorno himself described Benjamin's way of seeing as a "microscopic gaze." Buck-Morss, *Origin of Negative Dialectics,* 74.

10. Ibid., 73.

11. "The particular was not 'a case of the general'; it could not be identified by placing it within a general category, for its significance lay in its contingency rather than its universality . . . each particular was unique, yet each contained a picture of the whole, an 'image of the world,' which within a Marxist frame meant an image of the bourgeois social structure." Ibid., 76.

12. Ibid.

13. Bernstein, "Negative Dialectics as Fate," 39.

14. Bourgeois promenading and strolling as described here by Adorno bear little resemblance to the disruptive, adventurous, unsettling form of walking that Thoreau espouses. Adorno would approve of Thoreau's description of walking. For Thoreau, when we walk, we confront the "wild"—that which cannot be contained or controlled: Thoreau's notion of the wild bears strong resemblances to Adorno's notion of the

Nonidentical. See chapter 4 in this book, "Huckleberrying Toward Democracy: Thoreau's Practices of Withdrawal."

15. Tom Huhn, "Thoughts Beside Themselves," in *Cambridge Companion to Adorno*, ed. Tom Huhn (New York: Cambridge University Press, 2004), 5.

16. This general decay of experience is a primary indicator of the modern crisis: "There is, in short, an implied loss of something that once existed and has been seriously damaged, if not entirely destroyed, in the present. Variously attributed to the traumas of world war, modern technologies of information, and the 'atemporal, technified process of the production of material goods,' which seems another way to say capitalist industrialization, the decay of something called experience is for Adorno an index of the general crisis of modern life." Martin Jay, "Is Experience Still in Crisis? Reflections on a Frankfurt School Lament," in *Cambridge Companion to Adorno*, ed. Tom Huhn (New York: Cambridge University Press, 2004), 131.

17. In the original German, the phrase translated as "has to pay dearly" is put much more strongly as "has to pay with a bitter sacrifice": "*hat fraglos mit bitterem Opfer an der qualitativen Mannigfaltigkeit der Erfahrung zu zahlen.*" Adorno, *Negative Dialektik*, 18.

18. The quote is from Ferdinand Kürnberger's *Der Amerika—Müde (Tired of America)*.

19. See my article "Damaged Life as Exuberant Health: Adorno, America, and the Sickness of Health," forthcoming in a special issue of *Telos* on the topic of "Adorno in America." I explore how Adorno's depiction of alienation as damaged life was influenced by and responds to the post–World War II psychoanalytic revolution in America.

20. The way to remedy the situation is not through a return to a previous, less damaged era. Change, if possible at all, is rooted in extending the possibilities that persist even within the landscape of damaged life. "Adorno understands the development of subjectivity as a dialectical, historical process. Therefore, what is required, according to him, is not a return to some earlier form of subjectivity but rather some forward movement from within what subjectivity has already become." Huhn, "Thoughts Beside Themselves," 4.

21. Stefan Müller-Doohm, *Adorno: A Biography*, trans. Rodney Livingstone (Cambridge, UK: Polity Press, 2005), 305.

22. The dictionary explanation for this idiomatic expression reads as follows: "*sich etwas hinter den Spiegel stecken* (fig.; *ursprünglich*) *zur täglichen Ansicht aufheben (allgemein) sich merken, einprägen (besonders Unangenehmes).*" Gerhard Wahrig, *Deutsches Wörterbuch* (Gütersloh/Munich: Bertelsman Lexikon Verlag, 2001), 1178.

23. Thanks to Samuel Frederick for pointing out this allusion to me and for his help with this section generally.

24. Müller-Doohm, *Adorno: A Biography*, 305–6.

25. Theodor Adorno, *Lectures on Kant's Critique of Pure Reason*, trans. Rodney Livingstone (Stanford, CA: Stanford University Press, 2001), 111. Hereafter cited in text as *Kant's Critique*.

26. "[H]uman beings have increasingly made the world in their own image, and the world has become increasingly theirs. At the same time, however, the world has

increasingly become a world that dominates them. It is a world in which they are hetero-geneous beings and with which they find it ever harder to cope" (*Kant's Critique,* 115).

27. Theodor Adorno and Max Horkheimer, *Dialectic of Enlightenment,* ed. Gunzelin Schmid Noerr, trans. Edmund Jephcott (Stanford, CA: Stanford University Press, 2002), 9.

28. Susan Buck-Morss states: "[E]ver since [Adorno's] first exposure to philosophy, when at age sixteen he read Kant together with Kracauer on Sunday afternoons, he had been struck by the significance of logical breaks. . . . The fractures, the ambiguities and contradictions, were the philosophical details upon which Adorno focused his interpre-tive efforts." These fractures were fissures through which an "unintentional truth" could shine out: "The bourgeois thinker expresses the truth in spite of himself; or, rather, like Freudian slips of the tongue, truth resurfaces in the inconsistencies of his theory, now more than ever, because of philosophy's 'disintegration.'" Buck-Morss, *Origin of Negative Dialectics,* 80.

29. Theodor Adorno, *Kierkegaard: Construction of the Aesthetic,* ed. and trans. Robert Hullot-Kentor (Minneapolis: University of Minnesota Press, 1989), 43. Hereafter cited in text as *Kierkegaard.*

30. Ultimately, Kierkegaard's thought was also "subjectivism without a subject," as Buck-Morss puts it: "For once objective reality was dismissed and left behind, in order to give life meaning Kierkegaard's individual ended up sacrificing itself, its own (first-nature) body as well as its critical consciousness, through a blind leap into a realm of mythic spirituality and submission to God." Buck-Morss, *Origin of Negative Dialectics,* 116.

31. Adorno's first published book was *Kierkegaard: Construction of the Aesthetic,* which had been his (second) *Habilitationsschrift.* As Robert Hullot-Kentor notes in his foreword, Adorno's book on Kierkegaard "appeared in bookstores on February 27, 1933, the day that Hitler declared a national emergency and suspended the freedom of the press, making the transition from chancellor to dictator" (*Kierkegaard,* xi).

32. Emerson famously says in his essay *Nature,* "Every spirit builds itself a house, and beyond its house a world, and beyond its world a heaven. . . . Build therefore your own world. As fast as you conform your life to the pure idea in your mind, that will un-fold its greatest proportions. A correspondent revolution in things will attend the influx of the spirit. So fast will disagreeable appearances, swine, spiders, snakes, pests, mad-houses, prisons, enemies, vanish; they are temporary and shall be no more seen." Ralph Waldo Emerson, *Nature, Addresses, and Lectures,* ed. Alfred R. Ferguson, vol. 1, *The Collected Works of Ralph Waldo Emerson* (Cambridge, MA: Belknap Press of Harvard University Press, 1971), 44–45.

33. Espen Hammer shows how Adorno was more engaged in the major political is-sues of his day than is sometimes thought and his analysis valuably corrects the (hope-fully now less dominant) view of Adorno as apathetic, apolitical, or elitist. Hammer ex-plores Adorno's understanding of theory as itself a form of praxis and concludes that Adorno's "vision of politics" is ultimately about an "ethics of resistance" that works against the logic of identity (179). Hammer also describes theory and art as the necessary

"placeholders" for politics, which Adorno thinks is no longer possible in the conventional sense (25). Espen Hammer, *Adorno and the Political* (New York: Routledge, 2005).

34. Müller-Doohm, *Adorno: A Biography*, 385.

35. This discussion is included in the most recent English translation of the essay, in Theodor Adorno, "Appendix 1: Discussion of Professor Adorno's Lecture 'The Meaning of Working Through the Past,'" in *Critical Models: Interventions and Catchwords* (New York: Columbia, 1998). Hereafter cited in text as "Discussion to Lecture."

36. Theodor Adorno, "The Meaning of Working Through the Past," in *Critical Models: Interventions and Catchwords* (New York: Columbia University Press, 1998). Hereafter cited in text as "Working Through the Past."

37. Thoreau uses the same imagery of clogging the machinery of government in "Resistance to Civil Government." He says "Let your life be a counter-friction to stop the machine" ("Resistance," 73).

38. Theodor Adorno, "Critique," in *Critical Models: Interventions and Catchwords* (New York: Columbia University Press, 1998), 281.

Chapter 2. Alienated Existence, Focal Distancing, and Emerson's Transcendental Idealism

1. Walter Harding, "Thoreau's Reputation," in *The Cambridge Companion to Henry David Thoreau*, ed. Joel Myerson (New York: Cambridge University Press, 1995), 1; James Russell Lowell, *A Fable for Critics* (Boston: Houghton Mifflin and Co., 1890), 46. This long poem, which reviewed many of Lowell's contemporary writers, refers to Thoreau but does not name him explicitly. As Walter Harding notes, "One of the earliest published evaluations of Thoreau's writing, James Russell Lowell's *A Fable for Critics* (1848), dismissed him as one who has 'stolen all his apples from Emerson's orchard' and urged him to strike out on his own. This was a charge that would haunt Thoreau's literary career, not only throughout his lifetime but well into the twentieth century, even though it would be difficult to think of an author more ruggedly independent, or one who prided himself on his distinct individualism more that Henry Thoreau." Harding, "Thoreau's Reputation," 1. The very idea that Thoreau stole his apples from Emerson's orchard is especially ironic, given that Thoreau wrote an essay on "Wild Apples." See chapter 4 in this book. See also Joel Porte, *Emerson and Thoreau: Transcendentalists in Conflict* (Middletown, CT: Wesleyan University Press, 1966), 4. Porte reexamines and calls into question this reading of the relationship between Thoreau and Emerson. But Porte ultimately agrees with Emerson's critique of Thoreau, making the familiar argument that Thoreau retreats away from politics to pursue aesthetic experiences alone in nature. See also Mark Van Doren, *Henry David Thoreau: A Critical Study* (Boston: Houghton Mifflin and Co., 1916).

2. Ralph Waldo Emerson, "Self-Reliance," in *Essays: First Series*, vol. 2, ed. Joseph Slater, *The Collected Works of Ralph Waldo Emerson* (Cambridge, MA: Belknap Press of Harvard University Press, 1979), 27. Hereafter cited in text as "Self-Reliance."

3. For more considerations of Emerson's place within democratic thought, see George Kateb, *The Inner Ocean: Individualism and Democratic Culture* (Ithaca, NY: Cornell University Press, 1992). See Judith N. Shklar, "Emerson and the Inhibitions of Democracy," *Political Theory* 18, no. 4 (1990). See also Hans Von Rautenfeld, "Thinking for Thousands: Emerson's Theory of Political Representation in the Public Sphere," *American Journal of Political Science* 49, no. 1 (2005), and Jack Turner, "Emerson, Slavery, and the Ethics of Citizenship," *Raritan: A Quarterly Review* 28, no. 2 (2008).

4. Stanley Cavell, *Conditions Handsome and Unhandsome: The Constitution of Emersonian Perfectionism* (Chicago: University of Chicago Press, 1990), 11, 8.

5. Although George Kateb, for example, does refer to Thoreau, Emerson, and Whitman as "The Emersonians" in his writings in ways that seem to collapse some important differences, other recent political theorists such as Jane Bennett and Bob Pepperman Taylor have been sensitive to differences of tone and substance in Thoreau and Emerson's writings. Jane Bennett sees Thoreau as more embodied, more corporeal than Emerson, who dwells in the realm of the mind: "Thoreau, whose sensibility is so embodied, so sensory, so alien to the notion of 'the mind itself' could not be this kind of Transcendentalism. The kind that he is is better approached by focusing not on the object of transcendence (intuitions of the mind itself) but on the *motion* of transcending. To trans-send, to soar, to cross the line, to get high, to go beyond, to fly away. . . . Thoreau's 'transcendentalism' is not about 'imperative forms' but about lines of flight, not about static perfections but about ever-changing, over-reaching aspirations." Jane Bennett, *Thoreau's Nature: Ethics, Politics and the Wild* (Thousand Oaks, CA: Sage, 1994), 109. Bob Pepperman Taylor focuses on how Thoreau locates himself in a specific historical context, whereas Emerson says we are above history, above context, and can create our own reality: "The freedom Emerson seeks is a freedom beyond history because in his view history gives us only thoughtless prejudices and habit, both enemies of an authentic independence. . . . It is tempting to think that Thoreau shares this understanding of freedom with Emerson. . . . There are good reasons to believe, however, that Thoreau's views are significantly different than Emerson's on these matters. . . . Once we are in a position to appreciate the degree to which Thoreau, unlike Emerson, accepts the necessity of locating our choices and freedoms within social contexts and historical time, we have taken the first step toward a reevaluation of the quality and significance of Thoreau's political thought as a whole." Bob Pepperman Taylor, *America's Bachelor Uncle: Thoreau in the American Polity* (Lawrence: University of Kansas Press, 1996), 17.

6. Emerson, *Nature* in *Nature, Addresses, Lectures,* vol. 1, ed. Alfred R. Ferguson, *The Collected Works of Ralph Waldo Emerson* (Cambridge, MA: Belknap Press of Harvard University Press, 1971), 45. Hereafter cited in text as *Nature.* In-text references to Emerson's essay of the same name, from his volume *Essays: Second Series,* will be cited as "Nature."

7. Robert D. Richardson, *Emerson: The Mind on Fire* (Berkeley: University of California Press, 1995), 104, 146.

8. The group of scholars and interested parties, which became known as the Transcendental Club, was first called the Hedge Club because it met at Frederic Hedge's home.

9. Later in his life, Emerson was reabsorbed into German idealism via Hegel. Richardson notes that Emerson found his own ideas reflected in Hegel's notion of the mind as the path to freedom: "The integrative energy of Hegelian thought, its assimilative power, and its fierce drive to grasp the *processes* of history and mind were deeply congenial to Emerson." Richardson, *Emerson: The Mind on Fire,* 472.

10. Ibid., 233. Emerson's Kant is very idiosyncratic and often his version of Transcendental Idealism bears little resemblance to Kant's. In one important respect in particular, something was lost in translation as Kant's ideas passed from Coleridge and Carlyle to Hedge to Emerson. Unlike Kant, Emerson seems to think that we can access Truth, that we can have knowledge of the thing-itself. He implies that Being itself is Spirit or Mind. Lawrence Buell notes in *Emerson* that this sublime experience of reality itself seems more possible for Emerson than for Kant: "Never mind for now that this was a wishful reading of Coleridge's version of the Reason-Understanding distinction, itself a wishful reading of Kant's German successors' wishful reading of Kant. . . . That Kant denies Reason can know the thing in itself, whereas Emerson granted Reason that knowledge invoking Kantian authority, is one of the ironies of intellectual history." Lawrence Buell, *Emerson* (Cambridge, MA: Belknap Press of Harvard University Press, 2003), 61. The later Emerson somewhat qualifies the optimism of the earlier Emerson. In "Experience," Emerson wonders whether we can truly know reality except at the moment of our death. A second difference from Kant concerns Emerson's unique emphasis on the passive over the active, the abandonment of the self, letting-go to the universal.

11. Emerson, "The Transcendentalist," in *Nature: Addresses/Lectures,* vol. 1, ed. Alfred R. Ferguson, *Collected Works of Ralph Waldo Emerson,* 206. Hereafter cited in text as "The Transcendentalist."

12. Emerson, "The Over-Soul," in *Essays: First Series,* ed. Joseph Slater, *Collected Works of Ralph Waldo Emerson* (Cambridge, MA: Belknap Press of Harvard University Press, 1979), 161. Hereafter cited in text as "The Over-Soul."

13. Ralph Waldo Emerson, "The Poet," in *Essays: Second Series,* vol. 3, ed. Joseph Slater, *The Collected Works of Ralph Waldo Emerson* (Cambridge, MA: Belknap Press of Harvard University Press, 1983). Hereafter cited in text as "The Poet."

14. Emerson, "Experience," in *Essays: Second Series,* ed. Joseph Slater, *Collected Works of Ralph Waldo Emerson,* 27. Hereafter cited in text as "Experience."

15. In his challenging and elegant text *Conditions Handsome and Unhandsome: The Constitution of Emersonian Perfectionism,* Stanley Cavell undertakes an interesting reading of this passage.

16. Emerson's first wife, Ellen Louise Tucker, died of tuberculosis only seventeen months after they were married in 1829. Emerson loved Ellen deeply and was haunted by her death. In his journal, he writes that he visited her tomb after she died and opened

the coffin, something that he also reports having done when his young son Waldo died. Richardson, *Emerson: The Mind on Fire*, 121.

17. Emerson, "Nature," in *Essays: Second Series*, ed. Joseph Slater, *Collected Works of Ralph Waldo Emerson*, 112. Hereafter cited in text as "Nature."

18. Emerson's idea of "focal distance" might draw upon the technology of photography. The focal distance (focal length) is the distance from a lens, in the eye or in a camera, for example, to the focal point. But the eye also has lens that focus, so Emerson's concept of focal distance seems at once both a technological and a naturalistic image, reflecting the harmony Emerson often describes between technological processes of modernization and naturalistic images of man's coming to maturity.

19. Emerson, "History," in *Essays: First Series*, vol. 2, ed. Joseph Slater, *Collected Works of Ralph Waldo Emerson*, 9. Hereafter cited in text as "History."

20. Emerson, "Self-Reliance," 28.

21. Emerson, "Heroism," in *Essays: First Series*, vol. 2, ed. Joseph Slater, *Collected Works of Ralph Waldo Emerson*, 148. Hereafter cited in text as "Heroism."

22. "The other terror that scares us from self-trust is our consistency; a reverence for our past act or word, because the eyes of others have no other data for computing our orbit than our past acts, and we are loath to disappoint them. . . . A foolish consistency is the hobgoblin of little minds, adored by little statesmen and philosophers and divines. With consistency a great soul has simply nothing to do. He may as well concern himself with his shadow on the wall" ("Self-Reliance," 33).

23. Nietzsche was a great admirer of Emerson and there are important sympathies between Nietzsche's notion of the will to power as a continual self-overcoming and Emerson's notion of Self-Reliance, as well as their thoughts on creativity and the artist. For further discussions of Emerson and Nietzsche connections, see Stanley Cavell's essays "Aversive Thinking: Emersonian Representations in Heidegger and Nietzsche" and "Old and New in Nietzsche and Emerson" in Stanley Cavell, *Emerson's Transcendental Etudes*, ed. David Justin Hodge (Stanford, CA: Stanford University Press, 2003). See also Lawrence Buell's discussion of echoes of Emerson in Nietzsche's writings in Buell, *Emerson*, esp. 218–27.

24. In his excellent essay "Political Theory for Losers," Thomas L. Dumm also draws upon "Experience" to explore how loss might be theorized. See Thomas L. Dumm, "Political Theory for Losers," in *Vocations of Political Theory*, ed. Jason Frank and John Tambornino (Minneapolis: University of Minnesota Press, 2000). See a revised version of this essay, and a more general treatment of these themes of grief and loss, in Dumm's book, *Loneliness as a Way of Life* (Cambridge, MA: Harvard University Press, 2008).

25. In "On the Passing of the First-Born Son: Emerson's 'Focal Distancing' and Du Bois's 'Second Sight,' and Disruptive Particularity," *Political Theory* 37, no. 3 (2009) I compare Emerson's essay "Experience" with W. E. B. Du Bois's strikingly similar essay "On the Passing of the First Born" in *The Souls of Black Folk*, exploring Du Bois's "subversion" and "revision" of Emerson through an analysis of the visual metaphors they

each employ and enact. By contrasting Emerson's practice of "focal distancing" with Du Bois's enactment of "second sight" and seeing through the "Veil," a tragic coincidence offers a unique field to compare their different ways of seeing: both of their first-born sons died at very young ages, an event that each explored in essay form. Both writers, literally, seem to be *looking* for answers, and both struggle over how keep the proper perspective between disruptive particular things, such as the death of a son, and more harmonious visions of a universal realm where we might dwell as sovereign souls. In "Experience," Emerson questions his prior practice of "focal distancing" and seems to recognize how it makes it difficult for him to stare directly at the disruptive particular loss of his son and grieve. His faith in the practice of "focal distancing" is ultimately restored, though on more tentative, cautious, chastened grounds.

26. Interestingly, Thoreau too idealizes "the West," but for entirely different reasons. The West for Thoreau is a metaphor figured in opposition to the industrial, domesticating, modernizing features of the East. The West is a frontier, for Thoreau, but it is imagined in opposition to specifically modern historical conditions, not as an eternal escape from more existential conditions of loss and estrangement.

27. Stanley Cavell, "Finding as Founding: Taking Steps in Emerson's 'Experience,'" in *Emerson's Transcendental Etudes,* edited by David Justin Hodge (Stanford, CA: Stanford University Press, 2003), 117.

28. Cavell, *Conditions Handsome and Unhandsome,* 39.

29. This is a very different attitude from the tones Thoreau will take on when he discusses the railroad or the post office.

30. Cavell, *Conditions Handsome and Unhandsome,* 47.

31. Ibid., xxi, 16.

32. Cavell, "Finding as Founding," 139.

33. Emerson, "Circles," in *Essays: First Series,* ed. Joseph Slater, *Collected Works of Ralph Waldo Emerson.* Hereafter cited in text as "Circles."

34. Cavell's readings of Emerson draw most heavily from "Circles" and "Experience" in ways that portray the continually upsetting Emerson as the "real," most philosophical Emerson.

35. Cavell sees the fact that Emerson vacillates between a sense of groundlessness and a desire to create foundation as a way of testifying to, giving evidence of, enacting, the skeptical encounter with reality, as responding (like J. L. Austin and Wittgenstein) "to the anxiety about our human capacities as knowers." For Cavell, "skepticism is a place, perhaps the central secular place, in which the human wish to deny the unsettled condition of human existence is expressed, and so long as the denial is essential to what we think of as the human, skepticism cannot, or must not, be denied. This makes skepticism an argument internal to the individual, or separate, human creature as it were an argument of the self with itself (over its finitude.) That this is expressed as a kind of argument of language with itself (over its essence) is how it came to look to me . . . as a response to what I have come to call the truth of skepticism (as if the problem of skepticism is expressed by its threat or temptation, by our sense of groundlessness." Emerson

is trying to recover a ground, trying to recover an intimacy with nature, and he expresses this desire for a return through his use of language. Circling is the nature of existence, and we must make the best of it, though. Emerson struggles with groundlessness and circling. We cannot know reality; we want to, but for Cavell, we can only "acknowledge" existence, cannot *know* it. Stanley Cavell, "The Philosopher in American Life: Toward Emerson and Thoreau," in *Emerson's Transcendental Etudes*, edited by David Justin Hodge. (Stanford, CA: Stanford University Press, 2003), 34–35.

36. Thanks to Jason Frank for pointing out the historical context of Emerson's thoughts on traveling.

37. Emerson, "Compensation," in *Essays: First Series*, ed. Joseph Slater, *Collected Works of Ralph Waldo Emerson*. Hereafter cited in text as "Compensation."

38. For further treatment of the theme of disruptive particularity in Emerson, see my essay "On the Passing of the First-Born Son."

39. Henry David Thoreau, *The Journal of Henry D. Thoreau*, ed. Bradford Torrey and Francis Allen, vols. 1–7 (New York: Dover, 1962), 41.

40. For example, in the conclusion to *Walden*, Thoreau calls our "dullest perception" "common sense" and says "the commonest sense is the sense of men asleep, which they express by snoring" (325). Alternately, he says "to be awake is to be alive" (90).

Chapter 3. Man as Machine

1. Ralph Waldo Emerson, "Experience," in *Essays: Second Series*, ed. Joseph Slater, *The Collected Works of Ralph Waldo Emerson* (Cambridge, MA: Belknap Press of Harvard University Press, 1983), 29.

2. Mary Hosmer Brown spent a great deal of time with Thoreau on childhood visits to her grandfather's farm in Concord. As an adult, she returned to Concord and collected many anecdotes about the town's inhabitants, compiled in her *Memories of Concord*. Mary Hosmer Brown, *Memories of Concord* (Boston: Four Seas Company, 1926), 88–89, also esp. chap. 8.

3. Thoreau to friend and admirer Daniel Ricketson, September 27, 1855. Henry David Thoreau, *Familiar Letters*, ed. F. B. Sanborn, vol. 6, *The Writings of Henry David Thoreau* (Boston: Houghton Mifflin and Co., 1906), 262.

4. For example, Thoreau expresses concern about various ways that nature was instrumentalized in the Concord of his era: farmers set fire to the shrubs and bushes in fields to prepare them for cultivation, drained swamps to prepare fertile farmland, and cut down trees for timber on a massive scale.

5. Perhaps every generation sees its own experience of modernity as the most intense. Indeed, Rousseau was raging against an increasingly inauthentic form of modernity in the eighteenth century. But in Thoreau's case, his lifespan almost exactly corresponds to the period historians have identified as an extremely rapid period of modernization and industrialization in the United States, especially in New England.

6. Richard D. Brown and Jack Tager, *Massachusetts: A Concise History* (Amherst: University of Massachusetts Press, 2000), 116–17.

7. These numbers are from the town census, recorded in Edmund Jarvis, *Traditions and Reminiscences of Concord, Massachusetts 1779–1878*, ed. Sarah Chapin (Amherst: University of Massachusetts Press, 1993), 200.

8. Brown and Tager, *Massachusetts: A Concise History*, 115–16, 119.

9. Ibid., 125, 165.

10. Ibid., 164.

11. In researching Concord's social history and in accessing these newspapers during the summer of 2005, I was greatly helped by and would like to thank Leslie Perrin Wilson, the curator of the William Munroe Special Collection at the Concord Free Public Library.

12. This is the railroad line that ran by Thoreau's cabin, paralleling the banks on one side of Walden Pond; he wrote at length about the whistle of the railroad. When I visited the site of Thoreau's cabin at Walden Pond in the summer of 2005, a train happened to go by on the still-active railroad line. The rumbling and whistle were easily heard as I stood on the site of Thoreau's cabin, and the railroad could be seen if you walked a little ways beyond the cabin site.

13. For another interesting social history, see Leslie Perrin Wilson, "A Concord Farmer Looks Back: The Reminiscences of William Henry Hunt," *Concord Saunterer* 10 (2002). See also James Kimenker, "The Concord Farmer: An Economic History, 1750–1850," in *Concord: The Social History of a New England Town, 1750–1850*, ed. David Hackett Fischer (Waltham, MA: Brandeis University Press, 1984). For other texts that give a sense of what Concord was like during Thoreau's time, see Paul Brooks, *The People of Concord: One Year in the Flowering of New England* (Guilford, CT: Globe Pequot Press, 1990), Allen French and Lester Hornby, *Old Concord* (Boston: Little, Brown and Co., 1915).

14. Jarvis began his book as a supplement to Lemuel Shattuck's classic book *A history of the town of Concord, Middlesex County, Massachusetts: from its earliest settlement to 1832 : and of the adjoining towns, Bedford, Acton, Lincoln, and Carlisle, containing various notices of county and state history* (Boston : Russell, Odiorne, and Co. 1835). But Jarvis found that he had too many corrections and supplementary information about Concord and ended up binding his work together in a separate volume, which was then given to the Concord Free Public Library and eventually published by University of Massachusetts Press at Amherst.

15. See Richard N. Weintraub, "Stratification and Mobility in Concord: A Sociological History, 1750–1850," in Fischer, *Concord: The Social History*. See also Marc Harris, "The People of Concord: A Demographic History, 1750–1850," in Fischer, *Concord: The Social History*.

16. Jarvis, *Traditions and Reminiscences*, 34.

17. Ibid., 37, 38, 40.

18. Ibid., xxxiv.

19. Ibid., xxxv.

20. Ibid., 4.

21. Ibid., 56.

22. Henry David Thoreau, *Walden*, ed. J. Lyndon Shanley, *The Writings of Henry David Thoreau* (Princeton, NJ: Princeton University Press, 2004), 9. Hereafter cited in text as *Walden*.

23. Henry David Thoreau, "Life without Principle," in *The Higher Law: Thoreau on Civil Disobedience and Reform*, ed. Wendell Glick (Princeton, NJ: Princeton University Press, 2004), 160. Hereafter cited in text as "Life."

24. Here, Thoreau sounds like Sigmund Freud, where he describes how civilization sets up an agency within the individual, to watch over this enemy territory, "like a garrison in a conquered city." Sigmund Freud, *Civilization and Its Discontents* (New York: W. W. Norton, 1961, 1989), 84.

25. Emerson began writing his famous essay *Nature* in this house, which was also later inhabited by Nathaniel Hawthorne and his wife, Sophia. Hawthorne's book of short stories, *Mosses from an Old Manse*, gets its title from this house. If you tour the Old Manse, you can still see the bridge easily from this window of the study upstairs. In fact, as the pamphlet notes, it would have been much easier to see the bridge in those days because there were far fewer trees in Concord then than there are now.

26. Hannah Arendt, *The Human Condition* (Chicago: University of Chicago Press, 1958).

27. Hannah Arendt, *On Revolution* (New York: Penguin, 1963, 1965). See especially chapter 6, "The Revolutionary Tradition and Its Lost Treasure."

28. This passage is directly taken from Matthew, 6:19–20: "Do not store up for yourselves treasures on earth. Where moth and rust consume and where thieves break in and steal; but store up for yourselves treasures in heaven, where neither moth not rust consumes and where thieves do not break in and steal. For where your treasure is, there your heart will be also." *New Oxford Annotated Bible*, ed. Michael D. Coogan, 3rd ed. (New York: Oxford University Press, 2007).

29. Henry David Thoreau, "Wild Apples," in *Collected Essays and Poems*, ed. Elizabeth Hall Witherell (New York: Library of America, 2001). Hereafter cited in text as "Wild Apples."

30. Michael T. Gilmore, *American Romanticism and the Marketplace* (Chicago: Chicago University Press, 1985), 38–39.

31. Ibid., 39.

32. The "failures of "Civil Disobedience" and *A Week* strengthen his anti-market resolution, but at the same time force him to retreat from his ambition to reform the polity. Since he cannot shape public opinion without large sales, he effectively abandons his civic project by striving to make *Walden* a difficult text at which the reader has to labor — hence a text which is inaccessible to the great majority of the public." Ibid., 50.

33. Ibid., 35.

34. Ibid., 36, 44–45.

35. In her book *Thoreau's Nature,* Jane Bennett calls the conventional and complacent social self that Thoreau tries to displace "the They," in an allusion to Heidegger: "Only in a setting that surprises and is in some way unfamiliar can Thoreau live deliberately. . . . Extraordinary measures must be taken to disrupt the state of dependence on others, to jar oneself away from the They. . . . The task will be to locate and then regularly expose oneself to Wild sites and sights, to maximize opportunities for shock and disorientation" (3). Unlike my reading, Bennett does not tie this conventional "default mode" of subjectivity to Thoreau's unique experience of nascent modernity. Furthermore, she sees Thoreau's practices as aimed toward "disrupting" the default mode of subjectivity, but not as a way of *regaining* the critical capacities that I see as central to Thoreau's notion of selfhood. For Bennett, "For the sake of the noble self (the I), steps must be taken to disrupt the familiar self (the They)" (5). Bennett continues, "My Thoreau is a sculptor" (xxiv). She claims to offer "a kind of art criticism" of Thoreau's "art of the self" or "technologies of the self" (xxiv). She reads Thoreau as attempting to escape powers of normalization by *creating* an alternate self from the ground up: "These exercises are to be practiced daily until they become second nature" (17). Bennett understands Thoreau's work as centrally about "self-fashioning" and "self-creation" (xxiv). But her notion of subjectivity does not seem to allow for a discourse of alienation where loss figures prominently and where excursions in nature aim at recuperating critical capacities lost at the hands of modernity. Jane Bennett, *Thoreau's Nature: Ethics, Politics, and the Wild* (Thousand Oaks, CA: Sage, 1994).

36. Richard D. Brown, *Modernization: The Transformation of American Life 1600–1865* (New York: Farrar, Straus and Giroux, 1976), 128.

37. Brown and Tager, *Massachusetts: A Concise History,* 125, 124.

38. In his biography of Emerson, Robert Richardson lends further credence to the suspicion that the "friend" Thoreau names was Emerson. As Richardson notes, the two neighbors grew apart as Emerson became more famous and spent more time abroad (while Thoreau stayed at Emerson's house and helped out the family in Emerson's absence): "Emerson's return from England also marked the beginning of a serious rift between him and Henry Thoreau. . . . Thoreau was skeptical about English success, materialism, steam, speed, talk, and books, and he was contemptuous of Emerson's apparent relish of it all" (461). At the same time, Emerson became critical of Thoreau for his *lack* of worldliness: "It is a misfortune of Thoreau's that he has no appetite . . . he neither eats nor drinks. What can you have in common with a man who does not know the difference between ice cream and cabbage and who has no experience of wine or ale?" (463). This must all be taken in context, though, as Richardson rightly notes: despite their "terrifyingly high" expectations and despite some difficulties, "Emerson at the end of his life still thought of Thoreau as having been his best friend" (464). Robert D. Richardson, *Emerson: The Mind on Fire* (Berkeley: University of California Press, 1995).

39. Henry David Thoreau, *The Journal of Henry D. Thoreau,* ed. Bradford Torrey and Francis Allen, vols. 1–7 (New York: Dover, 1962), 290 (italics mine).

40. "To manage the small talk of a party is to make an effort to do what was at first done admirably, because naturally, at your fireside." Ibid., 25.

41. Walter Harding, *The Days of Henry Thoreau: A Biography* (Princeton, NJ: Princeton University Press 1962), 315.

42. Ibid., 315, 314–19. See Harding's discussion for more instances of Thoreau's involvement with the Underground railroad.

43. Emerson was also stimulated into greater abolitionist action when slavery came home to Massachusetts in the form of this law. For a deeper exploration of Emerson and the Fugitive Slave Law, see Jack Turner, "Emerson, Slavery, and the Ethics of Citizenship," *Raritan: A Quarterly Review*, 28 no. 2 (2008).

44. Harding, *The Days of Henry Thoreau*, 317.

45. For further exploration of the modern condition of loneliness, see Thomas Dumm's *Loneliness as a Way of Life* (Cambridge, MA: Harvard University Press, 2008).

46. In the beginning, the factories were populated by American-born women who moved off of the farms. But by the mid-nineteenth century, factories were increasingly filled with immigrant workers. As one historian notes, "The names on the factory lists in Chicopee, Massachusetts, changed from Lucinda Pease and Wealthy Snow to Bridget Murphy and Patrick Moriarty. In Fall River in 1826 only twenty-six out of 612 operatives were foreign, but by 1846, the majority of the plant was Irish. . . . Looking at the mill weaving rooms in Lowell as a whole, in 1845 they were more than 95 percent Yankee; in 1855 they were more than 60 percent Irish. Moreover, as the ethnic composition of the workplace changed, so did its gender make-up. By 1860, roughly 30 percent of the workers in Lowell were male." Robert Heilbroner and Aaron Singer, *The Economic Transformation of America: 1600 to the Present,* 4th ed. (New York: Harcourt Brace and Company, 1999), 111–12.

47. Ibid., 110.

48. Joel Porte, "Emerson, Thoreau, and the Double Consciousness," *New England Quarterly* 41, no. 1 (1968), 42, 45.

49. He expands on this anecdote more in "Resistance to Civil Government," where he says he was asked to lead a huckleberry party that was in need of a captain. The political significance of the berry picking as well as Thoreau's explicit juxtaposition of the jail (an arm of the State) with the huckleberry fields represent this particular action as a political practice that offers an alternative to politics as commonly understood.

Chapter 4. Huckleberrying toward Democracy

1. Stanley Cavell, *The Senses of Walden* (San Francisco: North Point Press, 1981), 3, 110.

2. Ibid., 85–86.

3. Thanks to Jack Turner for pointing out this biblical allusion. Here, Thoreau references Luke 14:26, which reads "Whoever comes to me and does not hate father and mother, wife and children, brothers and sisters, yes, and even life itself, cannot be my

disciple." *New Oxford Annotated Bible,* ed. Michael D. Coogan, 3rd ed. (New York: Oxford University Press, 2007). Similarly, in "Self-Reliance," Emerson writes, "I shun father and mother, and wife and brother when my genius calls me."

4. As Thoreau says in *Walden,* "I fear chiefly lest my expression may not be *extra-vagant* enough, may not wander far enough beyond the narrow limits of my daily experience, so as to be adequate to the truth of which I have been convinced. *Extra vagance!* . . . I desire to speak somewhere without bounds; like a man in a waking moment, to men in their waking moments; for I am convinced that I cannot exaggerate enough even to lay the foundation of a true expression" (324).

5. Henry David Thoreau, "Thomas Carlyle and His Works," in *Collected Essays and Poems,* ed. Elizabeth Hall Witherell (New York: Library of America, 2001).

6. *New Shorter Oxford English Dictionary,* s.v. "moss-trooper": "A pillager or marauder of the Scottish Borders in the middle of the 17th cent.; any bandit or raider." (Oxford: Clarenden Press, 1993).

7. In his essay "Thoreau and Emerson," Robert Sattlemeyer gives another example of how Emerson failed to understand the significance of Thoreau's project and the symbolic importance of the notion of a swamp. As Sattlemeyer says, in his diary Emerson records his frustration over Thoreau's "account of living a hermit's life in the Maine wilderness 'with despair' and he wonders if the hermit 'has found it foolish & wasteful to spend a tenth or a twentieth of his active life with a muskrat & friend fishes." As if to emphasize their disagreement, Emerson writes on the next page a mock letter to Thoreau summarizing his exasperation: 'My dear Henry, A frog was made to live in a swamp, but a man was not made to live in a swamp. Yours ever, R." Robert Sattlemeyer, "Thoreau and Emerson," in *The Cambridge Companion to Henry David Thoreau,* ed. Joel Myerson (New York: Cambridge University Press, 1995), 35.

8. Here, Thoreau alludes to John the Baptist: "Now John wore clothing of camel's hair with a leather belt around his waist, and his food was locusts and honey" (Matt. 3:4, NOAB). John is described in these same terms in Mark: "Now John was clothed with camel's hair, with a leather belt around his waist, and he ate locusts and honey" (Mark 1:6, NOAB).

9. Today, when walking, one does not enjoy such freedom. Thoreau foresaw these limitations: "At present, in this vicinity, the best part of the land is not private property; the landscape is not owned, and the walker enjoys comparative freedom. But possibly the day will come when it will be partitioned off into so-called pleasure grounds, in which a few will take a narrow and exclusive pleasure only,—when fences shall be multiplied, and man-traps and other engines invented to confine men to the *public* road, and walking over the surface of God's earth shall be construed to mean trespassing on some gentleman's ground" ("Walking," 233).

10. For a different kind of exploration of how the ordinary man can reclaim a measure of autonomy thought walking in the city, see chapter 7 of Michel de Certeau's *The Practice of Everyday Life* (Berkeley: University of California Press, 1984, 2002).

11. For an interesting description of the experience of walking and the ways the mind works at "3 mph," see Rebecca Solnit's *Wanderlust: A History of Walking* (New York: Penguin, 2001).

12. For another comparison of Rousseau and Thoreau, see Melissa Lane's "Thoreau and Rousseau: Nature as Utopia," in *A Political Companion to Henry David Thoreau*, ed. Jack Turner (Lexington: University Press of Kentucky, 2009).

13. Jean-Jacques Rousseau, *Reveries of the Solitary Walker*, trans. Peter France (New York: Penguin Classics, 1979), 35.

14. Ibid., 95, 103, 101.

15. Ibid., 88–89.

16. Ibid., 90.

17. See my article "Thoreau, Adorno, and the Critical Potential of Particularity," in Turner, *Political Companion to Henry David Thoreau*.

18. As Robert Sattlemeyer says "each came to represent to the other a problem in American society, raising their quarrel to the level of cultural criticism. After Emerson's return from England and his increased involvement in social activities like the Town and Country Club, he came to represent to Thoreau the conventional man of the world who observed proprieties and etiquette rather than essentials." Sattlemeyer, "Thoreau and Emerson," 35.

19. As Robert Sattlemeyer and other scholars have noted, Emerson seemed to use his now famous eulogy to Thoreau as a chance to settle some scores with Thoreau and remind everyone that he thought Thoreau has wasted his life by not being more of a traditional social or political leader. "Emerson's eulogy seems particularly designed to present Thoreau's life as one of renunciation and withdrawal. . . . Emerson's account of Thoreau makes him a renouncer, an iconoclast . . . and a hermit and scetic." Ibid., 37.

20. Ralph Waldo Emerson, introduction to *Walden and Other Writings* (New York: Modern Library, 2000), xxviii.

21. Henry David Thoreau, "Huckleberries," in *Collected Essays and Poems*, ed. Elizabeth Witherell (New York: Library of America, 2001), 468. Hereafter cited in text as "Huckleberries."

22. In "The Bean-Field" chapter of *Walden*, Thoreau describes another instance where his ability to know the object could have been threatened by the profit motive and the logic of exchange. At Walden Pond, Thoreau had a bean field, but he makes it clear that his aim was not profit, but that he was "determined to know beans" (161). But Thoreau implies that if profit had been his motive, he should never have gotten to know either beans or himself. The experience of planting, hoeing, weeding, threshing, and picking over would not have been rich if he had had his eye only on the goods he could buy with his bean-money: "it was a singular experience that long acquaintance which I cultivated with beans" (161). Instead of just seeing the beans as a means to profit, Thoreau speaks of "knowing" them, of "cherishing" them, and of "cultivating" a relationship with the beans themselves. He did eventually sell the beans, though not for a profit, and taking them to market "was the hardest of all," because of his intimacy with them (161).

23. James L. Colwell, "Huckleberries and Humans: On the Naming of Huckleberry Finn," *PMLA* 86, no. 1 (1971), 74.

24. In his essay "Thoreau's Later Natural History Writings," Ronald Wesley Hoag also notes the democratic tendencies of Thoreau's "Huckleberries." However, Hoag focuses only on the democratic tone of the piece and the democratic imperative to preserve more natural spaces to be held in common, as public spaces. "Even Thoreau's tone in this essay is unusually democratic, as when he assures his reader's that "It is my own way of living that I complain of as well as yours" (30) or speaks companionably as "we dwellers in the huckleberry pastures" (26). Thoreau's friendliness is tactical, for in this essay the target of reform is entire communities rather than individuals." Hoag sees "Huckleberries" as a plea to preserve wild spaces in a democracy, but he doesn't explore why maintaining this space is valuable, for Thoreau. Hoag doesn't explore how, for Thoreau, the practice of huckleberrying itself as educating us toward being more critical and independent democratic citizens. He also doesn't describe the huckleberry fields themselves as a political space for the formation of a new type of citizen; in his reading, Thoreau is simply saying that a democracy need to maintain and preserve wild spaces, but these spaces themselves are not a new ground for politics but more of a space of retreat. Ronald Wesley Hoag, "Thoreau's Later Natural History Writings," in Myerson, *Cambridge Companion to Henry David Thoreau*, ed. Joel Myerson (New York: Cambridge University Press, 1995), 162.

25. For an earlier version of my argument regarding wild apples, with a focus on particularity, see my article "Thoreau, Adorno, and the Critical Potential of Particularity," in Turner, *Political Companion to Henry David Thoreau*.

26. Compare Thoreau's critique of imperialism here with Emerson's statement at Thoreau's funeral: "Pounding beans is good to the end of pounding empires one of these days; but if, at the end of years; it is still only beans!" This is the kind of statement that highlight's Thoreau's far more wary and tempering attitude toward self-assertion. More than Emerson, Thoreau seems to appreciate the connections between the projection of the self outward onto the world and taming, domestication, even imperialism. Emerson, introduction to *Walden*, xxviii.

27. Jane Bennett, *Thoreau's Nature: Ethics, Politics, and the Wild* (Thousand Oaks, CA: Sage, 1994), xxi, 35.

28. Henry David Thoreau, *The Maine Woods*, ed. Joseph J. Moldenhauer, *The Writings of Henry D. Thoreau* (Princeton, NJ: Princeton University Press, 2004), 69. Hereafter cited in text as *Maine Woods*.

29. For a fascinating look at the transformations New England's landscapes, see William Cronon's classic *Changes in the Land: Indians, Colonists and the Ecology of New England*. Cronon writes a history of transformations that fields, forests, plant, and animal communities underwent as Native American populations declined and European populations increased. Cronon describes a dialectical relationship between the people and the land, where differing views between the Indians and the colonists concerning nature, ownership, value, trade, and even time had dramatic consequences for the New

England ecology. William Cronon, *Changes in the Land: Indians, Colonists and the Ecology of New England* (New York: Hill and Wang, 1983, 2003).

30. Brian Donahue, "The Forests and Fields of Concord: An Ecological History, 1750–1850," in *Concord: The Social History of a New England Town 1750–1850*, ed. David Hackett Fischer (Waltham, MA: Brandeis University Press, 1984), 30, 52, 32, 57, 60.

31. Ibid., 57, 53.

32. Henry David Thoreau, "Paradise (to Be) Regained," in *The Higher Law: Thoreau on Civil Disobedience and Reform*, ed. Wendell Glick (Princeton, NJ: Princeton University Press, 2004), 115. Hereafter cited in text as "Paradise."

Chapter 5. Traveling Away from Home

1. For an excellent discussion of this poem and the concept of home, see John Hollander, "It All Depends," *Social Research* 58, no. 1 (1991).

2. Robert Frost, *The Poetry of Robert Frost: The Collected Poems, Complete and Unabridged*, ed. Edward Connery Latham (New York: Henry Holt and Co., 1969).

3. The epigraph is from Henry David Thoreau, "Wild Apples," in *Collected Essays and Poems*, ed. Elizabeth Hall Witherell (New York: Library of America, 2001), 461.

4. Bonnie Honig, "Difference, Dilemmas, and the Politics of Home," in *Democracy and Difference: Contesting the Boundaries of the Political*, ed. Seyla Benhabib (Princeton, NJ: Princeton University Press, 1996), 260. In a related study, Honig's *Democracy and the Foreigner* considers the valuable work the image of the "Foreigner" plays in contemporary democracy. The symbolic presence of the Foreigner (alienated, distanced from home) works to highlight the unnaturalness of democratic law and illuminate anxieties about popular sovereignty, but foreignness can also be invoked to soothe these anxieties: "What can that foreigner, the iconic foreign-founder, teach us about the insufficiencies, challenges, dramas, and dreams of democracy?" (14). Bonnie Honig, *Democracy and the Foreigner* (Princeton, NJ: Princeton University Press, 2001).

5. Honig, "Difference, Dilemmas, and the Politics of Home," 258, 270.

6. Thomas Dumm, "Joyce Brown, or Democracy and Homelessness," in *united states* (Ithaca, NY: Cornell University Press, 1994), 155, 177.

7. Thoreau's desire to "travel," to seek displacement, and avoid feeling "at home" carries elements of what George Kateb calls "moderate alienation." I have used alienation differently, to indicate a loss of critical capacities, an unthinking conformity. This is not a valuable state for any of us: our ideas are sympathetic but not our terminology. Like my notion of displacement, Kateb's idea of moderate alienation is helpful because it also works against a sense of being "at home," an unthinking conformity. For Kateb, "alienation or estrangement is good, and hence that wanting to be at home mentally or spiritually is questionable, and ought to be questioned" (135). People crave to be "at home," even if they are already there: "What is their desire? They crave that the self be made of answerable questions. They want no real self-process. They want an identity, a self-same self. They want to be defined, known and understood by those around them. Others are

their furnishings and they do not believe in the right of self trust" (137). George Kateb, "Introduction: Exile, Alienation, and Estrangement," *Social Research* 58 (Spring 1991).

8. For two interesting considerations of the tyrannical possibilities of the "model home" and the "nice" home, see Gwendolyn Wright, "Prescribing the Model Home," *Social Research* 58 (Spring 1991), and Mary Douglas, "The Idea of Home: A Kind of Space," *Social Research* 58 (Spring 1991).

9. See the introduction, note 55, where I discuss the origin of this passage, and Thoreau's refusal to explain it.

10. Stanley Cavell, *The Senses of Walden* (San Francisco: North Point Press, 1981), 53.

11. Ibid., 51–54.

12. Henry David Thoreau, *The Journals of Henry D. Thoreau*, vols. 8–14 (New York: Dover, 1962), 81.

13. Walter Benn Michaels, "*Walden*'s False Bottoms," in *Critical Essays on Henry David Thoreau's Walden*, ed. Joel Myerson (Boston: G. K. Hall and Company, 1988), 146.

14. Ibid., 145.

15. Ibid.

16. Ibid., 132.

17. Henry David Thoreau, "The Landlord," in *Collected Essays and Poems*, ed. Elizabeth Hall Witherell, 108. Hereafter cited in text as "Landlord."

18. During Thoreau's time, the post office was often the primary form of direct contact people had with the state. This makes it even more significant that the innkeeper can read his mail with such equanimity.

19. See *The New Shorter Oxford English Dictionary*, s.v. "Publican." (Oxford: Clarendon Press, 1973, 1993).

20. Frost, *Poetry of Robert Frost*, 33.

Conclusion

1. Susan Buck-Morss, *The Origin of Negative Dialectics* (New York: Free Press, 1977), 85.

2. To name a few texts concerned with alienation: Herbert Marcuse's *One Dimensional Man* was originally published in 1964; Bertell Ollman's *Alienation: Marx's Conception of Man in Capitalist Society* was published in 1971; Marshall Berman's *The Politics of Authenticity: Radical Individualism and the Emergence of Modern Society*, which deals with themes of authenticity and alienation in the work of Montesquieu and Rousseau especially, was published in 1970; John Patrick Diggins's "Thoreau, Marx, and the 'Riddle' of Alienation" was published in 1972; Sartre's *Nausea*, published in 1938, gained new popularity in the 1960s; Camus' *The Stranger* won the Nobel Prize for Literature in 1957; Erich Fromm's *Escape from Freedom*, first published in 1941, also gained new popularity in the 1960s and was reissued with a new forward by the author in 1965; Lukács' *History and Class Consciousness* was translated into English in 1971.

3. For an analysis of the links between Adorno's critique of alienation and the state of American psychology (both in the 1940s and in the contemporary era), see my

"Damaged Life as Exuberant Vitality: Adorno, America, and the Sickness of Health," forthcoming in a special issue of *Telos* dedicated to the topic of "Adorno in America."

4. Theodor Adorno, *Lectures on Kant's Critique of Pure Reason*, trans. Rodney Livingstone (Stanford, CA: Stanford University Press, 2001), 112.

5. Certainly new brain-imaging technologies account for part of why this era is referred to as "the age of the brain." But, as Peter Kramer notes in *Listening to Prozac*, the "new biological materialism" also reflects cultural needs in more complex ways: "My sense . . . is that the new biological materialism is a cultural phenomenon that goes beyond the scientific evidence. There have always been observations favoring nature over nurture. What changes, in response to the spirit of the times, is the choice of evidence to which we attend . . . cultural needs influence the evidence that scientists attend to. During the American civil rights struggle, for example, the proposition that biology is destiny became unthinkable. Today, in a society filled with the material fruits of the new biology—PET and CAT and MRI scanners . . . the proposition may seem incontrovertible." Peter Kramer, *Listening to Prozac* (New York: Penguin Books, 1993), xiv.

6. Satcher's quote comes from an interview on Jim Lehrer's *Newshour*, December 13, 1999, where he discussed his surgeon general's report on mental health. Also quoted in Elio Frattaroli, *Healing the Soul in the Age of the Brain* (New York: Penguin Books, 2001), 7.

7. For challenges to the "medical model" and "biological materialism," see T. M. Luhrmann's anthropological study of American psychiatry. T. M. Luhrmann, *Of Two Minds: An Anthropologist Looks at American Psychiatry* (New York: Vintage Books, 2001). See also Carl Elliot and Tod Chambers, eds., *Prozac as a Way of Life* (Chapel Hill: University of North Carolina Press, 2004). See also Frattaroli, *Healing the Soul in the Age of the Brain*, and Kramer, *Listening to Prozac*.

Bibliography

Abbott, Philip. "Henry David Thoreau, the State of Nature, and the Redemption of Liberalism." *Journal of Politics* 47, no. 1 (1985): 182–208.

Adorno, Theodor. "Aldous Huxley and Utopia." In *Prisms*. Cambridge, MA: MIT Press, 1983.

———. "Appendix 1: Discussion of Professor Adorno's Lecture 'The Meaning of Working through the Past.'" In *Critical Models: Interventions and Catchwords*. New York: Columbia University Press, 1998.

———. "Critique." In *Critical Models: Interventions and Catchwords*. New York: Columbia University Press, 1998.

———. *The Culture Industry*. Edited by J. M. Bernstein. New York: Routledge, 1991.

———. *Kierkegaard: Construction of the Aesthetic*. Translated and edited by Robert Hullot-Kentor. Minneapolis: University of Minnesota Press, 1989.

———. *Lectures on Kant's Critique of Pure Reason*. Translated by Rodney Livingstone. Stanford, CA: Stanford University Press, 2001.

———. *Minima Moralia: Reflections from Damaged Life*. Translated by E. F. N. Jephcott. London: Verso, 1974.

———. *Minima Moralia: Reflexionen aus dem beschädigten Leben*. Edited by Rolf Tiedemann et al. Gesammelte Schriften Band 4. Darmstadt: Wissenschaftliche Buchgesellschaft, 1997.

———. *Negative Dialectics*. Translated by E. B. Ashton. New York: Continuum, 1973.

———. *Negative Dialektik*. Edited by Rolf Tiedemann et al. Gesammelte Schriften Band 6. Darmstadt: Wissenschaftliche Buchgesellschaft, 1998.

———. "On Subject and Object." In *Critical Models: Interventions and Catchwords*. New York: Columbia University Press, 1998.

———. "Resignation." In *The Culture Industry*. New York: Routledge, 1991.

Adorno, Theodor, and Max Horkheimer. *Dialectic of Enlightenment*. Translated by Edmund Jephcott. Edited by Gunzelin Schmid Noerr. Stanford, CA: Stanford University Press, 2002.

Arendt, Hannah. *Between Past and Future: Eight Exercises in Political Thought*. New York: Penguin Books, 1954.

———. "Civil Disobedience." In *Crises of the Republic*. New York: Harcourt, Brace and Jovanovich, 1969.

———. *The Human Condition*. Chicago: University of Chicago Press, 1958.

———. *On Revolution*. New York: Penguin, 1963, 1965.

Bellah, Robert, et al. *Habits of the Heart: Individualism and Commitment in American Life*. Berkeley: University of California Press, 1985, 1996.

Benhabib, Seyla. *Critique, Norm, and Utopia*. New York: Columbia University Press, 1986.

———, ed. *Democracy and Difference: Contesting the Boundaries of the Political*. Princeton, NJ: Princeton University Press, 1996.

———. "The Democratic Moment and the Problem of Difference." In *Democracy and Difference: Contesting the Boundaries of the Political*, edited by Seyla Benhabib. Princeton, NJ: Princeton University Press, 1996.

Benjamin, Walter. *Illuminations*. Translated by Harry Zohn. Edited by Hannah Arendt. New York: Schocken Books, 1968.

Bennett, Jane. *The Enchantment of Modern Life: Attachments, Crossings, Ethics*. Princeton, NJ: Princeton University Press, 2001.

———. *Thoreau's Nature: Ethics, Politics, and the Wild*. Thousand Oaks, CA: Sage, 1994.

Bercovitch, Sacvan. *The American Jeremiad*. Madison: University of Wisconsin Press, 1978.

———. *The Puritan Origins of the American Self*. New Haven, CT: Yale University Press, 1975.

Berman, Marshall. *The Politics of Authenticity: Radical Individualism and the Emergence of Modern Society*. New York: Atheneum, 1970.

Bernstein, J. M. *Adorno: Disenchantment and Ethics*. New York: Cambridge University Press, 2001.

———. "Negative Dialectics as Fate." In *Cambridge Companion to Adorno*, edited by Tom Huhn. New York: Cambridge University Press, 2004.

Bridgman, Richard. *Dark Thoreau*. Lincoln: University of Nebraska Press, 1982.

Brooks, Paul. *The People of Concord: One Year in the Flowering of New England*. Guilford, CT: Globe Pequot Press, 1990.

Brown, Mary Hosmer. *Memories of Concord*. Boston: Four Seas Company, 1926.

Brown, Richard D. *Modernization: The Transformation of American Life, 1600–1865*. New York: Farrar, Straus and Giroux, 1976.

Brown, Richard D., and Jack Tager. *Massachusetts: A Concise History*. Amherst: University of Massachusetts Press, 2000.

Buck-Morss, Susan. *The Origin of Negative Dialectics*. New York: Free Press, 1977.

Buell, Lawrence. *Emerson*. Cambridge, MA: Belknap Press of Harvard University Press, 2003.

Buranelli, Vincent. "The Case against Thoreau." *Ethics* 67, no. 4 (1957): 257–68.

Camus, Albert. *The Stranger*. Translated by Matthew Ward. New York: Vintage International, 1988.

Cavell, Stanley. *Conditions Handsome and Unhandsome: The Constitution of Emersonian Perfectionism.* Chicago: University of Chicago Press, 1990.

———. *Emerson's Transcendental Etudes.* Edited by David Justin Hodge. Stanford, CA: Stanford University Press, 2003.

———. "Finding as Founding: Taking Steps in Emerson's 'Experience'." In *Emerson's Transcendental Etudes,* edited by David Justin Hodge. Stanford, CA: Stanford University Press, 2003.

———. "The Philosopher in American Life: Toward Emerson and Thoreau." In *Emerson's Transcendental Etudes,* edited by David Justin Hodge. Stanford, CA: Stanford University Press, 2003.

———. *The Senses of Walden.* San Francisco: North Point Press, 1981.

Certeau, Michel de. *The Practice of Everyday Life.* Berkeley: University of California Press, 1984, 2002.

Claussen, Detlev. *Theodor W. Adorno: One Last Genius.* Translated by Rodney Livingstone. Cambridge, MA: Belknap Press of Harvard University Press, 2008.

Colwell, James L. "Huckleberries and Humans: On the Naming of Huckleberry Finn." *PMLA* 86, no. 1 (1971): 70–76.

Connolly, William E. *The Ethos of Pluralization.* Minneapolis: University of Minnesota Press, 1995.

———. *Identity/Difference: Democratic Negotiations of Political Paradox.* Minneapolis: University of Minnesota Press, 1991.

Cronon, William. *Changes in the Land: Indians, Colonists and the Ecology of New England.* New York: Hill and Wang, 1983, 2003.

Dahl, Robert A. *On Political Equality.* New Haven, CT: Yale University Press, 2006.

Diggins, John P. "Thoreau, Marx, and the 'Riddle' of Alienation." *Social Research* 39 (1972): 571–98.

Donahue, Brian. "The Forests and Fields of Concord: An Ecological History, 1750–1850." In *Concord: The Social History of a New England Town 1750–1850,* edited by David Hackett Fischer. Waltham, MA: Brandeis University Press, 1984.

Douglas, Mary. "The Idea of Home: A Kind of Space." *Social Research* 58 (Spring 1991): 287–307.

Dubiel, Helmut. *Theory and Politics: Studies in the Development of Critical Theory.* Translated by Benjamin Gregg. Cambridge, MA: MIT Press, 1985.

Dumm, Thomas L. "Joyce Brown, or Democracy and Homelessness." In *united states.* Contestations Series. Ithaca, NY: Cornell University Press, 1994.

———. *Loneliness as a Way of Life.* Cambridge, MA: Harvard University Press, 2008.

———. "Political Theory for Losers." In *Vocations of Political Theory,* edited by Jason Frank and John Tambornino. Minneapolis: University of Minnesota Press, 2000.

Elliot, Carl, and Tod Chambers, eds. *Prozac as a Way of Life.* Chapel Hill: University of North Carolina Press, 2004.

Emerson, Ralph Waldo. "The American Scholar." In *Nature, Addresses and Lectures,* vol. 1, edited by Alfred R. Ferguson. Cambridge, MA: Belknap Press of Harvard University Press, 1971.

————. "Circles." In *Essays: First Series,* edited by Joseph Slater. Cambridge, MA: Belknap Press of Harvard University Press, 1979.

————. "Compensation." In *Essays: First Series,* edited by Joseph Slater. Cambridge, MA: Belknap Press of Harvard University Press, 1979.

————. *The Conduct of Life.* Edited by Joseph Slater. Vol. 6, *The Collected Works of Ralph Waldo Emerson.* Cambridge, MA: Belknap Press of Harvard University Press, 2003.

————. "The Divinity School Address." In *Nature, Addresses and Lectures,* vol. 1, edited by Alfred R. Ferguson. Cambridge, MA: Belknap Press of Harvard University Press, 1971.

————. *English Traits.* Edited by Joseph Slater. Vol. 5, *The Collected Works of Ralph Waldo Emerson.* Cambridge, MA: Belknap Press of Harvard University Press, 1994.

————. "Experience." In *Essays: Second Series,* edited by Joseph Slater. Cambridge, MA: Belknap Press of Harvard University Press, 1983.

————. "Heroism." In *Essays: First Series,* vol. 2, edited by Joseph Slater. Cambridge, MA: Belknap Press of Harvard University Press, 1979.

————. "History." In *Essays: First Series,* vol. 2, edited by Joseph Slater. Cambridge, MA: Belknap Press of Harvard University Press, 1979.

————. "Introduction." In *Walden and Other Writings,* by Henry David Thoreau. New York: Modern Library, 2000.

————. "Manners." In *Essays: Second Series,* edited by Joseph Slater. Cambridge, MA: Belknap Press of Harvard University Press, 1983.

————. *Nature, Addresses, and Lectures.* Edited by Alfred R. Ferguson. Vol. 1, *The Collected Works of Ralph Waldo Emerson.* Cambridge, MA: Belknap Press of Harvard University Press, 1971.

————. "Nature." In *Essays: Second Series,* edited by Joseph Slater. Cambridge, MA: Belknap Press of Harvard University Press, 1983.

————. "The Over-Soul." In *Essays: First Series,* edited by Joseph Slater. Cambridge, MA: Belknap Press of Harvard University Press, 1979.

————. "The Poet." In *Essays: Second Series,* vol. 3, edited by Joseph Slater. Cambridge, MA: Belknap Press of Harvard University Press, 1983.

————. "Self-Reliance." In *Essays: First Series,* vol. 2, edited by Joseph Slater. Cambridge, MA: Belknap Press of Harvard University Press, 1979.

————. "The Transcendentalist." In *Nature, Addresses and Lectures,* vol. 1, edited by Alfred R. Ferguson. Cambridge, MA: Belknap Press of Harvard University Press, 1971.

Frattaroli, Elio. *Healing the Soul in the Age of the Brain.* New York: Penguin Books, 2001.

French, Allen, and Lester Hornby. *Old Concord.* Boston: Little, Brown, 1915.

Freud, Sigmund. *Civilization and Its Discontents.* New York: W. W. Norton, 1961, 1989.

Fromm, Erich. *Escape from Freedom.* New York: Henry Holt, 1965.

Frost, Robert. *The Poetry of Robert Frost: The Collected Poems, Complete and Unabridged.* Edited by Edward Connery Latham. New York: Henry Holt, 1969.

Gilmore, Michael T. *American Romanticism and the Marketplace*. Chicago: Chicago University Press, 1985.

Goldman, Emma. *Anarchism and Other Essays*. New York: Dover Publications, 1969.

Habermas, Jürgen. *The Structural Transformation of the Public Sphere*. Translated by Thomas Burger with Frederick Lawrence. Cambridge, MA: MIT Press, 1989.

———. *The Theory of Communicative Action*. Vol. 1, *Reason and the Rationalization of Society*. Translated by Thomas McCarthy. Boston: Beacon Press, 1984.

———. *The Theory of Communicative Action*. Vol. 2, *Lifeworld and System: A Critique of Functionalist Reason*. Translated by Thomas McCarthy. Boston: Beacon Press, 1987.

Hamilton, Alexander, James Madison, and John Jay. *The Federalist Papers with Letters of "Brutus."* Edited by Terence Ball. New York: Cambridge University Press, 2003.

Hammer, Espen. *Adorno and the Political*. New York: Routledge, 2005.

Harding, Walter. *The Days of Henry Thoreau: A Biography*. Princeton, NJ: Princeton University Press 1962.

———. "Thoreau's Reputation." In *The Cambridge Companion to Henry David Thoreau*, edited by Joel Myerson. New York: Cambridge University Press, 1995.

Harris, Marc. "The People of Concord: A Demographic History, 1750–1850." In *Concord: The Social History of a New England Town, 1750–1850*, edited by David Hackett Fischer. Waltham, MA: Brandeis University Press, 1983.

Heilbroner, Robert, and Aaron Singer. *The Economic Transformation of America: 1600 to the Present*. 4th ed. New York: Harcourt Brace, 1999.

Hoag, Ronald Wesley. "Thoreau's Later Natural History Writings." In *The Cambridge Companion to Henry David Thoreau*, edited by Joel Myerson. New York: Cambridge University Press, 1995.

Hollander, John. "It All Depends." *Social Research* 58, no. 1 (1991): 31–49.

Honig, Bonnie. *Democracy and the Foreigner*. Princeton, NJ: Princeton University Press, 2001.

———. "Difference, Dilemmas, and the Politics of Home." In *Democracy and Difference: Contesting the Boundaries of the Political*, edited by Seyla Benhabib. Princeton, NJ: Princeton University Press, 1996.

———. *Political Theory and the Displacement of Politics*. Ithaca, NY: Cornell University Press, 1993.

Honneth, Axel. *The Fragmented World of the Social: Essays in Social and Political Philosophy*. Edited by Charles W. Wright. Binghamton: State University of New York Press, 1995.

Horkheimer, Max. *Critical Theory: Selected Essays*. Translated by Matthew J. O'Connell et al. New York: Continuum, 1999.

Huhn, Tom. "Thoughts Beside Themselves." In *Cambridge Companion to Adorno*, edited by Tom Huhn. New York: Cambridge University Press, 2004.

Jäger, Lorenz. *Adorno: A Political Biography*. Translated by Stewart Spencer. New Haven, CT: Yale University Press, 2004.

Jameson, Frederic. *Late Marxism: Adorno, or the Persistence of the Dialectic*. New York: Verso, 1990.

Jarvis, Edmund. *Traditions and Reminiscences of Concord, Massachusetts, 1779–1878*. Edited by Sarah Chapin. Amherst: University of Massachusetts Press, 1993.

Jay, Martin. *Adorno*. Cambridge, MA: Harvard University Press, 1984.

———. *The Dialectical Imagination*. Berkeley: University of California Press, 1973.

———. "Is Experience Still in Crisis? Reflections on a Frankfurt School Lament." In *Cambridge Companion to Adorno*, edited by Tom Huhn. New York: Cambridge University Press, 2004.

Jenco, Leigh Kathryn. "Thoreau's Critique of Democracy." *Review of Politics* 65 (Summer 2003): 355–81.

Jenemann, David. *Adorno in America*. Minneapolis: University of Minnesota Press, 2007.

Kalyvas, Andreas. "Back to Adorno? Critical Social Theory between Past and Future." *Political Theory* 32, no. 2 (2004): 247–56.

Kaplan, Morris B. "Queer Citizenship: Thoreau's Civil Disobedience and the Ethics of Self-Making," in *Sexual Justice: Democratic Citizenship and the Politics of Desire*. New York: Routledge, 1997.

Kateb, George. *The Inner Ocean: Individualism and Democratic Culture*. Ithaca, NY: Cornell University Press, 1992.

———. "Introduction: Exile, Alienation, and Estrangement." *Social Research* 58 (Spring 1991).

———. "The Moral Distinctiveness of Representative Democracy." *Ethics* 91, no. 3 (1981): 357–74.

———. "Walt Whitman and the Culture of Democracy." *Political Theory* 18, no. 4 (1990): 545–71.

Kimenker, James. "The Concord Farmer: An Economic History, 1750–1850." In *Concord: The Social History of a New England Town, 1750–1850*, edited by David Hackett Fischer. Waltham, MA: Brandeis University Press, 1984.

Kramer, Peter. *Listening to Prozac*. New York: Penguin Books, 1993.

Lane, Melissa. "Thoreau and Rousseau: Nature as Utopia." In *A Political Companion to Henry David Thoreau*, edited by Jack Turner. Lexington: University Press of Kentucky, 2009.

Lowell, James Russell. *A Fable for Critics*. Boston: Houghton Mifflin, 1890.

Luhrmann, T. M. *Of Two Minds: An Anthropologist Looks at American Psychiatry*. New York: Vintage Books, 2001.

Lukács, Georg. *History and Class Consciousness*. Cambridge, MA: MIT Press, 1971.

———. *The Theory of the Novel*. Cambridge, MA: MIT Press, 1994.

Marcuse, Herbert. *One Dimensional Man*. Boston: Beacon Press, 1991.

Mariotti, Shannon. "Critique from the Margins: Adorno and the Politics of Withdrawal." *Political Theory* 36, no. 3 (June 2008): 456–65.

———. "Damaged Life as Exuberant Vitality: Adorno, America, and the Sickness of Health." *Telos* (forthcoming).

———. "On the Passing of the First-Born Son: Emerson's 'Focal Distancing' and Du Bois's 'Second Sight' and Disruptive Particularity." *Political Theory* 37, no. 3 (2009): 351–74.

———. "Thoreau, Adorno, and the Critical Potential of Particularity." In *A Political Companion to Henry David Thoreau,* edited by Jack Turner. Lexington: University Press of Kentucky, 2009.

Marx, Karl. "Economic and Philosophic Manuscripts of 1844." In *The Marx-Engels Reader,* edited by Robert C. Tucker. New York: W. W. Norton, 1978.

Marx, Leo. *The Machine in the Garden: Technology and the Pastoral Ideal in America.* New York: Oxford University Press, 1964, 2000.

McCarthy, Thomas. *The Critical Theory of Jürgen Habermas.* Cambridge, MA: MIT Press, 1978.

Meyers, Michael. *"Several More Lives to Live": Thoreau's Political Reputation in America.* Westport, CT: Greenwood Press, 1977.

Michaels, Walter Benn. "*Walden*'s False Bottoms." In *Critical Essays on Henry David Thoreau's Walden,* edited by Joel Myerson. Boston: G. K. Hall, 1988.

Miller, Perry. *Consciousness in Concord: The Text of Thoreau's Hitherto "Lost Journal" (1840–1841) Together with Notes and a Commentary.* Boston: Houghton Mifflin, 1958.

Moldenhauer, Joseph J. "The Extra-Vagant Maneuver: Paradox in *Walden.*" In *Critical Essays on Henry David Thoreau's Walden,* edited by Joel Myerson. Boston: G. K. Hall, 1988.

Moller, Mary Elkin. *Thoreau in the Human Community.* Amherst: University of Massachusetts Press, 1980.

Morris, Martin. *Rethinking the Communicative Turn: Adorno, Habermas and the Problem of Communicative Freedom.* Albany: State University of New York Press, 2001.

Mouffe, Chantal. "Democracy, Power, and the 'Political.'" In *Democracy and Difference: Contesting the Boundaries of the Political,* edited by Seyla Benhabib. Princeton, NJ: Princeton University Press, 1996.

Müller-Doohm, Stefan. *Adorno: A Biography.* Translated by Rodney Livingstone. Cambridge, UK: Polity Press, 2005.

New Oxford Annotated Bible. Edited by Michael D. Coogan. 3rd ed. New York: Oxford University Press, 2007.

Ollman, Bertell. *Alienation: Marx's Conception of Man in Capitalist Society.* New York: Cambridge University Press, 1971.

Polanyi, Karl. *The Great Transformation: The Political and Economic Origins of Our Time.* Boston: Beacon Press, 2001.

Porte, Joel. *Consciousness and Culture: Emerson and Thoreau Reviewed.* New Haven, CT: Yale University Press, 2004.

———. *Emerson and Thoreau: Transcendentalists in Conflict.* Middletown, CT: Wesleyan University Press, 1966.

———. "Emerson, Thoreau, and the Double Consciousness." *New England Quarterly* 41, no. 1 (1968): 40–50.

Porte, Joel, and Saundra Morris, eds. *The Cambridge Companion to Ralph Waldo Emerson.* New York: Cambridge University Press, 1999.

Putnam, Robert. *Bowling Alone: The Collapse and Revival of American Community.* New York: Simon and Schuster, 2001.

Richardson, Robert D. *Emerson: The Mind on Fire*. Berkeley: University of California Press, 1995.

———. *Henry Thoreau: A Life of the Mind*. Berkeley: University of California Press, 1986.

———. "The Social Ethics of Walden." In *Critical Essays on Henry David Thoreau's Walden*, edited by Joel Myerson. Boston: G. K. Hall, 1988.

———. "Thoreau and Concord." In *The Cambridge Companion to Henry David Thoreau*, edited by Joel Myerson. New York: Cambridge University Press, 1995.

Rose, Gillian. *The Melancholy Science: An Introduction to the Thought of Theodor W. Adorno*. New York: Columbia University Press, 1978.

Rosenblum, Nancy. *Another Liberalism: Romanticism and the Reconstruction of Liberal Thought*. Cambridge, MA: Harvard University Press, 1987.

———. "The Inhibitions of Democracy on Romantic Political Thought: Thoreau's Democratic Individualism." In *Lessons of Romanticism: A Critical Companion*, edited by Thomas Pfau and Robert F. Gleckner. Durham, NC: Duke University Press, 1998.

———. "Thoreau's Militant Conscience." *Political Theory* 9, no. 1 (1981): 81–110.

Rousseau, Jean-Jacques. *Reveries of the Solitary Walker*. Translated by Peter France. New York: Penguin Classics, 1979.

Sandel, Michael. *Democracy's Discontents: America in Search of a Public Philosophy*. Cambridge, MA: Belknap Press of Harvard University Press, 1998.

———. *Liberalism and the Limits of Justice*. New York: Cambridge University Press, 1982, 1998.

———. *Public Philosophy: Essays on Morality in Politics*. Cambridge, MA: Harvard University Press, 2006.

Sartre, Jean-Paul. *Nausea*. Translated by Lloyd Alexander. New York: New Directions, 1964.

Sattelmeyer, Robert. "Thoreau and Emerson." In *The Cambridge Companion to Henry David Thoreau*, edited by Joel Myerson. New York: Cambridge University Press, 1995.

Schlosberg, David. "The Pluralist Imagination." In *The Oxford Handbook of Political Theory*, edited by Bonnie Honig, John S. Dryzek, and Anne Phillips. New York: Oxford University Press, 2006.

Shattuck, Lemuel. *History of the Town of Concord, Middlesex Co., Mass. From Its Earliest Settlement to 1832*. Boston: Russell, Odiorne and Co., 1835.

Shklar, Judith N. "Emerson and the Inhibitions of Democracy." *Political Theory* 18, no. 4 (1990): 601–14.

Solnit, Rebecca. *Wanderlust: A History of Walking*. New York: Penguin, 2001.

Taylor, Bob Pepperman. *America's Bachelor Uncle: Thoreau in the American Polity*. Lawrence: University of Kansas Press, 1996.

Teichgraeber, Richard F. *Sublime Thoughts/Penny Wisdom: Situating Emerson and Thoreau in the American Market*. Baltimore, MD: Johns Hopkins University Press, 1995.

Thoreau, Henry David. *The Correspondence of Henry David Thoreau*. Edited by Carl Bode and Walter Harding. Westport, CT: Greenwood Press, 1974.

———. *Familiar Letters.* Edited by F. B. Sanborn. Vol. 6, *The Writings of Henry David Thoreau.* Boston: Houghton Mifflin, 1906.

———. "Huckleberries." In *Collected Essays and Poems,* edited by Elizabeth Witherell. New York: Library of America, 2001.

———. *The Journals of Henry D. Thoreau.* Vols. 8–14. New York: Dover, 1962.

———. "The Landlord." In *Collected Essays and Poems,* edited by Elizabeth Hall Witherell. New York: Library of America, 2001.

———. "Life without Principle." In *The Higher Law: Thoreau on Civil Disobedience and Reform,* edited by Wendell Glick. Princeton, NJ: Princeton University Press, 2004.

———. *The Maine Woods.* Edited by Joseph J. Moldenhauer. Princeton, NJ: Princeton University Press, 2004.

———. "Paradise (to Be) Regained." In *The Higher Law: Thoreau on Civil Disobedience and Reform,* edited by Wendell Glick. Princeton, NJ: Princeton University Press, 2004.

———. "Resistance to Civil Government." In *The Higher Law: Thoreau on Civil Disobedience and Reform,* edited by Wendell Glick. Princeton, NJ: Princeton University Press, 2004.

———. "Slavery in Massachusetts." In *The Higher Law: Thoreau on Civil Disobedience and Reform,* edited by Wendell Glick. Princeton, NJ: Princeton University Press, 2004.

———. "Thomas Carlyle and His Works." In *Collected Essays and Poems,* edited by Elizabeth Witherell. New York: Library of America, 2001.

———. *Walden.* Edited by J. Lyndon Shanley. Princeton, NJ: Princeton University Press, 2004.

———. "Walking." In *Collected Essays and Poems,* edited by Elizabeth Hall Witherell. New York: Library of America, 2001.

———. *A Week on the Concord and Merrimack Rivers.* Edited by Carl A. Hovde, William L. Howarth and Elizabeth Hall Witherell. Princeton, NJ: Princeton University Press, 2004.

———. "Wild Apples." In *Collected Essays and Poems,* edited by Elizabeth Hall Witherell. New York: Library of America, 2001.

———. *Wild Fruits: Thoreau's Rediscovered Last Manuscript.* Edited by Bradley P. Dean. New York: W. W. Norton, 2000.

Tocqueville, Alexis de. *Democracy in America and Two Essays on America.* Translated by Gerald E. Bevan. New York: Penguin Books, 2003.

Turner, Jack. "Emerson, Slavery, and the Ethics of Citizenship." *Raritan: A Quarterly Review* 28, no. 2 (2008): 127–46.

———. "'Performing Conscience': Thoreau, Political Action and the Plea for John Brown." *Political Theory* 33, no. 4 (2005): 448–71.

———, ed. *A Political Companion to Henry David Thoreau.* Lexington: University Press of Kentucky, 2009.

Van Doren, Mark. *Henry David Thoreau: A Critical Study.* Boston: Houghton Mifflin, 1916.

Villa, Dana. *Socratic Citizenship.* Princeton, NJ: Princeton University Press, 2001.

Von Rautenfeld, Hans. "Thinking for Thousands: Emerson's Theory of Political Representation in the Public Sphere." *American Journal of Political Science* 49, no. 1 (2005): 184–97.

Walker, Brian. "Thoreau on Democratic Cultivation." *Political Theory* 29, no. 2 (2001): 155–89.

Warner, Michael. "Thoreau's Bottom." *Raritan: A Quarterly Review* 11, no. 3 (1992): 53–79.

Weber, Samuel. "Translating the Untranslatable." In *Prisms*, by Theodor Adorno. Cambridge, MA: MIT Press, 1981.

Weintraub, Richard N. "Stratification and Mobility in Concord: A Sociological History, 1750–1850." In *Concord: The Social History of a New England Town, 1750–1850*, edited by David Hackett Fischer. Waltham, MA: Brandeis University Press, 1983.

West, Cornel. *The American Evasion of Philosophy: A Genealogy of Pragmatism*. Madison: University of Wisconsin Press, 1989.

Wilson, Leslie Perrin. "A Concord Farmer Looks Back: The Reminiscences of William Henry Hunt." *Concord Saunterer* 10 (2002).

Wolin, Sheldon S. "Fugitive Democracy." In *Democracy and Difference: Contesting the Boundaries of the Political*, edited by Seyla Benhabib. Princeton, NJ: Princeton University Press, 1996.

———. *Politics and Vision: Continuity and Innovation in Western Political Thought*. Princeton, NJ: Princeton University Press, 2004.

Wright, Gwendolyn. "Prescribing the Model Home." *Social Research* 58 (Spring 1991): 213–25.

Young-Bruehl, Elisabeth. *Hannah Arendt: For Love of the World*. 2nd ed. New Haven, CT: Yale University Press, 2004.

Index

abandonment: Adorno and the dangers of passivity, 72–73; and dangers of "home," 45–51, 75, 164–65; Emerson and self-abandonment, 66–71, 73, 187n10; fascism and, 73; Thoreau and abandonment to "the wild," 139–40

Abbott, Philip, 3, 5

abolitionism, 106–7

abstract exchange: Adorno and, 11, 15, 22, 29, 33–34, 36, 115–16; Emerson and, 61, 77–78; and identity, 36, 77–78; logic of, 133–34; and market economy, 99–100, 115–16; Thoreau and the link between loss and, 77–78, 99–101, 133–36, 159

abstraction: Adorno on, 33–36; alienation and, 61; Emerson as proponent of inward creation and, 51, 64; Emerson's "focal distancing" as, 23, 60; idealist dialectic and, 35–36; identity linked to, 36; the particular as resistant to, 37; particularizing the abstract, 78; Thoreau and opposition to, 79–81; and Transcendental gaze, 22; as violation, 34–36, 133–37. *See also* abstract exchange

Adorno, Theodor W.: biographical information, xi, 45, 173n1, 184n31; as interlocutor for Thoreau, 8, 35, 56–57, 167–68; negative dialectics as practice of (*see* negative dialectics)

Adorno and the Political (Hammer), 51–52

The Adventures of Huckleberry Finn (Twain), 134

advice, Thoreau and, 4, 118–19

"After Auschwitz" (Adorno), 173n1

agonistic theories of democracy, xv–xvi, 174n15

alienation, 6, 198n7; Adorno's use of term, 12, 178n29; biological materialism and perspectives on, 168–69; "damaged life" and, 34, 41–50, 51; and deadening of critical consciousness, 44, 134; as deadening of experience, 34, 51, 92–94; Emerson on, 29, 62–64, 71; existential despair or angst confused with, 12; Habermas on democracy and resistance of, xiv; health and, 43–44; immediacy/intimacy (loss of distance) and the creation of estrangement, 16; Kateb's "moderate alienation," 198n7; loss and, 44; mechanization and, xvii, 12, 29, 42–44, 71, 170; and melancholy, 11–12, 49–50; modernity and, xii, 11–13, 108–9, 148; negative dialectics as resistance to, 29, 40–41, 170–71; political consequences of, 34, 51–56; psychology and psychoanalysis and, 43–44; reification contrasted with, 102, 178n29; as response to social and political condition, 11, 13; "self-alienation of society," 54; similarities between Adorno's and Thoreau's constructions of, 115–16; social theories of, 30; subjectivity and, 170–71; Thoreau on, 44, 71, 113–14, 132; Thoreau's "common sense" as, xiii, 27, 81, 93–94, 113, 138, 144, 181n58; Thoreau's Concord as context for his, 86–92; withdrawal and resistance to, xviii, 40–41, 167–68, 171

Americanism, 59

American Romanticism and the Marketplace (Gilmore), 5, 101–3

211